The Orders of Discourse

The Orders of Discourse

Philosophy, Social Science, and Politics

JOHN G. GUNNELL

ROWMAN & LITTLEFIELD PUBLISHERS, INC.
Lanham • Boulder • New York • Oxford

ROWMAN & LITTLEFIELD PUBLISHERS, INC.

Published in the United States of America
by Rowman & Littlefield Publishers, Inc.
4720 Boston Way, Lanham, Maryland 20706

12 Hid's Copse Road
Cumnor Hill, Oxford OX2 9JJ, England

British Library Cataloguing in Publication Information Available

Library of Congress Cataloging-in-Publication Data

Gunnell, John G.
      The orders of discourse : philosophy, social science, and politics
/ John G. Gunnell.
              p. cm.
      Includes bibliographical references and index.
      ISBN 0-8476-9202-7 (alk. paper). — ISBN 0-8476-9203-5 (pbk. :
alk. paper)
         1. Political science—Philosophy. 2. Social sciences—Philosophy.
I. Title
JA71.G88 1998
320'.01—dc21   98-18013
                                          CIP

ISBN 0-8476-9202-7 (cloth : alk. paper)
ISBN 0-8476-9203-5 (pbk. : alk.paper)

Printed in the United States of America

(∞)™ The paper used in this publication meets the minimum requirements of American National
Standard for Information Sciences—Permanence of Paper for Printed Library Materials, ANSI
Z39.48-1984.

Now the two masters, *theory and practice,* you cannot serve.

—*Charles S. Peirce*

Contents

Preface

This volume expands, refines, and synthesizes arguments about the nexus of philosophy, social science, and politics that I have advanced in a number of contexts over a considerable period of years. My aim, however, is to liberate the claims from the constraints of some of the particular conversations in which they have intervened, especially those distinctly intraspecific to the discipline and profession of academic political theory and political science (see Nelson 1986). Although the emphasis is still, at least for exemplary purposes, on political theory, the discussion is directed toward the broader area of social theory and the social sciences in general.

In earlier works, I sought to deconstruct specific myths about both science and history that had defined and, in my view, constrained much of the self-image and practice of political theory and political science (Gunnell 1975, 1979a). I subsequently joined these criticisms to a more comprehensive analysis of the field of academic political theory (1986a). I argued that much of it had become dominated by theoretically unanchored epistemological discourses that served to alienate it from politics as both a theoretical and practical object. The theoretical dimension of social science had been impoverished, if not displaced, by metatheoretical images of the nature of inquiry, and this impoverishment had, in turn, contributed to a retreat from an authentic consideration of the practical relationship between political theory and politics. It became increasingly apparent, however, that these problems had a genealogy. In a more recent work, and less critical vein, I explored the intellectual history of political theory in the United States, which I presented as a case study of the relationship between academic and public discourse, or at least social science's understanding of that relationship (Gunnell 1993).

Although from my analysis of political theory I wished to draw some general conclusions about the relationship between social science and its subject matter, political theory has occupied a somewhat unique, if not anomalous, place in the annals of the American academy. It was once an integral dimension of the discourse of American political science, as well as an institutionalized subfield, and it was also the locus of the discipline's abiding concern, and conversation, about its relationship to political life. When many political theorists by the late 1960s turned against what they perceived as the increasing scientism and political quietism of mainstream "behavioral" political science, they predicated a reformation of political theory on a dedication, or rededication, to the task of speaking to and about politics. The difficulties that have attended that project exemplify many of the issues that I wish to confront, and they represent the broader dilemma of the relationship between social science and politics as well as that of the general relationship between the academy and public life.

Much of the present work is devoted to an analytical examination of what I refer to as *the orders of discourse*. My fundamental concern is with what I will speak of as *metapractices*, that is, those practices that have other practices as their subject matter. I have coined this term to avoid the ambiguities that sometimes attach to the words *metatheory* and *metatheoretical*, which I will use more generically to refer to claims that are not per se theoretical. Metapractices, and their cognitive and practical relationship to their object of inquiry, are the basic subject of this volume, but a prominent theme is the issue of the relationship *among* metapractices, particularly the complex relationship between philosophy and social science.

Although in a few instances I engage in extended discussions of certain authors, this work is not in any primary sense about, or an interpretation of, particular individuals, texts, or schools of thought. I refer to various authors principally to situate my arguments, and even though I occasionally either endorse or take issue with their claims and parse the genres to which those claims belong, I do not, for the most part, attempt to offer any novel or contentious account of what they do in fact say. Many of the usual suspects in the mystery of contemporary political and social theory inevitably appear in the following pages, but I assume that the last thing we need is another extended summary of, and critical gloss on, their work. One of the pathologies of contemporary academic discussion is the regressive tendency to advance a claim by filtering it through the arguments of someone else. This, in turn, invites oblique criticism directed toward the individual or persuasion with whom the claim is identified.

My arguments cannot be understood by locating them in some particular philosophical school. This is not to say that certain aspects of my analysis have not been inspired by the ideas of others or cannot be reasonably categorized. The figure who most fundamentally lurks behind much of what I have to say is Ludwig Wittgenstein. Although this work is in no way presented as "Wittgensteinian analysis," whatever that might mean or entail, what I take to be the implications of his philosophy are reflected both in my focus on conventional phenomena and in my doubts about the epistemological enterprise in philosophy. As Stanley Cavell has noted, what Wittgenstein pointed to was "the depth of convention in human life," the extent to which convention was not simply a matter of society but constitutive of what we think of as "human nature" itself (1979:111). With respect to the enterprise of philosophy, Wittgenstein spoke of such things as philosophical problems disappearing; the manner in which much of philosophical discourse had become like a great "house of cards," an "engine idling," or language on "holiday"; returning language from its metaphysical to ordinary uses; the impossibility of finding grounds for our beliefs outside the practices in which they are embedded; how the picture that held us captive was that of philosophy as an enterprise that sought the foundation or essence of everything empirical, some phantasm or ontological principle beyond space and time; and how it might be necessary to give up certain philosophical habits just as we might be forced to give up the habit of driving if automobiles were found to cause illness. The basic message behind many of these remarks was, I believe, that the traditional transcendental and epistemological habits in philosophy should be broken. I would stress, however, that the effects and consequences of these habits outside philosophy, and particularly in the social sciences, have been even more pathological and consequential. Much of what I have to say can reasonably, and correctly, be construed as in the spirit of Cavell and Richard Rorty in that I unequivocally reject all truth-conditional philosophical ventures. There are, however, some very distinct differences. Their work is, I believe, still bound to the historical image of contemporary academic philosophy as part of a tradition reaching from Plato to the present, and while they seek to undermine certain tendencies in modern philosophy, they have not fully come to grips with the issue of how academic philosophy, or any second-order discourse, relates to the practices it talks about. What we might think of as "postanalytic" philosophy (Rajchman and West 1985) has, on the whole, not satisfactorily confronted this problem.

I introduce some elements of jargon and neologism that some may find jarring, such as the concept of metapractice and references to various (first, second, third, fourth) levels of discourse, but they are crucial to the structure of my analysis and are designed to produce specificity and clarity. The general themes that define this book are, I believe, explicit and unambiguous, and each chapter pursues a relatively distinct and narrowly defined argument. It is probably fair to say that these arguments tend to move against the grain of dominant opinion, but it is important to indicate accurately what is at issue. There has, for example, been considerable misunderstanding of both the content and purpose of my earlier claims about the "alienation" of political theory (Gunnell 1986a), and since the present work continues to address many of the same problems and extend the analysis to metapractices in general, the basic claims deserve some brief recapitulation.

There is, first of all, what I have called the "innocent," or structural, alienation of political theory from politics. This alienation is simply a function of the fact that politics and the academic study of politics are existentially, that is, historically and institutionally, different activities no matter how much the latter may be directed toward understanding or affecting the former and notwithstanding the extent to which there may be various forms of interaction between these spheres. The contemporary failure of political theory to confront the pragmatic dimension of this relationship, however, as well as its propensity to seek metatheoretical answers to what is actually a practical problem, engender a less innocuous estrangement. At the core of the alienation of political theory has been the tendency, born of a search for intellectual identity and authority, to subscribe and become hostage to various philosophical doctrines—particularly those involving the foundations of scientific and normative judgment. This has encouraged the construction of abstract images of both the activity and object of inquiry and of the relationship between them. Such philosophical mortgaging has also hampered discussion among discursive enclaves within the field. Although one can point to distinct controversies, such as that among varieties of liberalism, there is very little real confrontation among arguments in political theory or between this field and its estranged parent discipline of political science, in which it still professionally resides. This state of affairs has both distanced political theory from what might be called the particularities of politics and inhibited an engagement with the crucial theoretical issue of the generic constitution of social phenomena.

When, in 1986, I characterized the work of individuals such as Jürgen Habermas and John Rawls as representing the "end of political theory," I was playing on the ambiguity of the phrase. These abstract universalistic endeavors, devoted, in the one case, to the epistemological foundations of a critical social science and, in the other, to providing a philosophical ground for liberalism, had to a large extent been embraced as the *purpose* of political theorizing. In my view, this work also signaled the *exhaustion* of a certain mode of academic discourse and a retreat from any serious contextualized confrontation with the issue of what has traditionally been called theory and practice. I was, however, less concerned with such paradigmatic works than with the cottage industries of commentary that they had inspired and that had come to dominate the literature in the field. Now, more than a decade later, the situation remains much the same. For the most part, academic political theory continues to be defined by debates that revolve around abstract self-referencing issues with only the most tenuous ties to situated political phenomena. The production of knowledge, whether theoretical, analytical, or empirical, has fallen aside as the conversation of political theory has devolved into a churning of the ideas of a handful of contemporary authors and into a chase for new philosophical authorities.

My arguments have sometimes prompted the criticism that I am, in principle, hostile to philosophy and to theory. Although I would strenuously resist any such general characterization, I do not wish to back away from the claim that there are severe problems both with certain elements of contemporary philosophy and with social science's often uncritical appropriation and application of philosophical ideas. Some have suggested that my arguments amount to a call for political theorists to engage in political action; others read me as implying that academicians neither can nor should have an impact on political practice. I have never, however, embraced either position. The principal object of my criticism has been the pretension to be practically engaged and the failure to confront the complex issues involved in the relationship between academic and public discourse. How social science actually relates, and should relate, to its subject matter is a complex historical problem for which there are no easy answers.

Once in a forum where I was criticizing political theorists for retreating to epistemology and transcendentalism instead of talking directly about concrete political things, a well-known scholar and sometime publicist asked incredulously if I expected "theorists" to address such mundane matters as how much money a mother on welfare should receive. In a similar circumstance, a younger scholar bridled and insisted I recognize that "after all, we are philosophers." My goal has been, and in this book remains, less to suggest that we should be other than "theorists" and "philosophers" or that we have a duty, or ability, to speak to concrete issues of ethics and public policy than to urge that we, that is, metapractitioners, think more realistically and authentically about our role. If what I have to say points in any specific direction, it is toward an intellectual engagement of concrete particulars whether they be actions, practices, texts, or historical artifacts. Cavell has characterized John Austin and Wittgenstein as taking up "the cause of what they call the ordinary" against "philosophy's metaphysical flight from the ordinary" (1995:46), and what I have to say amounts in many ways to a plea that political and social theory return to the ordinary, which would include both thinking theoretically about the essence of the ordinary in human life and confronting the situated practical problem of the relationship between metapractices and the modes of ordinariness that they address.

Many of the difficulties in the contemporary social scientific enterprise are rooted in its past. The philosophy of social science is inseparable from the history of social science (Manicas 1987). Social science was once, even within the university setting, an activity that conceived of itself as defined

The Orders of Discourse

by a practical mission. Its cognitive goals were driven by its search for political authority or authority over politics. While the social sciences eventually became largely quintessential scholarly activities, shaped principally by the demands of university life, they retained, much like moral philosophy and the philosophy of science, the idiom of their origin. This prescriptive and evaluative style, however, became ever more anomalous and paradoxical in the context of the modern academy and in a situation where practical authority seemed to depend increasingly on a claim to objectivity and scientific purity. It is the implications of this development that constitute the focus of much of what I examine in the following chapters. Many political theorists foster an image of themselves as public moralists and of political theory as a kind of moralism. This attitude is in part the residue of the nineteenth-century origins of political theory and social science in general. It is also, however, more recently a product of taking seriously some of its own legitimating claims, namely that this academic enterprise is the heir to a tradition extending back to Plato and that it has special philosophical access to some transcendental ground of judgment.

Despite its historical peculiarities and vagaries, however, the situation of a field such as political theory is, in the end, generically defined by the issues and dilemmas that necessarily attend metapractices and by the historical context of social science. To understand the condition of political theory requires grasping the nature of these activities and the complex character of their relationship to their subject matter. As I will stress at several points, a metapractice does not lack a theoretical dimension, and this is one reason I avoid the designation "metatheoretical" when locating social science in the orders of discourse. Although exploring and charting the orders of discourse are not themselves what I take to be a theoretical endeavor, they at certain points presuppose a theoretical account of human activity, and one distinct purpose of this book is to further explicate such a theory. Yet on the whole, the following chapters are still the product of the metatheoretical voice even if the purpose is often to dissolve persistent metatheoretical issues and dilemmas.

It has sometimes been suggested that there is a fundamental paradox, or even a logical contradiction, involved in speaking metatheoretically while criticizing certain metatheoretical claims. This putative Munchausenian dilemma, this "it takes one to know one" type of criticism is, however, based on a conflation of type and token. There is no way to engage metatheoretical claims except in metatheoretical terms, and to argue, for example, "against epistemology" or against certain manifestations of it is not to condemn metatheory as such. It can, however, reasonably be asked, if my work deals with such issues and if much of my analysis is devoted to explicating the character of metapractices, what, precisely, is its own identity? My short answer is that much of it belongs to the category of what I will call third-order analysis. It is not politics, and it is not about politics. It is rather about the study of politics and about claims about the study of politics. I suppose that one might still reasonably ask whether this project succeeds in extricating itself from the very problems it identifies, whether it lives up to the standard of practicing what one preaches, and whether it exemplifies a "return to the ordinary." There are, I am sure, several dimensions of irony manifest in this book, but they are not of the Socratic variety.

My intellectual debts in fashioning this work are difficult to specify, since they are often primarily, although indirectly, to my critics—both those who have forced me to respond to specific critiques of my position and those who have challenged me in various informal forums. Much of what I am saying in this volume has been nuanced in light of my experience with how earlier versions of these claims have been understood and received. It is only through criticism and misunderstanding and consequent attempts at defense and clarification that they have evolved, and their further development requires that same dialectical context. In most instances, I am more interested in commencing a conversation about the issues discussed and the arguments advanced than achieving closure. My most explicit and systematic attempts at clarification and emendation have arisen in response to students in graduate seminars at the University at Albany and more recently at the University of California at Davis and the University of California at Irvine. The penultimate draft benefited from systematic and detailed criticisms by John Nelson and Christopher Robinson, as well as helpful comments by Peter Breiner.

During the course of writing this book, which was begun in 1992 and which has undergone several revisions, I have received and am grateful for support from a variety of sources. A fellowship from the National Endowment for the Humanities provided both the time to complete my work on the history of academic political theory and to formulate a portion of the initial draft of this volume. This was followed by a Fulbright lectureship in the Institute of Politics at the University of Copenhagen, which allowed me more directly to engage recent trends in Continental political and social theory and to present some of the basic arguments to an audience outside the United States. These opportunities were coupled with generous sabbatical and research leaves from the State University of New York at Albany. Although this book has evolved as a work of one piece, expressions of the principal themes have appeared in various places during the past few years. Most notably, abbreviated versions of chapters 3 and 4 have been published in *Political Theory* and the *Journal of Politics*, respectively.

Introduction

Philosophy is this tyrannical drive itself, the most spiritual will to power. . . .
—Friedrich Nietzsche

Philosophy is the discipline that involves creating *concepts.*
—Gilles Deleuze and Felix Guattari

A locus classicus of the issues that I am engaging is Michael Oakeshott's essay "On Understanding Human Conduct" (1975). Unlike, for example, H.-G. Gadamer (1975), Oakeshott was concerned not with a general account of human understanding but with the situation of one practice attempting to understand another and with the cognitive and practical relationships between them. The subtext of the essay revolved around the distinctiveness of the "doings" that constitute human conduct. Oakeshott depreciated the naturalistic pretensions of sociology and psychology, and he criticized their failure to approach instances of human conduct as intelligible actions and utterances informed by "reflective intelligence" and manifest in rules, beliefs, intentions, and choices. The study of human conduct, he argued, required a more appropriate "idiom of inquiry." Understanding "understanding" and understanding the general nature of what is understood must, however, be supplemented, Oakeshott insisted, by a consideration of what is involved in the process of actually going about the business of understanding a particular event or action. He stressed particularity and context and urged that the narratives of "historical understanding" represented the paradigm case of understanding human conduct (107).

Oakeshott argued that while free agency and an agent's understanding of self and the world are the ultimate source of the acts and utterances constituting the practices and artifacts of human conduct, individual performances are responses to particular circumstances and entail transactions with other agents. Conduct is *"inter homines."* Human actions are not merely subjective and a matter of personal enactment but rather involve self-disclosure through communication and the invocation of public conventions of language and "moral converse." Although concepts such as deliberation and motive are essential for describing conduct, they do not necessarily imply consciousness in the narrow sense of calculation or explicitly adhering to rules, since much conduct is a matter of habit, custom, and traditions. But despite Oakeshott's emphasis on the holistic and social character of human conduct, he insisted on the ontological priority of individual agents. Although Oakeshott did not deny that understanding might have practical purposes and effects, just as the Greek image of *theoria* arose from practical concerns, he wished to differentiate sharply, as he had in previous work (1962), between theory and practice and to penetrate what was involved in theorizing as itself a particular kind of activity that was distinct from the phenomena that were being theorized. Theorizing, he claimed, is an exploration that constitutes an unconditional critical engagement that goes beyond the familiar in order to achieve a deeper intelligibility.

While Oakeshott's analysis represents what by now has become a familiar genre of postpositivist claims regarding the nature of social scientific explanation, the exact character of that genre is elusive. Although he made a number of general claims about the nature of human conduct, he did not present any detailed theory of such phenomena. What he actually provided was an image or intimation of such a theory that in turn served to support his more immediate objective of giving an account of what was involved in understanding human conduct and differentiating between such understanding and the explanation of natural phenomena. Neither can his account be construed as either an approach or a method. His essay presented what can be best characterized as an epistemology rather than a theory and a methodology rather than a method. It was a metatheoretical exercise in the philosophy of social science and what, more generally, I will refer to as third-order analysis. Finally, while Oakeshott stressed the difference between understanding and what was understood and offered dicta on the relationship between them, he did not explore in any systematic manner the logical and historical character of, and relationships between, these realms.

Although Oakeshott insisted on the need to lay down some basic postulates regarding human conduct and to consider the nature and purposes of social inquiry, he, as well as most of his postpositivist contemporaries and successors (e.g., Winch 1958; Taylor 1971), were diverted from fully embracing this task. Their accounts of social scientific explanation were theoretically underdetermined. This was in part because their principal agenda was a defense of the cognitive autonomy of social inquiry. It was this agenda, as well as that of their naturalist and positivist opponents, that increasingly drew the philosophy and often the practice of social science into the orbit of epistemology and, consequently, led it in the direction of theoretical impoverishment. Epistemology became the theology of social science. And despite the underlying assumption, and claim, that the activity of understanding was not a "doing" or was at least a very different kind of "doing" than that involved in human conduct in general, these analyses of the nature of inquiry and of its cognitive and practical relationship to its object were limited in depth and scope. Whether, as in the case of Oakeshott, there were reservations about the utility and viability of practical interaction or whether, as in the case of Charles Taylor, a more rationalist interventionist image of social inquiry emerged or whether, as in the case of Peter Winch, there was skepticism about the cognitive priority of social science (1964) as well as its practical role, the claims were seldom fully explicated. Winch rejected both the "master-scientist" and "underlabourer" view of philosophy and, by implication, social science, leaving a fundamental ambiguity about the practical role of second-order discourses—an ambiguity that would be seized upon by critics such as Jürgen Habermas who wished to defend a stronger position with respect to both the cognitive authority and practical role of philosophy and social inquiry. But this ambiguity is hardly a recent concern. The history of the social sciences has largely been driven by the issue of how to vindicate its cognitive claims and translate them into a basis of practical authority.

Although my general sympathies are with these postpositivist accounts of the cognitive character of social science, one of my purposes is to remedy their deficiencies and to put theory and epistemology in their proper relationship. The first task is to provide a fuller discussion of the character of what I call metapractices or what Oakeshott and many others have referred to as theorizing. For reasons that I will develop more fully later, I wish to avoid the phrase "theory and practice." However one construes the nature of the "doings" that constitute human conduct, there are certain logical dimensions of metapractices that require elaboration. Second, if the "idiom" of inquiry and understanding is fundamentally predicated on the nature of the phenomena that constitute its object, then more than truncated theoretical claims about that object are necessary. Third, there is a need to analyze more fully the cognitive and practical relationship between inquiry and its object. Although I have doubts both about the possibility of establishing philosophical grounds for the cognitive superiority of metapractical claims and about the possibility and desirability of social science wielding practical authority, my principal concern is to examine critically some of the often extravagant assertions about these matters.

The social sciences, like all metapractices, stand in a distinctive discursive space. It would be too strong to say that they are parasitic, but as a species of human practice, they are at least commensal with respect to their relationship to their object of inquiry. They often wish to identify with it, but at the same time, they tend to exhibit an endemic, and sometimes paradoxical, wish to distinguish themselves from it. In both cases, however, there is an attempt to establish authority over it. It is not possible to conceive of the social sciences, or understand their history, apart from their perceived relationship to the practices they study. It might well be argued that the history of their actual relationship to those practices is more important, but to a large extent, the discourse of social science has been shaped less by its interaction with its object of inquiry than by its aspirations regarding such interaction. Although the basic fact of this dependence of metapractices on their object is, in many respects, too obvious to merit comment, the implications, both generic and specific, are indeed complex.

Finally, it is not only the relationship between metapractical inquiry and its object that is at issue but the relationship among metapractices—particularly that between philosophy and social science. When speaking of philosophy, I am talking about the formal institutionalized academic practice and not some general dimension of reflective thought. While social science's concern about its relationship to its subject matter might be expected to be, in a variety of ways, determinative with respect to both its self-image and the conduct of inquiry, the genesis and basis of its connection to the literature of formal philosophy is less transparent. The connections, however, are both historical and functional. The idea still persists that the origin of modern natural science is to be found in its differentiation from the intellectual mother-body of philosophy. As I will suggest later, this account, despite some element of truth, is often based on a retrospectively contrived preinstitutional image of philosophy and does not provide a very accurate representation of the relationship between philosophy as a distinct academic practice and the evolution of the natural sciences. The social sciences, however, were rooted to a significant degree in nineteenth-century philosophical discourses, and they have never cast off either the imprint of their birth or the latent authority of their parentage. But the attachment to philosophy has bases other than familial.

The social sciences share with much of philosophy a certain structural position in the metapractical universe and an attending set of problems. As metapractices, they are enmeshed in the dimensions of a problematic involving their cognitive and practical relationship to their object. Notwithstanding this parallel and functional similarity—and despite Winch's provocative and in many ways illuminating suggestion—social science is not simply "misbegotten" philosophy (1958). Winch was attempting to undermine social scientific pretensions of employing the methods of natural science, but viewing social science generically as philosophy in light of what amounts to its status as a metapractice obscures its distinctive character and history as well as its close relationship to philosophy. Philosophical discourse has often had little, or at least an oblique, impact on other activities—including those that have constituted its subject matter.

Neither common sense nor natural science, for example, appears to be very directly beholden to philosophical dicta. Thus it is important to explain the philosophical enchantment that has characterized social science and more specialized fields such as political theory.

Social science has been drawn to philosophy in part because the two share dilemmas common to metapractices and because philosophy has had a great deal to say about these matters, but social science has also characteristically turned to philosophy for validation. What social science has traditionally sought from philosophy has been cognitive identity and authority, and it has also sought practical significance by appropriating arguments from philosophy concerning the ground of both empirical and normative judgment. This search has, however, carried a price. Because social science has in this manner, so often unreflectively, articled itself to philosophy, it has surrendered much of its intellectual autonomy, and the fate of various philosophical doctrines has often become the fate of social science. While appearing robust, social science has sometimes suddenly found its identity, like that of Dorian Gray, bound to an obsolete and degenerating image. This was the situation with its attachment to positivism, but it is no less the case with more recent examples of philosophical indenture. As various dimensions of philosophy have been transfigured, social science and political theory have found themselves aged and infirm. There is, in principle, nothing wrong with seeking aid and comfort from philosophy. One can, for example, hardly denigrate broadening the conceptual horizons of social science. But these attachments are, nevertheless, in several respects *liaisons dangereuses*. The problem is in part relational. Social scientists have, for example, not only tended to accept unreflectively the authority of philosophical claims but often not sorted out the differences between such things as methodology, that is, philosophical accounts of scientific procedure, and method, that is, the application of procedures. But the problem is also one of content.

Philosophy as an academic field is hardly of one piece, and in the following chapters, I draw upon it as well as criticize it. I wish, however, to express and engender a fundamental skepticism about some of the elements of the project, if it can be viewed at all generically, of modern philosophy. For more than twenty-five years, before the popularity of various forms of antifoundationalism (e.g., Rorty 1979) and the postmodernist depreciation of "metanarratives" (Lyotard 1984), I have maintained doubts about the form and content of what Stanley Cavell (1979) has called the "epistemological quest" and the "transcendental illusion." The full implications of Wittgenstein's critique have not, despite the work of Thomas Kuhn, Cavell, Rorty, and others, yet been manifest in either philosophy itself or in the fields that have drawn upon it for support. Although my primary concern is to put into relief the problem of what social scientists and political theorists are doing when they call upon philosophy for assistance or attach themselves to the career of various doctrines, I also want to achieve a little consciousness-raising with respect to what much of philosophy is still all about. We need not go as far as Paul Feyerabend, who at the end of his life suggested that "there are now two types of tumors to be removed—philosophy of science and general philosophy (ethics, epistemology, etc.)," but we might take seriously his claim that there are "two areas of human activity that could survive without them— science and common sense" (1995:142).

Even though various elements of postpositivism and postmodernism constitute a challenge to traditional epistemology and transcendentalism, some of the motives and motifs of philosophy have remained remarkably persistent. Although the work of Michel Foucault, for example, may represent a challenge to the content of much of traditional philosophy, it, like much of poststructuralism, is hardly free of the imperialistic world-historical spirit that has animated the enterprise. While many who might be thought of as "constructivists" see various first-order discourses as creating order in the world, they tend to reserve for philosophy, and second-order intellectuals in general, a special place. The attitude may not be always baldly articulated, but it is still immanent in much of the literature of contemporary philosophy, especially in Europe. Gilles Deleuze and Felix Guattari, for example, claim that "the exclusive right of concept creation secures a foundation for philosophy" and that "the concept's baptism calls for a specifically philosophical *taste*," unlike "other modes of ideation that, like scientific thought, do not have to pass through concepts" (1994:5–8).

Many social theorists who embrace claims associated with contemporary critics of traditional philosophy have not managed to extricate themselves from the more general problems revolving around the status of philosophy and the relationship between philosophy and social science as well as around the character of metapractices as a whole. There has been a tendency simply to substitute one set of philosophical authorities for another. Whatever might be said in defense of the intrinsic worth of various philosophical projects, my principal concerns revolve around the impact of philosophy on social science and political theory. Social scientists tend uncritically to approach and adopt philosophical arguments about such things as normative judgment and scientific explanation. This problem is exacerbated by the fact that philosophical issues are frequently internally generated and parochially defined as well as by the fact that philosophers seldom adequately recognize the impact of their formulations on other fields.

Sometimes there is a problem of truth in advertising. Philosophy often seems to promise more than it can deliver when it speaks abstractly about matters of truth, right, and meaning. Yet philosophers are often not actually attempting to sell the commodities that social scientists have acquired at the epistemological emporium. While the philosophy of natural science has, for example, exercised negligible direct and consistent influence on the practices of natural science, its accounts of the logic and epistemology of scientific explanation have continuously been a source of models, and contrast-models, for the social sciences as the latter have gone about the business of constructing and underwriting their identities. And at certain points, dependence on these accounts has, as in the case of political science, significantly shaped the actual conduct of inquiry. Similarly, ethics and other normative dimensions of philosophy have been mined for criteria of prescriptive and evaluative claims. While there is no reason to condemn intercourse with philosophy, caution should be exercised by the monogamous as well as the promiscuous.

Although philosophical seduction has created a range of specific difficulties, some of the most prominent of which I explore in the following chapters, the most basic problem is the manner in which it has produced an inverted relationship between theory and epistemology. Whereas epistemology properly construed is, I will maintain, a post hoc enterprise contingent on substantive theory and scientific practice, political and social theorists have attempted to ground social science and social scientific explanation and judgment on a priori epistemological foundations. And often these metatheories have been both borrowed on dubious grounds and problematically related to their subject matter. The issue, however, is not so much one of assigning blame as explaining the dilemmas that have been generated. There are, for example, few who would today defend the original version of the hypothetico-deductive model of scientific explanation as either a satisfactory philosophical account of the logic of science or as an appropriate object of emulation for social science. But the problem represented in this well-known case of social science's allegiance to a philosophical doctrine is deeper than the content of this particular formulation. Carl Hempel (1965), for example, probably the most important propagator of the "covering-law" model, quite explicitly stated that his account of scientific explanation was neither a reconstruction of nor a guide to actual scientific practice. Yet this was generally how such analyses were interpreted by social scientists. But while social scientists might be faulted for not more carefully examining this model and its intellectual context, Hempel not only largely spoke in descriptive and normative terms but pressed the thesis of the unity and hierarchy of science.

In such cases, there is, first, the problem of the intrinsic, that is, philosophical, validity of the claims to which social scientists are attracted but often do not confront. Second, there is the problem of the extent to which a philosophical claim about practical judgment in science or other spheres relates descriptively to that realm of judgment. Third, there is the problem of the extent to which such a philosophical account can, in principle, either provide criteria of judgment or be translated into applicable procedures of decision. But the most significant problem is, once again, the implications for substantive theory in social science. What has suffered is not only the autonomy of social science but concrete and detailed arguments about the nature of social phenomena and social reality. These have been either neglected or uncritically accepted and driven underground as metatheoretical claims about social scientific knowledge, pursued as part of a search for cognitive and practical potency, have occupied the space.

Chapter 1 presents what might be called a taxonomy and natural history of metapractices and metadiscourses that, in turn, frame the discussion of more specific issues in the succeeding chapters. Since there is no distinct academic conversation in which this analysis intervenes, the discussion admittedly presents a challenge to both myself and the reader that exceeds even the most dense portions of the subsequent chapters. Although I offer a general analytical examination of metapractices and their relationship to their subject matter, the principal focus is on second-order practices such as philosophy and social science and their cognitive and practical relationship to first-order practices such as science and politics. One purpose of chapter 1 is to stress that there is no philosophical or metapractical answer to the practical problem of what has traditionally been called the relationship between theory and practice. Another principal argument advanced in this chapter is that there is a need to reverse the commonly accepted contrast between natural and social science, which has been based on the assumption that natural, as opposed to social, objects or facts are in some manner more objectively given and discursively independent. This assumption has transcended the transition from positivism to postpositivism and is deeply implicated in the failure of social science to advance theoretically. Maybe the most contentious dimension of this chapter, particularly in light of persistent attempts to ontologize politics and transform *political* into a noun, involves an argument about the nature of theory and about why there cannot be a *theory* of politics. Both of these issues are explored further in succeeding chapters, but the essence of the claim is simply that politics is a particular historical conventional configuration that does not admit to independent theoretical treatment. My concern is neither to devalue politics nor to deny its autonomy but rather to clarify its theoretical and epistemological status.

Since much of my discussion involves valorizing what I legislate as "theory," chapter 2 points to the deficiency of theory in various dimensions of social scientific practice such as that represented in social choice analysis and the new "institutionalism." The principal content of this chapter, however, is devoted to an elaboration of the basic theses composing what I call the *theory of conventional objects*. This in turn entails or amounts to a theory of language and action as well as texts, institutions, and other artifacts. It is what is often called a theory of social reality, but the concept of social as I use it here is employed with some reservation as a generic reference to the phenomena of human interaction. It does not imply, for example, the priority of social over political phenomena. Although I have, over a period of years, advanced versions of this theory, my concern here is to present a yet more developed form and at the same time to deal further with the implications of this theory for both social scientific inquiry and certain perennial issues in the philosophy of social science. Although much of the discussion in this chapter employs a language derived from analyses of these matters in the literature of both philosophy and social science, my argument requires to some extent, as in the case of chapter 1, forging an idiom that does not always accord with standard usage.

In the late 1960s and early 1970s, I began to develop what at that time I called a "phenomenology" of action (1968b, 1973). This originally was an intervention in the debate about behavioralism in political science that centered around the discipline's commitment to emulating what it believed to be the methods of natural science. My challenge to the dominant positivist account of social scientific explanation was influenced by a range of postpositivist arguments about the nature of social scientific inquiry, particularly those of Winch and Alfred Schutz as well as Max Weber's discussion of understanding meaningful action. The specific argument, however, was eventually at its core largely based on an extrapolation and emendation of J. L. Austin's analysis of speech acts and performative utterance (1962), certain aspects of Wittgenstein's account of linguistic meaning and intention, and more recent philosophical claims about action and speech such as those advanced by John Searle. It is probably quite correct to say that Austin, no more than Wittgenstein, "set forth, or even held at all, anything like a general *theory* of action" (Forguson 1969:128), but his formulation of the structure of speech acts seemed to me to offer a basis for solutions to some of the most difficult issues attending social scientific inquiry.

I cannot, outside the specific literature of political science and political theory, claim any particular originality for a general position that included the propositions that there is a fundamental logical and epistemological difference between the modes of inquiry characteristic of natural and social science; that there is a parallel between understanding action and understanding speech; that much of social inquiry is necessarily interpretive or hermeneutical in character; and that there is a conceptual convergence between the English analytical and Continental philosophical traditions with respect to implications for the philosophy of social science (e.g., Winch 1958; Skinner 1969, 1970, 1971; Taylor 1970a, 1970b, 1971; Ricoeur 1971; Bernstein 1976; Giddens 1976, 1977; Dallmayr and McCarthy 1977; Rabinow and Sullivan 1979). I did, however, very early on, begin to diverge in significant ways from some of the basic concerns and assumptions represented in much of this literature, and that divergence constitutes a central theme in this book. My quarrel with many of the individuals with whom I shared this general postpositivist orientation revolved around the substance of certain theoretical claims, but more generally, I was convinced that many of these arguments, to the extent that they were theoretical, were severely undernourished and often enunciated in the context of an epistemological position to which the theoretical claims were subservient or even instrumental. While there were intimations of a *theory* of action, the arguments were primarily about the *understanding* or *explanation* of action and/or about the *uses* of social science.

In a "prolegomena" (Gunnell 1979b) to a revision and elaboration of my theoretical argument, I continued to stress, as I had at greater length earlier (Gunnell 1973, 1975), the inhibitions to theorizing induced by social science's attachment to doctrines in the philosophy of science and particularly the commitment to the positivist instrumentalist account of theory and of the relationship between theory and fact. I also criticized the more general propensity of social theorists to embrace eclectically a variety of epistemological and transcendental claims rather than directly confronting concrete issues in the theory of human action. I subsequently offered a further and more detailed version of my substantive theory of action that was less tied to the specifics of Austin's formulation (Gunnell 1981). Although Habermas had been working in this area (e.g., 1970) and subsequently did explicitly embrace elements of the theory of performative speech in developing his widely discussed argument about communicative action (1984), this argument turned out, I claimed (Gunnell 1986a), to be yet another case of the inversion of theory and epistemology. Selective theoretical appropriation served to underwrite images of the nature and purpose of social inquiry and to support claims about the universal foundations of practical judgment. There was little elaboration or defense of the particular claims about the phenomena of action, and there was little historically situated consideration of the issue of the relationship between social science and politics. It is significant that in the extensive scholarly commentary that has followed in the wake of Habermas's work, there has been almost no attention to the specific, and often philosophically contentious, elements of his theory of action. This lack is a clear indication on the part of both Habermas and commentators on his argument that the substantive theoretical issues were not, and have not been, the primary concern.

By the mid-1980s, it seemed evident to me that there were limits to the common analogy between speech and action, that is, to attempts to move from a theory of speech to a more general account of human action—as well as to an account of artifacts such as institutions and texts—or to view speech as a form of action. It also seemed to me that conceptions of the relationship of speech and action to thought and other mental predicates had become increasingly anomalous. I concluded that speech, action, and thought should be conceived as modes of conventions (Gunnell 1986a). My account of what I now referred to as "conventional objects" was, however, still extremely compressed and designed primarily to demonstrate how epistemological problems were theoretically derivative and admitted only to theoretical solutions and how many of the specific perennial issues in social science and the philosophy of social science, such as that of the relationship between fact and value, could be theoretically resolved. Claims about the nature of scientific explanation are, I maintained, the ghosts of old theories, and most epistemological issues are shades of contending theories.

During the next decade, I continued to follow the development of the theory of action in the literature of philosophy and attending issues in the philosophies of language and mind, and I became increasingly dissatisfied with the direction of the discussion. This led me to the work of the philosopher Donald Davidson, who maybe more than any other single individual has influenced the contemporary conversation and has contributed to the persistence, or resurrection, albeit in new form, of the idea that actions are behavioral events initiated by prior mental states. My theory of conventional objects posits an autonomous ontology of conventions that is grounded neither in mentalities nor in some dimension of what Searle, Taylor, and others refer to as the "brute facts" of behavior. Mind, persons, social wholes, and practices are among the things that might, and have been, advanced as the basis of a social ontology or theory, but I am pursuing the claim that conventions must be construed as the essence of social reality. Although conventions are often viewed as ephemeral, I pursue an argument that despite its oxymoronic overtones I label *conventional realism*. The exposition of my theory in chapter 2 remains relatively brief if compared with the vast and diverse literature devoted to theories of action, speech, and mind. Since I assume that few social scientists have the interest and patience to find their way through this literature, my goal has been to cut through the complexities of much of this material, isolate certain

basic and relevant issues, and enunciate as cleanly and compactly as possible some constitutive theoretical principles. While it may be futile to ask
social scientists to become deeply involved with specific issues in the theory
of action, it is often forgotten that some very basic theoretical assumptions about such matters as the nature of ideas and their relationship to
human behavior are deeply embedded in the practice of social science as
well as in claims about the uses of social science. Although much of this
chapter is devoted to quite technical issues dealing with such matters as
the individuation of action, I offer a further elaboration of my argument
about why there cannot be a *theory* of politics and an argument about why
many approaches to social scientific inquiry are not truly theoretical.

One of the concerns, and fears, shared by philosophy, social science,
and other second-order metapractices has been the issue of relativism.
My argument in chapter 3 is that this issue, in its various intellectual manifestations, is a metatheoretical displacement of the practical problem of
the relationship between metapractices and their subject matter. Discussions of relativism point up the problems of both the relationship of
metapractices to their object and the relationship of social science to philosophy. The underlying issue is not, as it is usually professed to be, the
status of truth and objectivity in first-order activities such as politics and
science but rather the cognitive, and practical, authority of metapractical
claims. Relativism, as imaged in the language of philosophy, has no real
practical counterpart. Relativism is a defining problematic of contemporary philosophy, but this dis-ease admits of no authentic philosophical
solution and only drives metapractices in the direction of foundationalist
epistemologies. In this chapter, I return again to Davidson, since his work
has been significantly implicated in recent attempts, in both philosophy
and social science, to find an answer to the perceived problem of relativism. His work and its reception also exemplifies some of the general problems in the relationship between social science and philosophy as well as
in the philosophical enterprise itself. The uses of Davidson's work in certain dimensions of social theory is yet another example of how a complex
philosophical corpus has been unreflectively and selectively, and often in-
sensitively, simplified and employed. His arguments, which seem to aim at
reassuring us about the existence and accessibility of the external world,
are also a primary example of a genre that, while fitting nicely into the
internal discursive universe of professional philosophy, would seem from
a more distant perspective to require some sort of explanation and justification.

The issue of relativism is again encountered in chapter 4, which both
explores one paradigm case of the relationship between a metapractice
and its object and examines one crucial instance of the relationship

between metapractices. My purpose in this chapter is in part to hold the philosophy of science up as an object to be scrutinized, and this requires a degree of summarization of the literature that some readers familiar with these issues may find redundant. The relationship between the philosophy of science and natural science, however, reveals a great deal about the general character and evolution of metapractices, and the reliance of social science on the philosophy of science exemplifies the attachment of social science to epistemological doctrines and the consequent neglect of theory. In mainstream political science, as with other social sciences, this attachment was manifest in the adoption and deployment of theoretical instrumentalism and the deductive model of scientific explanation, which were derived from logical positivism and logical empiricism. This cognitive image of theory, as I have insisted in other works (1975, 1986a, 1997), has exercised a unique hold on the assumptions and practices of social science. The general tendency to assume an identity between the practice of natural science and philosophical accounts of scientific explanation has hardly, however, been confined to those committed to adopting what they construed, under the influence of positivism, as the logic and epistemology of explanation in natural science. Critical Theory, for example, in its persistent attack on scientific rationality has almost without exception failed to distinguish between philosophical images of science and the actual practice of natural science (e.g., Adorno et al. 1976).

During the revolution in the philosophy of science precipitated by Kuhn (1962) and others during the 1960s, the philosophical critique of logical positivism spilled over into social scientific doubts about the image of scientific explanation derived from what had become the orthodox, or "received," view in the philosophy of science. The problem, however, was that rather than undertaking a general reconsideration of the relationship between philosophy and social science, dissidents tended to embrace new philosophical images of scientific inquiry and postpositivist accounts of the nature of social scientific understanding and interpretation. While debates between positivist and postpositivist epistemological and methodological positions dominated the discourse of social science for some time, both internal changes in these disciplines and developments in the philosophy of science tended to lead to a dissipation of the discussion. They also led, however, to a neglect or repression of some of the fundamental problems manifest in those debates. What I explore in this chapter is the manner in which social science has continued, for a variety of reasons, to turn to the philosophy of science. The impetus springs from concerns about finding unity in the contemporary, and increasingly plural and specialized, universe of social inquiry and about providing epistemological backing for the idea of critical theory and dealing with the issue of relativism in matters of both empirical and normative judgment. The principal focus in the philosophy of science today is, arguably, the meaning and validity of various accounts of realism. The attempts of political and social theory to appropriate versions of this philosophy indicate that the same basic problems of the relationship between philosophy and social science are still very much with us.

There is no area in which the issue of relativism and the contest of epistemologies has been so evident as in debates about the nature of textual and historical interpretation. And there is no area in which the inversion of theory and epistemology is more pronounced. What makes the issue of interpretation particularly salient is that the concept of interpretation has become a metaphor for postpositivist claims about the nature of social scientific inquiry, but this has once again led social science to seek philosophical answers. Chapter 5 focuses on the manner in which various discussions of, and arguments about, the nature of interpretation have been detached from a theoretical ground. My argument is that the concept of interpretation, like explanation, gains substantive meaning only within a theoretical context and that my theory of conventional objects provides one such context. One purpose of this chapter is to suggest how the theory of conventional objects has implications for thinking about a particular area of inquiry, in this case textual and historical interpretation, but if social science is conceived generally as an interpretive endeavor, the implications are more far reaching.

One theme in chapter 5 involves what I refer to as the autonomy of the text, which in turn is closely related to my analysis of metapractices. This claim is not at all what someone such as H.-G. Gadamer or others such as Stanley Fish, who have been accused of wishing to banish the author, have in mind. Neither is it an attempt to defend a variation of the claim that texts possess some intrinsic meaning that is rooted in an author's mental intention. It is instead an attempt to further elaborate my argument in chapter 2 about the extent to which texts and other conventional artifacts have a certain dimension of giveness that is obscured by the contemporary emphasis on contextual explanation as well as by often opposing arguments about textual meaning as a function of interpretation. While I do not wish to suggest that contextual analysis is not relevant, the concept of context in many contemporary arguments tends to lack coherency, and while there is an obvious sense in which meaning is a creation of interpretation, there are definite limits to such a proposition.

Although I have considerable sympathy with some of the principal claims and products of the "new historicism" in political theory represented in the work of individuals such as Quentin Skinner and J. G. A. Pocock, as well as allied notions of social science as an interpretive mode of inquiry,

I also have some distinct disagreements with both the theoretical and prag-matic dimensions of that program and its scholarly issue. As in the case of others who have championed the idea of interpretive inquiry and have focused on linguistic meaning and analogies between language and social phenomena in general, the claims about historical understanding have been theoretically underdetermined, and there has been considerable confu-sion about the relationship between theories and methods.

My critique of the "myth of the tradition" (1979a, 1986a), a myth that dominated the study of the history of political theory for so many years, closely paralleled the criticisms contained in arguments by individuals such as Pocock and Skinner about the need for a more truly historical approach to the study of political thought. Pocock (1980), however, found it diffi-cult to understand how I could criticize past scholarship and yet quarrel with his historiographical claims. And Skinner, in his reply to his critics, noted that I "do not succeed in characterizing [his] views at all accurately" and that Pocock's discussion of my work was "surprisingly respectful" (1988:326). Since Skinner did not specify, or even indicate, how I had failed in my account of his work, reiterating and clarifying some of the central points of my disagreement seems in order. I take the opportunity to ex-plain more fully my sympathies with his position but also to contest his suggestion that my opposing claims make me, in his words, an "epistemo-logical anarchist," an advocate of "the complete separation of theory and practice in interpretation," and a defender of the view that an author's meaning and intention are both unavailable and irrelevant (232–33, 272–73, 281). It is precisely such epistemological Manichaeanism that obstructs dialogue.

I have already elaborated my theoretical and historiographical differ-ences with Skinner and with Pocock and other historians at some length (Gunnell 1979a, 1980, 1982, 1986b, 1986c, 1993). In this chapter I focus, for exemplary purposes, on Skinner's claims about historicity and on E. D. Hirsch's argument about interpretation as the recovery of an author's in-tentions as well as scrutinize what might seem to be the contrary argu-ments of individuals such as Gadamer, Paul Ricoeur, and Jacques Derrida. My purpose, however, is not simply to recount once more these now fa-miliar claims about the nature of interpretation or to provide yet another comparative overview but rather to isolate and identify problems that are characteristic of this genre, whatever the particular conception of inter-pretation that is defended. The individuals discussed are chosen because their work is representative of certain types of argument, because they have often been the subject of discussion within social science and the philosophy of social science, and because a confrontation with their work provides a medium for presenting my own argument about these matters.

My principal conclusion is that all of these positions amount largely to metatheoretical claims about the nature of textual and historical understanding and that the theoretical issues have once again been repressed. Although there are distinctly theoretical dimensions in, for example, Skinner's work, his critics, as in the case of Habermas, have not focused on this dimension. This neglect is, I suggest, in part because the issue of the theoretical status of texts is less the primary concern than a defense of a particular epistemology, method of interpretation, and mode of historical practice.

The concluding chapter 6 serves, in part, a summary function and returns to the theme that ultimately the so-called theory/practice problem is, indeed, itself a practical rather than an epistemological problem and that it must be historically situated. Part of my purpose in this chapter is to explore further the problematical relationship between philosophy and social science, but my principal concern is to examine more specifically the contemporary relationship between public and academic discourse and what it means, or could mean, for social science to "speak politically." In the case of the United States, the issue really is a function of the relationship between the university and politics. Although the argument is in no way a rejection of a political role for social science, it is a criticism of some of the pretensions of academic moralism and of the assumption that academic discourse is necessarily in some way a form of political action. I also suggest that there may be an inherent tension between a commitment to democratic values, on the one hand, and the search for metapractical authority, on the other.

Metapractices

The theorist of conduct is not, as such, a "doer," and the theoretical
understanding of conduct cannot itself be theorized in terms of doing.
—Michael Oakeshott

Distinguishing and characterizing the orders of discourse involves, initially, a conceptual analysis that is a prolegomenon to an examination of existential or historical relationships such as those among philosophy, social science, and politics. The following chapters deal with such relationships and consider more closely and systematically what is involved in particular cases. In this chapter I am concerned with sorting and clarifying the *kinds*, or classes, of things that I refer to as practices and discourses, that is, their generic, logical, or necessary character and relations rather than their pragmatic dimensions, and with pointing to some of the basic implications. The divisions within the orders of discourse, that is, first, second, and third, are neither ideal typifications nor analytical constructs. Although they may share some of the attributes and uses of such concepts, they represent natural realms of discursivity and a grammar of conventional practices. It may seem paradoxical to designate them as "natural," since they are conventional, but they are natural in the same sense that we speak about natural languages. The orders of discourse may be construed, in some respects, as equivalent to what Wittgenstein referred to as "forms of life." As I will make clear later, my purpose is not to elaborate a theory of human practice. What I am undertaking is more like an exercise in descriptive natural history or taxonomy. Practices and discourses are species of conventional objects and not per se the subject of theory. An account of conventionality is, however, a theoretical undertaking and the subject of the next chapter.

I

When speaking of *practices,* I am talking about relatively distinct conventionally determinate, and often disciplinized and professionalized, activities such as philosophy, the natural sciences, the social sciences, religion, and politics. There are many other concepts represented by the term *practice*—such as the practice of paying one's bills on time—that do not conform to my usage. *Practice* can also be employed as an analytical category (for example, I will sometimes refer to the sciences as practices of knowledge), but my primary reference is to historically discrete families of human activity. Although there is a considerable difference between, for example, a highly formalized practice such as political science and the more diverse and amorphous realm that we call politics, they both fall within the species of practices. Where they differ, essentially, is with respect to the logical order of discourse to which they belong. By referring to practices as conventional, I am not suggesting either that they are necessarily socially acceptable or that they are not innovative. Although a theory of convention is ultimately crucial in understanding practices, I am at this point simply maintaining that practices are historical, socially constructed, and discursive in character. The concept of discursive today carries a great deal of metatheoretical baggage often associated with poststructuralism and postmodernism, so it is necessary to be clear about what is involved in my application of the term. This issue will be discussed in chapter 2, but for the moment I am simply stressing the linguistic, or, more broadly, symbolic, character of human practices. By speaking of practices as determinate, I am indicating that despite their conventionality and, consequently, intrinsic capacity for change, they possess a certain self-constituted as well as socially acknowledged identity. To say that they are determinate does not imply that in specific cases the boundaries are impermeable or fixed or that their character and status are, from either an internal or external perspective, uncontentious. It is only to say that at particular times and places there is an explicit or tacit recognition of their identity and difference. Although it may be possible to give historical examples of how practices come into existence or are invented and how they are transformed and pass away or even to isolate some typical patterns regarding such matters, as in the case of Thomas Kuhn's analysis of the natural sciences, there is little that can be said in this regard that is definitive.

Although practices characteristically represent and are represented by certain orders of discourse, *discourses* and practice are not identical even though I will at times use the concepts interchangeably. As concepts, practice and discourse do not have the same logical extension. When we use the phrase "orders of discourse," *discourse* is a more generic term than practice, but certain practices are often identified with or subsume particular discourses, or what might be called *discursive regimes*. A particular practice, such as one of the social sciences, often contains more than one level or order of discourse, while a certain mode of discourse may not be especially associated with any distinct practice. There were, for example, discourses on nature before there were differentiated practices of natural science, and there were discourses about politics that antedated the practice represented in the discipline and profession of political science. Practices are distinguished from discourses primarily by the acquisition of institutional form. There are two fundamental types of discourses and practices—*first-order* and *meta*.

First-order practices (and discourses) are those modes of activity that are primordial and "given" in that their various forms and historical manifestations represent functionally necessary elements of human activity. Among first-order discourses can be counted what is loosely construed as the diffuse and variegated yet amalgamated and sedimented world of common sense or everyday life, which at various times and places constitutes that somewhat amorphous image of reality that Wilfrid Sellars has called the "manifest image" (1963). But distinct and differentiated first-order practices include the more circumscribed realms of myth, metaphysics, natural science, religion, music, art, and politics. What exact forms and varieties exist in historical time and space, the manner in which they are identified, how they relate to one another, and the extent to which they overlap and interpenetrate are historically and culturally variable. While it is probably correct to say that art, for example, did not emerge as a differentiated human practice until the Hellenic period in Western civilization, it would be difficult to imagine a society lacking the functional equivalent of what we today categorize as art.

The property of giveness, like that of determinacy does not signify that first-order discourses are transconventional but rather that they are unpredicated. They are not given in the sense of being unalterable, but they do not, despite what may be deemed the holistic character of society, gain their primary identity in terms of their relationship to and dependency on another practice. All human practices are given in that they are encountered, both by participants and observers, as preconstituted conventional discursive configurations, but what most fundamentally distinguishes first-order practices is that they not only define and conceptually and practically constitute themselves, reflectively or unreflectively, but in varying ways and degrees construct and project an image of the external world in which they are situated. Such practices are the medium through which the "world" is defined. It is such a construction, which I will later identify as *theory*, that involves the primary ontological claims and assumptions, tacit or explicit, that define a universe of phenomena, constitute a vision of reality, and create a domain of facticity.

This is not to say, however, that theory is the exclusive province of first-order discourse but rather that first-order theories are, in a special manner, constitutive of what is theorized. The relationship between a first-order practice of knowledge and its object, such as in the case of natural science and natural phenomena, is in many respects like that of the relationship between artists and their paintings. We might say that each produces a representation of the world, but what we take as that portion of the world that is *re-presented,* if other than the rendition presented in the language of art or science, is necessarily a construction of some other first-order discourse such as common sense. What distinguishes first order theories is that the "world" that is projected is an internally generated discursive artifact with no other criteria of existence and character. While it is possible for someone to embrace the philosophical position that first-order discourses such as those of natural science presuppose the existence of a reality external to them, such a claim, as I will argue more fully at a later point, has little import for understanding such practices, since that "world" is a conceptual construction of natural science. The "world" is only accessible through and articulated in first-order discourses. But to claim, from the perspective of philosophy, that the "world" does not exist apart from such constructions is also not to say anything of much substance.

First-order discourses are characterized by existence claims and other types of judgment that are not normally or logically open to metatheoretical arbitration even though those who study, address, and talk about such claims may seek, either by their actions or in principle, to arrogate to themselves the authority to make such judgments. The claims of first-order practices are, in effect, irreducible despite the attempt of some philosophers to privilege such accounts as the scientific image of the world or, on the contrary, the "natural" or commonsense vision. This is why there is, often overtly and always implicitly, tension between different spheres of first-order claims—such as in the case of science and religion—as well as between conflicting claims within a first-order practice. A particular first-order image, of itself or the world, might be disputed either internally or, by other first-order claims, externally, but such an image represents an incommensurable conceptual or symbolic hegemony and style that at any particular time and place is crucial to the identity of the practice.

Metapractices represent an order of discourse, often practices of knowledge such as philosophy and the social sciences that gain their primary identity in terms of the fact that they have another conventional activity as their subject matter. They are essentially *supervenient,* since they are predicated on the existence of other practices and discourses and since they are not, in a primary sense or the typical course of events, constitutive of their object. But they could also be understood as subservient both in the conventional sense of that term and in the sense that, in various ways and degrees, they may reflect what is happening in the world of their subject matter. Metapractices, however, are not necessary elements in human society no matter how salutary one may consider their existence to be. It might be difficult to find societies in which they are absent, but such a situation is not inconceivable. No matter how much metapractitioners may believe that their activities are essential for the salvation of their subject matter, metapractices are contingent. Although it would be quite easy to imagine politics without political science, it would be difficult, except possibly in a Borges novel, to imagine, for example, political philosophy or political science without the existence of the practice of politics as a conventionally distinct and recognized activity. One might argue that this was the irony, and fate, of Aristotle's treatise, that is, to have been formulated after the effective demise of the *polis,* and as I will suggest later, there are certainly examples of metapractices that have a tenuous relationship to their purported object; but the very idea of a metapractice presumes the existence and relative autonomy of its object. Their character is, consequently, in large measure a function of their logical and pragmatic relationship to their object of inquiry.

This relationship has often, and traditionally, been referred to as that of theory and practice, but this typology is often both prejudicial and rhetorically motivated. It suggests, first, either that a metapractice possesses some sort of inherent authority over its object or that it can make a claim to some form of identity with it. Second, it implies that practice is either devoid of theory or deficient and that theory is the province of another activity. Although my principal concern is to explore the general nature of metapractices and the problematics that surround them, the analysis moves in the direction of challenging the belief that metapractices have any intrinsically privileged status. My argument is not that metapractices, as a matter of principle, should not have or at times have not had such a status but only that there is no a priori basis for such status. Much of metapractical discourse, however, has been devoted to attempting to demonstrate that there is some such logical or epistemological ground for their claim to authority.

Since metadiscourses are simply those that are defined by the fact that they speak about other discourses, this realm is in principle infinite, like a hall of mirrors. Every set of claims within a practice or discourse allows, in principle, another set of claims *about* it. Metapractices, however, tend to be self-limiting even in a period of extreme disciplinary differentiation and specialization. Beyond noting that metapractices are contingent and supervenient and indicating certain general logical and historical implications, there is a limit to what can be said conceptually about them. We may generalize to some degree from historical instances about their character, but it is a mistake to reify such generalizations and take them to be essential features.

My principal focus is on *second-order* practices, whose object is a first-

order activity and which include the social sciences and much of philosophy. *Third-order* types are those that have another metapractice as their
object, and they include, for example, the philosophy of social science.
And the perspective in this chapter can be construed as belonging to the
fourth order. What is often confusing is the fact that while practices such as
the philosophy and history of natural science may have a certain functional and professional similarity to the philosophy and history of social
science, and while there may be intellectual connections between them,
they belong to different logical orders of discourse, that is, respectively,
second-order and third-order, and thus they are fundamentally different
in certain crucial respects.

I would emphasize that my distinctions between first-order practices
and metapractices and between types of metapractices do not imply any
hierarchy or prescriptive or evaluative assumptions. I might suggest various models or graphic representations of this scheme, but the partiality of
each would in some manner distort the basic conception. If we think of
practices in terms of vertically stacked levels, we might be inclined to put
first-order practices at the bottom to illustrate one dimension of the relationship, but the image could easily be reversed or cast in the form of a
network. Even though I have argued that at least in principle we could live
without metapractices, this argument does not entail the claim that we
would live better. A certain temporal and logical priority is, however, involved in this numerical order. The first-order practice of natural science,
for example, preceded the philosophy of natural science, and social science was preceded historically by the social practices that it studies. Although it may be possible to quibble with such general propositions, the
point is that second-order practices are identified, in terms of logic, function, and self-understanding, by the fact that in various ways they speak
about and sometimes *to* first-order activities. While first-order practices
conceivably can and sometimes do address second-order ones, this is not
a defining characteristic, even though in certain historical instances it may
be an important practical dimension of the relationship. While, for example, the philosophy of natural science has seldom been systematically
examined or practically engaged by natural scientists, political science has
sometimes been an object of political scrutiny (Gunnell 1993).

Among second-order practices are the social sciences, history, and certain aspects of philosophy (the philosophy of science, the philosophy of
religion, ethics, etc.), but they also include literary criticism, sportscasting,
and a variety of other enterprises. To say that second-order discourses are
metadiscourses is not to say that they are necessarily metatheoretical
except in the sense that they address practices that are theoretically
constituted. Second-order practices have, at least in principle, a theoretical

attitude toward, and conception of, their object. But while a first-order activity such as natural science gains its primary identity in terms of its theoretical constitution of its object, the identity of a second-order practice is usually more a function of its metapractical posture and character, that is, its relationship to its subject matter, than its particular theoretical construal of that subject matter. There may be a close connection between second-order theory and certain dimensions of its subject matter in that, for example, one might reasonably expect that the theoretical claims of political science have been influenced by the discipline's political context. It would, however, add little to our understanding of a first-order practice, such as natural science, to say that its character is determined by its relationship to the natural world, since the natural world is, in effect, a discursive construction of natural science. Second-order practices, however, cannot be understood apart from their historical relationship to their object of inquiry. This point has extensive conceptual implications.

When the philosophy of science, for example, addresses the issue of natural scientific knowledge, this is very different from asking a question about, for example, political science's knowledge of politics or philosophy's knowledge of natural science. There is a paradox built into the very notion of speaking about natural science's relationship to nature, since what we usually are referring to when speaking about nature derives from the constructions of natural science. Although politics and science are not, in the first instance, metapractical constructions, metapractices offer interpretations or reconstructions of these practices. This posture entails that unlike the relationship between a first-order practice such as a natural science and its object, there is an inherent *cognitive* and potential *practical* relationship, and tension, between second-order practices and their first-order objects—as well as between third- and second-order practices. This tension is between, on the one hand, both the theoretical and specific claims of a metapractice and, on the other hand, the theoretical self-understanding and account of itself, and maybe the world, manifest in the activity that constitutes its object.

Since the object of the philosophy of social science is a second-order activity and the object of the philosophy of natural science is a first-order activity, these dimensions of philosophy, despite the tendency to often think of them as parallel or laterally related endeavors, are not logically comparable. It is social science and the philosophy of natural science, on the one hand, and politics and natural science, on the other hand, that belong to the same orders of discourse. The philosophy of social science is a third-order enterprise, and as such it makes sense to speak of it as addressing the relationship, both cognitive and practical, between, for example, political science and politics, since they are conventional preconstituted activities. In talking about these practices, the philosophy of social science is presenting a reconstruction and interpretation, and there could reasonably be fourth-order discussions comparing these reconstructions with the practices that have been reconstructed.

It is important to stress again that a practice may include more than one order of the discourse. While it may be reasonable to suggest that there are metaphilosophical or third-order discourses devoted to thinking about the nature of the practice of the philosophy of natural science, they are usually part of that practice just as in the case of fourth-order reflection on the philosophy of social science. This is, for example, a characteristic feature of contemporary social science, where substantive discussions of its subject matter are often interwoven with a variety of functionally epistemological and methodological (third-order) claims about the nature of social scientific inquiry and knowledge as well as those drawn explicitly from the literature of other practices such as philosophy. But the presence of epistemological discourse in social science should not create any ambiguity with respect to the issue of whether it is possible to distinguish between social science and philosophy as practices—any more, for example, than the occasional presence of metaphysical reflection in natural science produces any real ambiguity about the discursive identity of such an activity. Similarly, as I will argue more expansively at a later point, the existence of what might be viewed as ideological claims or perspectives in social science does not, except in a metaphorical sense, transform social science into politics.

Epistemological (and methodological) discourses present a distinct problem. This will be more fully explored in subsequent chapters, but it is necessary to distinguish between what I will call *external* and *internal* epistemology. The latter, in either first- or second-order practices, might appropriately appear as post facto accounts of the grounds of knowledge and the mode of its acquisition, which might best be described as what John Nelson has called a "rhetoric of inquiry" (Nelson, Megill, and McCloskey 1987). Here they would be derivative, and often offered as justifications, of prior substantive theoretical and factual claims. External epistemologies or rhetorics of inquiry, however, such as in the case of the philosophy of natural science or the philosophy of social science, that is, epistemology as distinct practice or discourse, present a more problematical case. Epistemology's role could be construed as describing and clarifying assumptions characteristic of a certain practice of knowledge and the theories that sustain it at a particular time and place. As a more generalized project, however, devoted to speaking universally about such things as the nature of scientific knowledge and what constitutes authentic knowledge and its foundations apart from any substantive theory, it is a more anomalous enterprise. And when this kind of epistemological claim is appropriated by a practice of knowledge such as social science and even advanced as the basis of substantive inquiry, it becomes potentially pathological.

It is important to stress that distinguishing conceptually among levels of metapractice and between metapractices and their object, and noting instances of each, do not presume a lack of relations. On the contrary, the very concept of relationship implies difference and a degree of autonomy, and parsing kinds of practices is a prerequisite for considering the historical relationships between them. To distinguish between, for example, political theory (as an academic metapractice) and politics is not to suggest either that they are not, or should not be, related or that the existential boundaries of each are distinct and immutable, but neither does fluidity of boundaries and the existence of relationships produce an identity between these activities. It is important to distinguish between *effect, function,* and *identity.* If one order of discourse has, in some instance or general context, a practical effect or impact on another (for example, political science on politics), the first does not thereby become a form of the second even though in some sense we might be tempted, and reasonably, to think of political science as "acting" politically or "being" political. But to suggest, because political science may be construed as always in some sense political (in that it talks about politics, reflects ideological positions, or may possibly in some way affect political life), that there is no real distinction between the practices and discourses of politics, on the one hand, and political inquiry, on the other hand, is merely to obviate any serious attempt to understand the relationship. Or if, for example, within political science there is self-reflection and metatheoretical discussion, political science does not, despite its functional similarity, become the philosophy of social science. These may seem to be gratuitous observations, but it is often suggested, as I will more explicitly point out at a later juncture, that metapractical claims about the subject matter of these disciplines are either a mode of participating in them or their theoretical dimension.

Although the concept of the orders of discourse might encourage thinking in terms of "vertical" and "downward" relationships and although both the cognitive and practical relationships may tend to have such a vector, there are "upward" as well as "lateral" tendencies. Social scientists have, for various reasons, often engaged the third-order realm of the philosophy of social science, but the most important source of images of scientific identity in social science and political theory has been its "horizontal" appropriation of ideas from areas such as the philosophy of natural science and ethics even if those ideas have often been mediated through the philosophy of social science. Furthermore, what we are often confronted with is not simply the problem of determining the relationship among different orders of practice but that of sorting out modes of discourse that have penetrated, or been assimilated to, a practice. Although the social sciences as disciplines can be identified with a dominant order of discourse, that is, second-order, what has characterized the history of these fields is an interspersion of "foreign" discursive elements.

At this point, despite all my qualifications, one might still be inclined to ask if I have not imposed too strict a distinction between orders of discourse. Are not drama and art, for example, which I have designated first-order practices, really second-order in that they are often representations of human activity? My basic answer in this case would be to suggest that art, for example, is not usually defined by the fact that it re-presents other activities and that it, or its functional equivalent, is an element that is a requisite of what we take to be human intercourse. My basic point, however, is not to make a priori categorical judgments about discourses in terms of the labels that are characteristically applied to them but rather to indicate criteria for making distinctions. In response to the open question of whether there is really a sharp distinction between a first-order and second-order practice, there is no general answer but rather the need to point to an instance such as the distinction between actors and theater critics in contemporary society or, in the case of art, between Willem de Kooning and Robert Hughes. If anyone wants to persist in saying that on the basis of some criteria there is not a significant difference in such cases, the conversation comes to an end.

Since the potential relationship between a metapractice and its subject matter is not merely cognitive, there is always at least the intimation of a practical relationship, and this in turn entails, as I repeatedly emphasize, that there cannot be a unilateral metapractical solution to the so-called theory/practice problem. One mode of relation is conflictual and is rooted in cognitive differences such as those between knowledge *in* and knowledge *about,* that is, for example, the self-understanding of an activity such as science as opposed to philosophical claims about the nature of scientific explanation. Such cognitive dissonance implies the possibility of practical tension that may in some instances never be directly manifest but that in other cases may be a contentious issue. What characterizes metapractices is what might be called a dual rhetoric of inquiry, which is devoted not only to the internal justification of certain claims and approaches but to justifying itself to an external audience that is often its object of inquiry. The criticism and defense of political theories, for example, are not tailored simply for an audience of political theorists but for political actors. It is here, however, in such endemic problems of the relationship between first- and second-order practices, that we should look, as I have already suggested, for the essential difference between natural and social science.

II

The rhetoric of scientific demarcation, such as that involved in distinguishing between natural and social science, arises primarily out of cognitive and practical boundary disputes both within and among orders of discourse. Various aspects of this general problem will be confronted in the following chapters, but in postpositivist philosophy of social science, much attention has been devoted to arguing that the social and natural sciences are logically asymmetrical. The arguments of more recent asymmetricists are more sophisticated than earlier claims about the special nature of social scientific or historical understanding *(Verstehen)* or arguments such as that of Leo Strauss about the impossibility of separating fact and value in social science (1953). But the basic form of the argument has remained quite similar. The fundamental difference, it is claimed, is a function of the fact that the phenomena that constitute the object of social science do not admit to "theoretical" or nomothetic explanation (e.g., Winch 1958; Taylor 1971; Oakeshott 1975) and require an interpretive approach; that the human sciences do not address an objectified external reality and thus their conditions of possibility are in some way internal to them (e.g., Foucault 1979); that the mental causes of human action are always somewhat hidden (e.g., Searle 1983, 1992); or that it is impossible to "decontextualize" or dehistoricize social activity (e.g., Dreyfus 1986).

What all these familiar claims rely on is a supposition that in some basic dimension, the object of inquiry in social science, that is, what is often referred to as social reality, is theoretically nonidentical to the kind of phenomena studied by the natural sciences. If we consider the matter abstractly, it might seem puzzling that such a large amount of literature has been devoted to making this point, since the basic argument could be construed as amounting to little more than the truism that there are theoretical differences among sciences—both within and between natural and social sciences and between historical instances of each. Such specific differences do not really provide much basis for positing generic differences between the natural sciences and the social sciences. There have been a number of specific agendas, involving both cognitive and practical concerns, informing these exercises in demarcation, but in all instances what the asymmetricists were most essentially pointing to was, in the end, the conventional character of social phenomena. While I would agree that this is a crucial difference between natural and social science and although I will in the next chapter advance a theory of conventionality, the distinction between natural and social science cannot be grounded simply on a claim about conventionality as a theoretical domain. Even if the conventionality of social phenomena is rejected theoretically, as it is in various ways by behaviorists, certain structuralists, sociobiologists, and others, it nevertheless is a crucial desideratum. The very manner in which structuralism and behaviorism seek to go beyond conventionality is an indication of its ineluctable character.

The arguments of the antisymmetricists, in both philosophy and social science, were in large measure a response to positivist claims about the unity of scientific method, the hierarchy of scientific practices, and the general character of scientific facts, which amounted in effect to an argument that social science was either an inferior science or not really a science at all. And the antisymmetricist response was either that social science was a science but a science of a different kind with a different logic of explanation or that it was another kind of inquiry altogether. This response, however, took place largely within the framework of discussion created by positivist/empiricist philosophical doctrines. First, it tended to assume that the positivist account of natural science was adequate, and second, it accepted the view that a defense of social science must somehow pivot on that account. With the collapse of positivism in the philosophy of science during the last half of the twentieth century and the rejection of such doctrines as the unity and universality of scientific method and various dogmas of empiricism such as that involving the theory/fact dichotomy, much of the traditional debate about whether the social sciences are in some essential manner different from or similar to the natural sciences became obsolescent.

The traditional problem of distinguishing between natural and social science was, then, largely an artificial, or at least parochial, issue engendered and sustained by the positivist account of natural science. The remnants of that account, however, linger on in many venues in addition to those, such as certain practices of social science, in which it is still accepted as a general image of scientific explanation. Defenses of the autonomy of social inquiry, however, remained bound by premises that derived from the positivist framework. There is still a very widespread belief, for example, that the natural, as opposed to the human, sciences are less influenced by their social context. As a historical and sociological argument, grounded in claims about such matters as the degree of consensus among natural scientists and the social differentiation of the practices of natural science, this may be credible. But for a wide range of individuals, including Jürgen Habermas, Michel Foucault, and Charles Taylor, it is still based on the residue of a positivist account of theory and fact in natural science. In order to explore adequately this problem of the comparability of natural and social science, it is necessary to cast off the vestiges of positivism.

Although the problem of the demarcation of social science was, then, in part the product of a philosophical debate about the logic of natural science, it provided a framework and language for discussions about the nature of social science, and it reflected and was in some measure instigated and perpetuated by concerns about scientific identity in these disciplines. It was, in short, a manifestation of the dialectic between the philosophy and practice of social science, the relationship between social science and the philosophy of natural science, and controversies within each of these fields. The issue has, however, also sprung from the problem of the cognitive and practical relationship between social science and its object. Nearly all arguments about the demarcation of social science are tied to claims about the cognitive status of second-order practices and, at least by implication, about the practical relationship of these practices to their subject matter. Once we appreciate the rhetorical character and context of past arguments about demarcation, we are in a better position to think anew about what can be said conceptually about distinguishing between social science and natural science.

Although there are numerous possible historical and analytical bases for such a distinction, there is no general logical or epistemological criterion of the kind most characteristically advanced. The differences must, in the end, as I have already suggested, be theoretical, that is, predicated on how different sciences theoretically constitute their factual domain. If social phenomena are theoretically construed as conventional by certain social sciences, there must, ipso facto, be a difference between explanation in natural and social science. It is tempting to suggest that the whole issue of demarcation was a pseudoproblem spawned by debates surrounding positivism. Yet there still remains a propensity to ask, from a third-order perspective, if there is not something definitive that differentiates the social or human sciences, as a class of practices, from the natural sciences, no matter how reality is theoretically defined. Even after the demise of positivism, the most prevalent, and still persistent, kind of answer offered by all sides in this discussion is that there is *something* about all natural facts that makes them fundamentally different from social facts. There is a pervasive and seemingly almost intuitive presumption that natural facts represent a kind of phenomena that are somehow more obviously "there," more tangible, hard, objective, or permanent.

This attitude is defended philosophically by antisymmetrists such as Taylor who suggest that what distinguishes natural science is that its subject matter consists of "brute phenomena" (1971) that allow the application of certain techniques of inquiry and modes of explanation. Similarly, Winch posited attributes of natural phenomena, such as intrinsic regularity, that supported explanation in terms of the subsumption of individual instances under general laws (1958). Social phenomena, in contrast, it was claimed, are "meaningful" and require "understanding" and a "hermeneutic" approach. While this widely accepted type of account is promising, it is still mortgaged to a latent positivist image of natural science. The only "brute" facts are those studied by zoologists. There is no manner in which the phenomena confronted by the natural sciences can be distinguished as a class in terms of certain intrinsic transtheoretical properties or attributes such as brutish. As I will argue more fully at a later point, it is not that we should extend the concept of interpretation to accounts of physical objects but rather that the positivist idea of natural facts as nondiscursive must be rejected. While Kuhn challenged such a notion of natural facts, Taylor has continued to cling to this image (see Kuhn 1991). But now that we are divested of the positivist, and antipositivist, answers, the question of the difference between natural and social science still seems to beg for an answer—and even gains new urgency when the basis of demarcation seems more elusive than ever.

One reason the question persists is simply the inability to shake off the insecurity attached to the position of inferiority in the hierarchy of science that positivism attributed to social science. If living up to the positivist image of scientific explanation seemed either difficult or undesirable, then it was crucial, as a matter of principle, to establish the methodological autonomy of social science. The other basic concern, however, was practical. The very idea of a social science remained tied to its historical self-image of having an end in action and required establishing its cognitive credibility. Finally, the issue of professional and disciplinary identity and independence must be recognized. Once we get past these somewhat strategic motives, the whole question as traditionally conceived may lose much of its force, but it emerges once more as part of the problem of understanding the basic character of metapractices.

The only satisfactory criteria for generic demarcation between natural and social science are relational. The subject matter of social science, no matter how it is theoretically conceived and approached, entails practical and cognitive relational issues that do not obtain in the case of natural science. Social science is a second-order practice consisting of a set of claims about another conventional, symbolic, linguistically constituted, or discursive activity. Although I will in chapter 2 make a theoretical argument about social phenomena and attribute to them an irreducible conventionality, different theories of such phenomena that would construe conventionality as in some manner epiphenomenal do not, as I have already argued, alter the fundamental relational characteristics. The distinction between natural and social science does not turn on how social phenomena are theoretically conceived but rather on where social science stands in the orders of discourse.

Despite the persistent temptation to think of natural science as confronting a world of more objectively distinct facts and of social science as dealing with phenomena more inherently fluid and open to subjective interpretation, there is actually an important sense in which the reverse is the case. Since social or conventional phenomena are the product of human action in historical contexts, it is reasonable, in one sense, to say that they are not given, but this obscures the more fundamental sense in which they *are* given in relation to the practices that study them—and in a way that natural facts are not. In the case of first-order discourses—including practices of knowledge such as natural science—the "world" that they articulate, or their object of knowledge, is theoretically or conceptually produced and constituted in the language of the activity. While we might metaphorically speak of natural science interpreting nature, such a formulation cannot be literally defended. There is no "book of nature," and there is no external or unique vantage point from which it makes sense to ask what the natural world is as something lying outside the discursive constructions of natural science—or some logically lateral and incommensurable first-order discourse.

The facts of natural science are discursive by-products, and the "world," as we encounter it in natural science, is always a discursive configuration. Consequently, it is not possible to explain the activity of natural science in terms of its relationship to the natural world; nor would it make sense to write the history of a natural science from the perspective of its relationship to its subject matter. However, understanding social science or writing its history would almost inevitably entail addressing such relational issues. It would, for example, make little sense to talk about writing a history of the physical world that was separable from currently accepted geological theory. The histories of the earth written before and after the advent of the theory of continental drift are very different stories. Every transformation in the basic theories of geology entails a new history of the earth or else one faces the paradoxical conclusion that the history of the earth is equivalent to the history of geological theories. Similarly, from a second-order perspective, one could not credibly speak about the actions of god independent of how deity has been conceived in religion (Armstrong 1993) or give an account of citizenship that was not grounded on how citizenship was formulated and practiced in politics. All this is not to say that second-order discourses cannot critically examine first-order claims or even seek in some respects to substitute their judgment, but the philosophy of science does not give rise to quantum mechanics, the philosophy of religion is not where the image of god is conjured up, and political science is not the locus of citizenship.

The "world" as conceived in first-order discourses is not a piece of universal currency that can be cashed in at any knowledge bank. The world as such, abstracted from concrete human practices, is an empty concept, and as Nelson Goodman has suggested, it is "not worth fighting for or against" as philosophers have traditionally done as partisans of realism and idealism (Goodman 1978:20). The "world" as theoretically construed and descriptively addressed in the language of second-order discourses may, as in the case of first-order discourses, be identified and explained in various ways, but it is not, not merely or not in the first instance, a function of these discourses. In the case of second-order claims, something like the now maligned correspondence theory of truth may have a certain cogency. The attempt of positivism to posit a parascientific theoretically independent language of fact was an exercise in philosophical mythology, but there is an inherent positivity attaching to the world of social fact. It is only in the case of the social sciences or, more generally, metapractices that it makes sense to speak of a fundamental theory/fact dichotomy, but this is actually a theory/theory dichotomy. The facts of social science are, in the first instance, preconstituted by the theories of a first-order discourse and are discursively distinct from social scientific theories, that is, theories *about* those facts or what social science takes to be the reality of its subject matter. The facts described and explained by social science have an independent referent and signification outside the language of social science and other logically comparable practices and discourses.

It is possible, for example, as I will discuss later, to make a case for the idea that the meaning of a text is essentially a construction of its readers and of its interpretive history, and it may be reasonable to suggest that there is an important sense in which every rendition of a composer's musical score is a new work. There are, however, limits to these epistemological metaphors. Conventional phenomena may be interpreted by second-order discourses, but they are not fundamentally a product of interpretation. The very idea of interpretation implies the autonomy of what is interpreted. Certain claims about the autonomy of the text, while often presented as a challenge to the notion of the sanctity of authorial meaning, are really, or subtly, *denials* of the autonomy of the text by privileging the position of the reader. Part of what is involved in such claims is a manifestation of the search of second-order practices for authority over their object. The most fundamental issue, however, is not one of who properly owns meaning but of the nature of the object and the relationship between interpreters and objects. Natural science, for example, is not the discursive residue of the philosophy of science, and similarly, politics is not, in a primary sense, the invention of political science—even though the latter might have its own theoretical and empirical version of what politics is or should be. There is thus an important sense in which the facts of natural science are more fundamentally discursive phenomena than those in social science, since they have no criteria of existence outside the conceptual repertoire of natural science.

Natural science does not, literally, interpret or reconstruct nature. It constructs nature. This is not to say that nature and god are fictions but only that they are not conventionally preconstituted. This claim also entails the more radical one that it makes little sense to attempt, from a metatheoretical perspective, to posit any general cognitive relationship between natural science and nature, and this further claim raises some basic issues about the very character of the philosophy of science as traditionally practiced. To suggest that the philosophy of science can address this relationship would be to assume that it has some trans- or suprascientific access to natural phenomenon. Neither does it make sense to talk literally about a practical relationship despite the prevalence of phrases such as the "scientific domination of nature." There can be a practical relationship only among actors or activities. In most instances, claims about the cognitive and practical relationship between science and nature must be understood as metaphorical. Epistemological claims about science and its object and arguments about the practical relationship are not, however, simply anomalous curiosities. While they do not tell us anything about the relationship between science and nature, they do, as I will argue more fully in chapter 4, reveal something about the origins, character, and historical career of enterprises such as the philosophy of science and about second-order practices in general.

Second-order discourses characteristically, in a variety of ways, often seek to validate their object and underwrite it, but this also often involves a search for self-validation. This has typically been the case, for example, with practices such as the philosophy of science. At times, however, second-order discourses, as in the case of various forms of critical social inquiry, seek to deconstruct their object and demonstrate that its vision of the world, and itself, are illusory. Both attitudes represent a search for second-order cognitive domination, which often is viewed as a means of, and justification for, practical intervention. The inherent tension between a first-order practice and second-order claims about it is in the first instance between the self-understanding of the former and its reconstruction by the latter. This cognitive tension may involve both the historical identity of the object and its theoretical constitution—as in the case of an anthropologist studying an alien culture where the self-image of that culture as well as its representation of the world is at least implicitly called into question. The anthropologist embraces both a second-order understanding of society and a first-order account of the world in which it is situated. The extent to which the cognitive tension is manifest in practical terms is a matter of historical and cultural circumstances and is determined by such things as the aspirations of second-order practices and the cognizance of first-order activities.

It has often been stressed, from Weber to Winch, that since the objects of social scientific inquiry are conventional and preconstituted, explanation requires taking account of the self-understanding of social actors. This does not imply, however, as some critics of such a position have suggested (Rudner 1966), that social science does not or should not have a language or theories of its own. On the contrary, the point is precisely that social science and its object are discursively disjoined. Talking about another discourse logically requires a metalanguage and involves the difference between a first-order construction and a metapractical reconstruction. What cannot easily be avoided, however, is making reference to the language of the object. The reconstructions of, for example, social science will, therefore, always to some degree be cognitively at odds with their object. There is still, however, the practical issue of the implications, both intended and unintended, of that divergence. Is the philosopher of science, for example, to be construed as a master scientist or even in some sense as a scientific actor? Is there something about the cognitive relationship that determines or prescribes the practical one? Although much of the history of social science has been characterized by attempts to establish or justify the practical authority of second-order practices on a cognitive basis, the problem of the relationship between first- and second-order practices cannot be solved by metapractical claims to cognitive superiority. There can be metapractical claims about what the relationship is and what it should be, but there are, strictly speaking, no metapractical solutions.

III

Sorting out the orders of discourse offers not only perspective on issues such as the similarities and differences among various practices and the relationships among them but a basis for critical analysis as well. One implication is that the philosophy of social science might be construed as a more viable enterprise than the philosophy of natural science, at least if judged in terms of how the latter has traditionally been pursued. Much of the philosophy of natural science, as I will argue in more detail in chapter 4, has been devoted to attempting to answer the questions of how science can, in principle, have knowledge of nature and what constitutes valid scientific knowledge. To return to my earlier analogy, such questions are,

or would be, not unlike the philosophy of religion
beings can know god. These are really, respectivel;
logical issues, that is, issues internal to first-order pracᴛ.
they may seldom be posed in a general formal manner in ᴜ
quiry. Such issues can be described and in various ways discᴛ.
metapractical terms, but they cannot be adjudicated in any manner ᴜ
extends beyond the criteria adduced in metapractical discourse. Although
the philosophy of social science may not conventionally be assigned any
authoritative role in assessing the relationship between social science and
its subject matter, it is at least in a position to *speak* about the relationship
between these practices. The philosophy of science, however, when it
purports to speak about the relationship between science and nature, can
really speak only about a relationship internal to scientific practice. The
issue of the status of the philosophy of social science, however, returns
us to the general subject of *third-order* discourse.

Since third-order practices are those, such as the philosophy of social
science, that speak about, and potentially to, second-order practices, their
primary identity derives from their metapractical supervenient character
and, more specifically, their relationship to second-order activities. Although
the philosophy of social science has at times advanced claims to practical
significance for second-order inquiry and although social scientists have
often turned to this literature for purposes of legitimation, critique, and
even method, there has not been a conversation comparable to that surrounding the theory/practice relationship between second- and first-
order discourses. To the extent that there is, or characteristically has been,
a relationship between third- and first-order practice, it is usually a mediated one—mediated through second-order discourse and its claims about
social phenomena. The practice of the philosophy of social science is not,
for example, an investigation of first-order social practices. Second-order
practices such as philosophy, social science, and history, as institutionalized fields, are, however, hardly one-dimensional, and as already noted,
third-order discourses, both indigenous and appropriated from philosophy, are often entwined with these practices.

It is, again, important to distinguish, for example, between the philosophy and history of natural science and the philosophy and history of social science in that the latter are directed toward a second-order as opposed to a first-order activity—and to consider the implications of this
difference. One such implication is that there are, historically as well as
logically, some basic and interesting parallels between the social sciences
and an enterprise such as the philosophy of natural science. If we want to
understand, through analogy and example, something about the nature,
history, and contemporary situation of social science, we would, as

ndicated previously, be better advised to look at the philosophy of natural science rather than natural science itself. We should look, however, not for the purpose of finding out how social science is similar to or different from natural science, which has been the characteristic concern that has drawn social science to the philosophy of science, but rather for the purpose of understanding the character and problems of a second-order discourse. As I will argue at a later point, the origins of the philosophy of science were in scientific practice, and to a large extent the social sciences were born in the context of politics (Gunnell 1993).

The characteristic attachment of social science to ideas in the philosophy of natural science is, historically, easily explained, but it is also laden with paradox. Social science aspired to the cultural and cognitive status of natural science, but natural science, for the most part, provided no account of itself. Logical positivism and logical empiricism gained a hegemony and largely defined the field during the first half of the twentieth century, and these philosophies not only offered such an account but propagated the very idea of the unity and hierarchy of science on which emulation was predicated. This account of the logic and epistemology of science was also presented as definitive, and although its primary concern was not to provide models or guides for scientific practice or even to describe the actual practice of science, its normative claims about the nature of scientific explanation and methodology encouraged this assumption on the part of external audiences such as social scientists. The difficulties involved, however, in seeking the meaning of science from the philosophy of science were, and remain, as I will argue at length in chapter 4, manifold. First, the embrace of these doctrines was unreflective. There was little or no consideration of the extent to which these philosophical accounts were philosophically adequate even at the point when the dominate persuasion of positivism was being severely challenged. Second, the accounts were never intended, for the most part, as a description of scientific practice but rather as an explication of its underlying logical and epistemological structure. Third, even to the extent that the analysis might be construed as descriptive or as achieving some degree of verisimilitude, there was the fundamental problem of the extent to which a metapractical rendition of scientific explanation could be a guide to the practice of science any more than, for example, aesthetics could provide the basis for artistic practice. Yet of all the claims that have been advanced in favor of emulating the methods of natural science as well as arguments against such borrowing, it is probably fair to say that few, if any, have been grounded on any substantial firsthand acquaintance with the practices of natural science. They have been based on philosophical images, and this is particularly the case with regard to the concept of theory.

IV

There are few more highly legislated concepts than that of theory, and my concern is less to promulgate yet another statute than to isolate a certain functionally distinguishable realm of discourse that happens to coincide with what is often, but hardly always, referred to as theory. I also want to suggest that the manner in which the term has often been employed in social science and philosophy does not really correspond with what may more intuitively and commonly be thought of as theory in an area such as natural science. The actual word is not intrinsically important. It is the identity of a concept, and certain kinds of discourse, that are at issue. Attempting to capture the title "theory" and the approbation that now, as opposed to in the nineteenth century, surrounds it is, however, often an important dimension of contesting the concept, such as in the case of Max Horkheimer's distinction between "traditional" and "critical" theory (1972). It is, parenthetically, worth pointing out there are not, despite what some have maintained (Gallie 1955–1956), any truly "essentially contested concepts," but there are those, such as theory, that are characteristically contested.

In most of the natural sciences, the concept of theory, despite specialized designations of fields such as "theoretical physics," is not systematically employed. It is not really a substantive scientific term at all, that is, one belonging to the language of scientific practice, but largely a word that is used in talking *about* science. It is primarily a metapractical concept. It is because social scientists have become so accustomed to thinking about science in terms of the language and analytical categories of the philosophy of science that they have assumed that theory and theorizing refer to an internally distinct conventional component of scientific practice. The same kind of mistake has followed in the wake of Kuhn's work as social scientists have reified the concept of paradigm and attempted either to locate their paradigms or to construct and deploy them. It is this assumption that philosophical categories are somehow homologous with the terms and structure of scientific practice that has contributed to the idea that it was possible to move from methodology to method, that is, from philosophical reconstructions to substantive inquiry. It has also reinforced the more general belief that science and other substantive practices are grounded in epistemological principles. While it is perfectly reasonable to talk, generically, about epistemological assumptions in the practice of science, such talk should not imply that epistemology as a metadiscourse is logically prior to, or an element of, science.

If we attempted to engage in some systematic sociological survey of the manner in which the concept of theory is used by natural scientists, there would undoubtedly be some common patterns, but probably what would be most apparent would be a plurality of uses without a great deal of significance attached to them. Sometimes *theory* refers to speculations and conjectures of a cosmological dimension such as the "big bang" account of the universe, sometimes the word refers to localized claims such as the theory of continental drift and tectonic plates, and sometimes it designates much more specific hypotheses. At the south rim of the Grand Canyon there is a signpost describing the diverse "theories" about how this geological feature was formed. Yet on the contrary, on other occasions, *theory* refers to claims that have been largely accepted and structure conventional scientific belief and practice such as the theory of evolution, atomic theory, the theory of light, or the theory of relativity. The latter are close to one sense of what Kuhn meant by the concept of paradigm. Sometimes scientists simply talk about theories as general claims, or big ideas, as opposed to lower-level generalizations, and at times they use *theory* to refer to things that fall outside the realm of what they take, either at a particular time or essentially, to be directly observable. On occasion, they use the term as a synonym for generalizations as opposed to what they take to be facts or those singular statements for which there is, in their view, fully justified belief. *Fact,* however, is another term that, while used in scientific discourse, gains systematic meaning only in metatheoretical discussion. It has no distinct scientific meaning, and the general problem of the relationship of theory to fact is not a scientific issue, although scientists are certainly comfortable with the idea that some particular fact can be a problem for or supportive of a theory, just as they are comfortable with the notion that theoretical changes entail changes of fact.

All that this tentative sketch implies is that looking at the language of science does not provide very much positive help as far as confirming the assumption that theory is important in science and plays some crucial role. And looking at the language of philosophy often does not provide much in the way of a guide for exploring theory in science. But while the meaning of *theory* is a crucial issue in the philosophy of science, and (not coincidentally) in social science, very little turns on its meaning in natural science. If we asked scientists questions about the nature and uses of theory in science, we would probably in most instances receive disappointing answers. But at one level, this would seem entirely to be expected. After all, scientists know about the "world," not about science, and natural scientists are not for the most part particularly self-reflective, at least as long as they are engaged in creative, substantive work. When scientists do become reflective, what is often apparent is that lacking any systematic language of reflection, they repair, like social scientists, to some version of the language of the philosophy of science, which in various ways often significantly constrains their analysis and understanding of their own endeavor.

Social scientists, however, for at least two related reasons, have been absorbed with the issue of the nature of theory. First, they are characteristically in search of a scientific identity to which the concept of theory is crucial, and philosophy has provided schematic, even if at times conflicted, images of the logic of science. Second, philosophical accounts of science have usually turned on the issue of the character and role of theory. Although the philosophy of science is an enterprise devoted to understanding science, it is not, as I have already indicated and will further argue, always a very reliable guide. During the twentieth century, the philosophy of science has been engaged in explaining, and sometimes explaining away, what it calls theory, and the literature must be carefully sifted if one is to extract knowledge either about science as an activity or about how to conduct it. Two questions might well arise at this point: why continue to hold on to seeking a model of theory in natural science, and why pursue the issue of theory at all?

Traditionally natural science has been an object of emulation because of assumptions about its instrumental power and social authority, and it has been criticized on the same grounds. There is no need to recapitulate the arguments that have revolved around these assumptions, and my concern with natural science is quite different. Many of the natural sciences constitute distinct cases of autonomous and internally coherent practices of knowledge that tend to be internally hegemonic or paradigmatic. The functional key to this paradigmatic character is what I have called theory. Social science, for various reasons including its internal institutional structure, the nature of its subject matter, and its complex relations to that subject matter, might neither wish nor be able to aspire to such a condition, but the fact that social science is less likely to be paradigmatic need not mean that it is untheoretical. It is to some extent the at least latent theoretical pluralism of social science that inhibits hegemony. The prevalence of epistemological discourse in social science is not simply a manifestation of scientific insecurity and concerns about its practical relationship to its subject matter but in part a symptom of underlying, if not always explicit, theoretical tensions that push it toward seeking a language of legitimation and critique. The difficulty, however, is that justificatory ventures into epistemology have often had the effect of displacing theory and driving it underground. Consequently, what is often called theory in social science is largely a philosophical image, or something to which a philosophical image is attached, that bears little resemblance to the theoretical dimension of natural science. There is no reason to assume that theories of social science would, in terms of either form or content, look like those of natural science any more than those of evolutionary biology look like those of particle physics. Such an assumption is a prejudicial residue of positivism and assumptions about the unity of science. The core similarity relates to the *kind* of claims that are involved.

There is no particular reason we should accord any special authority to the classical use of the term *theoria,* but it provides a starting point for exploring the idea of theory and suggests some of the features that I wish to emphasize. For various reasons often having to do with the rise of modern empiricist philosophy, the term *theory* had, by the early nineteenth century, fallen into some disrepute and had taken on the often negative connotation of speculation and abstraction. This depreciation of theory was exacerbated at the end of the century when the Newtonian vision of the universe turned out to be only a "theory" and not a "fact." This was in an important sense the initiating dilemma in the institutionalization of the philosophy of science. The issue of the place of theory in science and its relationship to fact has, to this day, remained the defining problem of the field. The concrete character of the original Greek word and its cognates has often been noted. *Theoria* was "seeing"—often viewing the spectacle of games or a religious festival, and theorists were those who went abroad to report on religious ceremonies (Gunnell 1979a). Even though the term was adapted by Greek philosophy to represent contemplation, the oracular metaphor continued to dominate. In all of Plato's work, for example, there is scarcely a use of the term, or one of its forms, that does not refer to direct and concrete observation—whatever the object and the order of reality to which it belonged. Another characteristic of the classical usage was that the emphasis on the separation of subject and object, which we tend to associate with the modern idea of theory, did not obtain. There was a distinct implication that there was no fundamental difference between the act of seeing and the thing seen—sometimes indicated by the use of the same word.

By returning to this idea of the identification of theory with what is seen or, to put it another way, with those claims that are constitutive of or conceptualize facts, we have an account of theory that I will call *theoretical realism*—as opposed to what is often called "scientific realism," which I will discuss at length in chapter 4 and which refers to a genre of philosophical arguments about the reality of scientific objects and their autonomy with respect to the language of science. Theories are that species of claim that we can call an *empirical ontology.* They are generic or universal claims about what kinds of things exist and the basic manner of their existence no matter how or in what form particulars may be contingently manifest. Theories are that class of claim that constitutes and defines facticity and specifies the stuff identified as the object of inquiry.

Theories need not or may not always be reflectively explicit or formalized. Certainly in the case of social science they often have not been explicit, in part because a very different philosophically generated image of theory has largely held these fields captive. But whether theories are analytically distinguished in the discourse of science or any other practice, they are embedded in factual claims. Factual claims are, in effect, singular or particular theoretical claims just as theoretical claims are reflected in statements of fact.

What constitutes a theoretical or ontological concept is not, on its face, evident, and since the issue is less the word than the kind of claim that is being made, it is necessary to be wary of the manner in which abstract concepts that are used generically to designate categories of particulars—concepts such as agency, structure, authority, and so on—often are reified and accorded theoretical status. If, for example, we turn to some version of the Judaic/Christian account of the universe and speak about the authority of God, authority becomes an ontological concept. But to say, for example, that authority is an essential feature of social relationships is really usually only to state a tautology or specify an analytically distinguishable category or function. To elaborate an ontology or theory of social phenomena is not to provide a generalized account of historical particulars but rather to explicate what kinds of things the particulars are and, if any, the existentially necessary dimensions of their relationship to one another. What I am referring to as theory bears a certain similarity to what is called music theory. These formulations are not primarily metapractical accounts of music but rather a formalization of the assumptions embedded in musical practice whether or not practitioners are fully aware of the principles that inform that practice.

What has, in both principle and practice, most fundamentally and specifically inhibited theorizing in social science is the pervasive influence of the instrumentalist metatheoretical account of theory that, in its various manifestations, dominated the philosophy of science for so many years (Gunnell 1975, 1986a). This account of theory, and its philosophical residue, will be more fully discussed in chapter 4, but the core idea is that theories are conceptual or mental constructs that serve as instruments for selecting and economically organizing and explaining an ontologically distinct realm of facts that are in some way given and apprehendable through immediate experience. Since theories, according to this formulation, are primarily analytical devices that provide a perspective on factual phenomena, they are not to be judged so much in terms of their truth or falsity as in terms of their utility. There are several reasons that the hold of instrumentalist imagery in social science has been so strong. The most obvious explanation is that it was the dominant vision in philosophy, but it is also rooted in certain aspects of the history of the social sciences, which were concerned, from their beginnings, with effecting social change and viewed the social scientific enterprise itself as instrumental and pragmatically validated. It was when these disciplines began to attempt to justify themselves as pure sciences, albeit still often for quite practical motives, that the tension between cognitive and practical instrumentalism began to emerge (Gunnell 1997). Social science had also been characteristically defined in terms of its attachment to factual realism and similar empiricist images of science that depreciated speculation and theory. Finally, and maybe most important, for a group of disciplines attempting to emulate natural science, it was convenient and seductive to believe that scientific theories were basically arbitrary analytical constructions that were useful for organizing and explaining data.

Instrumentalism permeated the language and practice of social theory from the 1950s through the 1970s, and its residue remains deeply sedimented in the language and practice of political and social science. There were few explicit attempts by social scientists to articulate and defend this position in any extended manner, but this kind of tortured imagery of the cognitive process of inquiry is only one manifestation of a more general inversion of theory and epistemology in the social sciences. The rejection of positivism in social theory characteristically involved simply embracing an alternative epistemology as the basis of an interpretive or hermeneutic approach to inquiry. While epistemology might provide a critical explication of a practice of theoretically grounded inquiry or even a defense of a particular theory, there has been a tendency to make truncated theoretical claims in the course of elaborating and defending metatheoretical constructions about the nature of social scientific explanation. This inversion of theory and epistemology has not, however, been simply a matter of social science's attachment to philosophy but something rooted in the problematic of second-order discourses. It is precisely because the "facts" of social science are given or preconstituted that it is easy to assume that theorizing about them is ultimately a matter of constructing a metatheoretical framework. This assumption is reflected in both positivist and antipositivist positions, but metapractices, as I have already emphasized, presuppose, in principle, theoretical discourses.

The problem of recognizing and attending to matters of theory in second-order practices is, however, exacerbated by the fact that often second-order practitioners share the same object language as the activities they study. Thus there is a tendency to assume that individuals in their capacities as social scientists and social actors have different perspectives on a common universe of facts. And in one sense, of course, they do. The facts constituted in first-order practices are in one respect the objects of both first- and second-order discourses. In some instances, such as in the relationship between the philosophy of science and natural science, these facts are rarely disputed. But there is, at least potentially, a conflict of theories, often presented in second-order discourses such as social science as a distinction between appearance and reality or common sense and science. Part of the reason that controversy in anthropology often moves between the poles of an extreme idiographic orientation, which assumes the absolute singularity of the conventions it studies, and a deep structuralism, which treats them as epiphenomenal, is that anthropologists and the activities they study tend not to share a common language and theoretical construction. Even though there is theory *in* social phenomena, social science inevitably possesses a theory *of* social phenomena—however well or badly it is articulated.

Since theory is embedded in and constitutive of any practice, it is, as I have stressed, part of any practice whether first-order or metapractical. In the case of politics, it involves a conception of human interaction in general as well as of the units and boundaries of politics and a wider first-order vision of the world. It is, then, appropriate to speak of theory *in* politics in much the same sense that there are theories or paradigmatic reality claims in natural science, even if the former is less formalized. Within politics, there are also second-order discourses and metanarratives (e.g., historical) concerned with legitimating and criticizing political identities. The practices of political science, and political theory, make cognitive claims *about* politics and offer, at various levels of articulation, theoretical constructions of political reality or theories of politics—and often surround them with legitimating metatheories. Although it is common to think of political science or academic political theory as providing a theoretical account of politics, which may differ from what might be called the theoretical self-understanding of politics, and to construe the relationship as one between theory and practice, this, as I have already emphasized, can lead to a distorted image of the relationship.

Political theory as a second-order discourse is no more the theoretical dimension of politics than the philosophy of science is the theoretical dimension of natural science. To speak of it in this manner would be to obscure both the logical distinction among the orders of discourse and the practical relationships. Conceptual demarcation can eliminate a great deal of the confusion that abounds in the language of metapractices and attaches to terms such as *theory,* but this confusion, or conflation, is not always altogether innocent in either intention or effect. It is often a way of wishing or willing away, as well as creating, both cognitive and practical distance. It is evident, for example, in the uses of terms like *political theory, political thought,* and *political criticism.* The nouns often intimate separation from politics, while the adjectives indicate identity, and these dual strategies are common in the history of political science and political theory as academic activities. Each of these terms has been employed to specify claims in the practice of politics, claims about politics in second-order realms, descriptions or discussions of each, and arguments that are political in purpose. This diversity in usage, however, brings us to the characteristic ambiguity that the adjective *political* and the noun *politics* share in varying degrees with a family of other concepts such as religious/religion and scientific/science.

These concepts are often employed in various levels of discourse as generic, class, or functional concepts that gain their primary criteria of application from the purposes for which a second-order user employs them. In political science and political theory, *politics* is often used to distinguish a class of activities marked by stipulated criteria. In this sense, the concept can be applied universally to designate some structure or dimension of any actual past or present or any conceivable society. Yet there is another mode of the concept that is inherently more restrictive and prior. *Politics* and *political* are also self-ascribed terms that refer to, and have arisen within, culturally and historically specific first-order activities. What is political is, in this sense, not metapractically determined—any more, for example, than the character and contours of natural science are determined by the philosophy of science and its definition of science.

Most fundamentally, that is, both chronologically and logically, *politics* refers to a conventionally distinct and historically situated first-order practice. Politics is a conventional form of life that arguably had a beginning, evolution, and dispersion—not, in principle, unlike polo or Protestantism—and that has been characterized by an internal preconstituted self-understanding of its qualitative features as well as its operative elements. But there is a wide range of properties belonging or ascribed to historical forms of politics that are much more universalizable—such as conflict, power, and interest. From this perspective, that is, defining politics in terms of such characteristics, politics is ubiquitous, and so is political theory or any mode of thinking about politics. What often happens in second-order discourses is that specific attributes of indigenous meaning are universalized as ideal typifications and analytical generic categories that are then reified and often applied to activities, and periods and places, where they may be at variance with preconstituted social forms. It is easy to define *politics,* and terms such as *political theory,* in any number of ways that may be useful in some instance but that are nearly always at once too broad and too narrow to be sustained as the basis of descriptive accounts or as a way of analyzing political theory as an academic vocation and considering its relationship to historical forms of politics. The metapractical use of the concept of politics may be constrained by a recognition of the indigenous meaning, but the latter is a matter of internal conceptual relations and conventions rather than external categorization. Although there may be first-order disputes about the meaning of a concept such as politics, its fundamental binary character, which is a function of its use in both first-order and metapractical discourse, contributes to what is often understood to be its inherently contested status. But this raises the issue of whether there can be a second-order theory of politics.

What is often referred to as theory in social science is a variety of analytical constructs, empirical generalizations, and models of behavior. There is no need to restrict the use of the word *theory,* but is important to distinguish between this image of theory and what I have referred to as theory, that is, the fundamental reality claims and assumptions that define a practice. Second-order practices are theoretical, but if theory is a genre of claims that amount to fundamental existence protocols, there cannot be theories of historical forms of conventions—only of conventions as such. Since politics as a first-order practice is a conventional and histori-cally bounded configuration of human activity, *there cannot, literally speaking, be a theory of politics* any more than, for example, in a natural science such as geology, there can be a theory of how certain mountains came into exist-ence. These are all specific empirical claims and conjectures that are nec-essarily tied to and predicated upon theoretical claims about what kinds of things politics or mountains may be and the wider universe in which they exist. As I will argue more fully in chapter 2, there can be a theory of politics only in the sense that there is a theory of conventional phenom-ena of which politics is one historical manifestation. At this point, it is also necessary to return to the related issue of why there cannot be a theory of human practices.

In recent social theory, there has been an increased emphasis on historization and contextualization as well as allied concerns about tradi-tional images of the human subject and the limitations of choices be-tween individual and society as ontological alternatives. This emphasis has occasioned a move in the direction of claiming that practices and dis-courses should be the focus of theory (e.g., Bourdieu 1976, 1990). It is suggested that practices are where individuality, agency, and social order emerge (e.g., Schatzki 1996). While I agree with the latter assessment, I would nevertheless maintain that practices are a species of convention just as politics, for example, is a species of practice. Wittgenstein's work, as many have suggested, points toward focusing on understanding human practices and the internal conceptual relations that define them, but I will argue that in a more fundamental sense his work implies the need for a theory of conventional objects as such. A focus on practices has become fashionable and has tended to displace the concept of structure, but there can no more be a general theory of practices than of something such as institutions.

In my development of a general theory of conventional reality, my concern in chapter 2 is to step away both from philosophical claims about the explanation of social phenomena and from fragmented theoretical assertions and repressed and tacit theoretical assumptions. Instead, I will advance in a broad but systematic manner a theory of human action or, more broadly construed, what I call a theory of conventional objects. In thinking about both the cognitive and practical aspects of the relationship between social science and its subject matter, what is crucial is the conception of that subject matter. Whether the issue is one of specification, explanation, description, evaluation, or prescription, the predicate of these performances, the *kind* of thing in question, provides the ultimate criteria of judgment. Yet it is precisely this matter that, for various reasons, is so often elided.

Conventional Objects

By a noun we mean a sound significant by convention . . . because nothing is by nature a noun.

—Aristotle

And this may be properly enough called a convention or agreement betwixt us . . . since the actions of each of us have a reference to those of the other. . . .

—David Hume

. . . the action is what we have given us. It is our raw material.

—Arthur Bentley

What has to be accepted, the given, is—so one could say—forms of life.

—Ludwig Wittgenstein

What, exactly, is the nature of this stuff that we refer to as action or that I designate more broadly as *conventional objects,* this stuff that is both "given" and "betwixt" us? What is required is more than a categorization of this stuff and some broad generic distinction between it and other kinds of stuff. In social science, and the philosophy of social science, arguments abound with respect to the understanding and explanation of action, while the nature of what is to be explained has usually been little more than insinuated or summarily characterized. Postpositivist epistemologies of social inquiry have advanced beyond the dogmas of empiricism, but they have remained theoretically unredeemed. In this chapter, I focus on the nature of conventional objects and attempt to keep this concern separate from pragmatic issues such as how conventions can be understood, transmitted, and the like. Although theoretical claims have implications for these matters and judgments about them, there can be no theoretical account of such matters.

I

Although Winch made as bold a step forward as anyone else in addressing the general issue of social reality, his attempt to formulate an image of social phenomena as rule-governed was essentially a work of metatheory rather than theory. His account of the character of social phenomena pointed to important attributes of conventional objects, but an account of such attributes and what they may entail with respect to the nature of social inquiry is hardly a sufficient theory. Winch's project and concerns were, however, complex and, even after all these years, seldom accurately reported and described. A clarification of his analysis, which in many respects was representative of the postpositivist turn in the philosophy of social science, provides a bridge for traversing this territory.

Winch properly pointed out that there was a parallel between social science and philosophy, but he stated it in a manner that has continued to be confusing. The confusion arises largely from the fact that Winch did not, for whatever reason, distinguish between philosophy as an institutionalized practice and philosophy as representing a certain order of discourse. This may have been in part an analytical lapse, but it also reflected a rhetorical strategy. He wished, first, to challenge positivist accounts of social science that defended the unity of scientific method and to demonstrate that at least a significant dimension of social science was more like philosophy than experimental science, since it dealt with a conceptual subject matter. His argument was defined primarily by the issue of whether there is logical symmetry between explanation in natural and social science, and Winch was attempting to demonstrate that social science and natural science were "logically incompatible" (1958:72).

An important part of Winch's argument was to call attention to what I have termed the second-order character of social inquiry. He claimed that just as philosophy (epistemology) was concerned with, for example, how natural science defined the criteria of knowledge and conceived of reality, the cognitive mission of social science was to elucidate the assumptions about knowledge and reality in social activity in order to understand the meaning of such "discursive" interaction. Part of what was reflected in Winch's work, although obliquely, was a concern with defending the autonomy of philosophy, that is, epistemology and metaphysics. This was during a period when a somewhat deflated view of these enterprises was being championed by certain proponents of "ordinary language" analysis and when the positivist account of the methodology of natural science was widely accepted as a universal model of knowledge acquisition. The role of philosophy was viewed by many as basically parasitic and devoted to linguistic and conceptual clarification in more primary or first-order activities as opposed to a "positive understanding of the world." He agreed that understanding concepts and language was the special province of philosophy but that this was, in effect, a matter of understanding the world, since our grasp of the world was always linguistically or conceptually mediated.

The task of social science, Winch argued, was, like that of philosophy, to illuminate the "internal relations" between concepts that defined modes of social activity and the social construction of reality (1958:4–7). He maintained that while natural science was concerned with *"particular* real things," philosophy was concerned with "reality as such," its "nature and intelligibility," as well as with the very idea of "intelligibility." These matters, he argued, could not be settled by the experimental methods of natural science, since they involved "conceptual" rather than "empirical" questions (8, 18, 21). Thus philosophy and social science were functionally equivalent. This, in retrospect, was surely too narrow a view of natural science, but Winch was still a captive of the positivist/empiricist account of natural science, which was his contrast-model for distinguishing social scientific inquiry. His argument, however, did serve to point to the need for considering the theoretical dimension of social science, which positivist images of that activity had suppressed.

Winch claimed that "many of the more important theoretical issues which have been raised in those studies belong to philosophy rather than to science and are, therefore, to be settled by *a priori* conceptual analysis rather than empirical research." What was required, he argued, was "an elucidation of the *concept* of social behavior," of social reality and social phenomena in general, or in Wittgensteinian terminology, the very idea of a form of life as such (17–18). Winch claimed that this task belonged to epistemology. This was, however, an ambiguous assertion, since he was not clear about whether the reference was to epistemology as a discipline or to a functional category, but he suggested that despite the difference in standpoint between social science and philosophy, an account of social reality as such was an essential dimension, even the "central problem," of social science. He then concluded that "this part of sociology is really misbegotten epistemology . . . because its problems have been largely misconstrued . . . as a species of scientific problem" (41–43) when they are actually foundational or constitutional issues that cannot be settled by empirical investigation.

The moral that we can extract from Winch's analysis, despite his particular agenda and the occasional (and sometimes rhetorically induced) awkwardness of his formulation, is that social science has neglected what might be referred to as its theoretical dimension. In its assumption that social facts were simply there to be studied by universal methods of science, social science obscured the basic theoretical issues. Designating this dimension epistemology or philosophy, however, only clouded the issue and did little to advance his underlying message that theory and empirical inquiry are integrally related. The *kinds* of claims that I am referring to as theoretical happen to be found predominately in the literature of academic philosophy, but there is little reason to suggest that philosophy, as

an institutionalized field, is or should be the theoretical dimension of social inquiry or the source of its cognitive identity. While, as things stand at
the moment, we must look largely to the discipline of philosophy to find a
discourse that frontally addresses issues about such things as the nature of
human action, it is necessary to avoid the error that characterized the reception of both positivism and postpositivism in the social sciences—that
is, assuming that various philosophical claims, either theoretical or
metatheoretical, can simply be accepted as authoritative. Theoretical issues in social science must be joined in the conversation of social science.
Winch, then, was quite correct in pointing to the poverty of theory in
social science, but his own work belongs to the third-order realm of the
philosophy of social science, which has largely been devoted to projects
such as seeking the difference between natural and social science and defining the cognitive and practical task of the latter. From Winch to
Habermas, claims about the nature of human action have themselves not
precipitated any significant debate because the primary concerns were really situated elsewhere. What has been reaped from this literature is what it
sowed, that is, arguments about the cognitive nature and practical role of
social science.

   Even though it is indisputable that human activity and its products are
the subject matter of the social sciences, it would be a mistake to suggest
that everything falling within the purview and horizon of these disciplines
is theoretically identical. Seldom is a practice of knowledge defined by
one theoretical/factual domain. But language, action, and their artifacts,
including texts and institutions, constitute a, and probably the, fundamental dimension of the object of social scientific inquiry. One might substitute the concept of artifact for my concept of conventional object, since
language can, for example, be construed as an artifact (Dipert 1993), but
the word *artifact,* used in this manner, does not have a ready equivalent in
other languages such as French and German. And in common English
usage, it tends to imply a narrower class than the category of convention
I am employing to encompass phenomena that I take to be theoretically
identical.

   There have been few systematic attempts by social scientists to develop a theory of such phenomena or even directly address the issue of
the theoretical constitution of social reality. Talcott Parsons's work (Parsons 1937; Parsons and Shils 1949) represented a distinct move in this
direction, but it was based on behavioristic psychology and justified in
terms of a positivist account of scientific explanation (Gunnell 1973,
1986a). Its subsequent evolution has been bound to a similar perspective (Parsons 1977, 1978; Munch 1987). The theory of action has remained largely the province of formal philosophy, but despite the rich

and extensive literature that has evolved in the past few decades, it has been pursued with limited awareness of its implications for other fields as well as significantly constrained by narrowly and internally defined disciplinary issues. Social scientists and political theorists have rarely engaged this material in any detail, and when they have done so, the concerns and efforts have often been selective and strategic.

The work that has gained the most attention in political and social theory in recent years is surely Habermas's account of communicative action. The principal problem involved in confronting his analysis, however, is that it has been substantially driven and shaped by his search for standards of rationality that would support a critical social theory, that is, for "conditions of rationality inherent in communicative action" (1984:ix). Although Habermas draws on the theory of language, and particularly the work of Austin, and touches on certain core problems in the theory of action, he avoids many of the hard issues, and the matters that are confronted are treated in a derivative and summary fashion that makes it difficult, and futile, to engage the argument in any detail. His concern with a theory of action is secondary, and his claims are part of an eclectic composite of philosophical and sociological themes that are often partially explicated and selectively deployed with little attention to a defense of either their own internal character or their compatibility with each other. Although Habermas states that his theory of action was a distinct turn away from his earlier "methodological interest" and from "metatheory" in favor of an interest in "substantive" theory, the project on the whole remains in the category of metatheoretical rationalism—"a social theory concerned to validate its own critical standards" (xxxix).

I am not suggesting that a theory of action has no bearing on or implications for prescriptive and evaluative claims. Such claims, like all others, must, as I have already stressed, ultimately be predicated on a theoretical conception of the kind of phenomena the claims are about. But as I have also emphasized, it is a mistake to assume that the practical historically situated relationship between social science and politics can be reduced to a theory of action conceived as the instrument of a self-validating rationalism. Habermas adopts many elements of, not always commensurable, rationalist programs in contemporary philosophy designed to demonstrate that modern "scientific rationality belongs to a complex of cognitive-instrumental rationality that can certainly claim validity beyond the context of particular cultures" (1984:65). He then seeks to project a normative social theory and an image of theorists, and actors, as gaining objectivity and a basis of critical judgment as virtual but reflective participants in the validity claims of various discourses. Notwithstanding all the dubious premises that may attach to past arguments about the

impossibility of deriving an "ought" from an "is," there is still a logical
jump involved in this attempt to move from a theory of social phenomena
to standards of moral validity. Whatever value some may view as attaching
to this project, it cannot be construed as providing a theory that can resolve either the abstract epistemological dilemmas that govern so much
of the discourse of social science and the philosophy of social science or
controversies about the practical role of social inquiry.

The question of the nature of social action has also recently received
considerable, even if somewhat derivative, attention in public and social
choice theory, but there are at least two fundamental problems attached to
the treatment in this literature. First, the orientation in many instances
remains fundamentally informed by the instrumentalist image of theory.
Jon Elster, for example, notes that *"social choice theory* is a useful tool for
stating the problem of how to arrive at socially optimal outcomes on the
basis of given individual preferences" (1983:30). Second, there really is
very little attention to the concept of action. Although this approach depends heavily on certain very basic assumptions about the nature of human action and rationality, regarding such matters as agency and the status
of mental states and their relationship to behavior, there is little in the way
of either a defense or elaboration of such assumptions. Even when someone such as Elster, who is among the most critical and reflective commentators on this scheme of inquiry (1986), offers a general account of action, it is largely a brief, porous, stipulated, and undefended discussion of
behavior and its relationship to such things as reasons, beliefs, and desires.
Rational choice "theory" is largely conceived as an external construct for
explaining the facts of human choice and behavior. Anthony Downs (1957),
one of the founders of social choice analysis, explicitly embraces Milton
Friedman's instrumentalist account of theory (1953). But it is precisely
this realm of facticity that requires elaboration. This literature offers less a
theory of action than models or ideal typifications of actions and social
situations, of actors and structures, that are broad enough to be used in
many instances by various people for various purposes—from Marxists to
classical liberals, from those who assume that human nature is self-inter-
ested to those who believe it is altruistically inclined. There are certainly
theoretical assumptions reflected in these models and their uses, but they
can be interpreted and applied in an "optional" manner, that is, they need
not entail individualistic psychological explanations in terms of causal
mental states and instead can be used in explanations that refer to an "agent's
environment" (Satz and Ferejohn 1994:71–72). The very concept of choice
is also often nebulous (Hauptmann 1996), and if by "theory" we are talking about something logically comparable to theory in natural science, rational choice models are not good candidates (Green and Shapiro 1994).

Although varieties of social choice analysis have come to play a dominant role in both empirical political science and the philosophy of social science, there has been at least an incipient but strong challenge from the standpoint inspired by the recent "return to the state" and other directions in institutional analysis. The claim of what some call the "new institutionalism" is that the focus since the 1950s on aggregate political behavior, based on self-interest and utilitarian estimates of consequences, must be at least complemented, if not somewhat displaced, by studies of how institutions determine political action. The concern is to provide "a more independent role for political institutions" by turning away from a perspective in which they are considered as just an arena for political behavior and as "mirrors of political forces" and by examining the manner in which institutions are in fact "political actors" (March and Olsen 1989:17). One of the purposes reflected in this general orientation is to rescue politics, or the idea of the "political," from approaches that did not "differentiate the polity from the rest of society," reduced it to the "aggregate consequences" of individual behavior, or viewed it functionally as a process of decisions for allocating resources and achieving equilibrium (3). The argument is that institutions and the political realm have "autonomy" and "coherence" and, in effect, make choices just as much as do individuals. The focus is on the manner in which political action is guided by rules and institutions that determine "appropriateness" and "constrain and shape politics through the construction and elaboration of meaning" for actors. Institutions, James March and John Olsen claim, "enact social reality" and give symbolic meaning to life and thus play a large role in what people do and in fostering both stability and change (38–39). They hold that "political actors are driven by institutional duties and roles" and by "routines, rules, and forms" and that they find their identity and purpose through the institutional "construction and interpretation of meaning." Only by understanding this can there be a "positive theory of politics" or a notion of the polity as more than a functional element in society (159–60).

The "new institutionalism" raises, at least implicitly, important theoretical issues such as the extent to which institutions can be understood as actors, the nature of the interaction between institutions and individuals, and, particularly, the theoretical status of politics. But like rational and social choice theory, it incorporates a number of unexamined meta-theoretical arguments, and it neither confronts theoretical issues very directly nor presents any analysis of the basic nature of human action. Its claims do not, in any significant manner, deviate from gross commonsense notions (e.g., acting in accordance with interests and preferences in view of consequences, conforming to rules and adopting institutional identity, etc.) or indicate a distinct theoretical perspective. If institutionalism is something more than a different distribution of emphasis in terms of research strategy, it demands some kind of theoretical underpinning or clarification.

Approaches in second-order inquiry, such as rational choice and institutionalism, emphasize explaining but without much attention to the nature of what is explained. Much the same can be said about third-order analysis in the philosophy of social science, which focuses on the problem of social scientific explanation. In both instances, the focus is misplaced. Explanations are particular context-bound moves in inquiry and presuppose a theory, but if we are looking for explanations, we should not look to theories directly. Despite the prevalent view to the contrary, theories, whether in natural science or the social sciences, do not literally explain anything. This imagery of theories as unexplained explainers is a residue of the language of positivism and theoretical instrumentalism. Theories tell us what kind of thing is to be explained and, thereby, what kinds of explanations are adequate and by what criteria particular explanations are to be judged.

John Searle has recently attempted to extend his influential analysis of speech-acts (1969, 1979) and intentionality (1983), which was based on his understanding of Austin, into a general account of the nature of social phenomena (1995). In this work, he moves beyond epistemology to what I have designated as theory, and he develops an argument that is directly relevant to social scientific inquiry and that goes beyond the summary claims that characterized the work of individuals such as Winch and Charles Taylor. This work, in principle, represents the kind of intersection between philosophy and social theory that I commend and recommend, and his position must be given serious consideration. There are, however, significant differences with regard to both theoretical content and intellectual agenda between his analysis and my account of conventional objects.

Searle seeks to develop an "ontology of social facts and institutions" and thereby address what "might be thought of as problems in the foundations of social sciences" but ones that "have not been satisfactorily answered in the social sciences" themselves (1995:xii). He emphasizes that social science has not accepted the burden of explicating its own theoretical grounds, and he presents what I would call a strong theory of social and institutional facts in that he both gives priority to collective or conventional intentionality over individual intentionality and refuses to reduce it to either biological structures or the innate universals posited by various versions of cognitive science associated with the work of individuals such as Noam Chomsky (Searle 1992). Social facts, including both actions and institutions, exist, he argues, within a holistic system and process of language-dependent "constitutive rules" that create a collective symbolic world and universe of power, rights, and obligations that can, in principle at least, be codified. Yet in the end, Searle backs away from conventionality as theoretically autonomous, and his underlying philosophical and ideological agenda leads him, as in the case of so many others, away from engaging some of the difficult issues raised by a theory of conventions. His concern, much like that of rationalist philosophers of social science such as Martin Hollis, is that claims about the "construction of social reality" spill over into an image of the "social construction of reality" (e.g., Berger and Luckmann 1966) or what Hollis (1982) claims amounts to the "social destruction of reality." Like so many others, such as Taylor and Habermas, Searle's epistemology is tied to an ideological program, in this case a conservative one. As I will indicate in chapter 3, it is, as Karl Mannheim noted long ago, philosophical rationalism that binds together academic radicals and conservatives. Whatever the political agenda, the underlying commitment is to transcendental truth, and as I will suggest in chapter 6, this commitment may, in the end, reflect more an attempt to vindicate the academy than any particular political position.

Searle begins by identifying social and institutional facts in contradistinction to what he calls, following G. E. M. Anscombe (1958), Winch, Taylor, and others, "brute facts," or those facts that "exist independent of any human institution"—even if they must be articulated in language. Although such a claim could be construed as a weak version of the argument that there are two basic categories of claims—those relating to physical objects and those relating to human practices—Searle pursues a stronger version. He argues, much like unreconstructed positivists, that there is a variety of things such as mountains and "sheer physical possession" that are independent of human intentionality or representation. Furthermore, they are, he argues, the foundation (sounds, marks, power, etc.) upon which social and institutional facts are ultimately constructed by the imposition of symbolization. Despite Searle's emphasis on the conventionality of social facts, he is worried that this view, if carried too far, makes the social world a somewhat shaky structure. "One of the most fascinating—and terrifying—features of the era in which I write is the steady erosion of acceptance of large institutional structures around the world" (1995:117). For Searle, this is the danger inherent in philosophical trends such as desconstructionism as well as in concrete social practices. And he sees a connection between the two.

Searle attempts to prop up our institutional universe by opting for metaphysical realism and the correspondence theory of truth, which he believes has been given new life by recent work on the semantic account of truth by philosophers such as Alfred Tarski. There is, he maintains, "a reality totally independent of us," and "true statements correspond to facts" (119–20). He does not want to collapse truth and reality, as in the case of Davidson and W. V. O. Quine, since he believes the former is always "aspectual" and that this quality confirms realism. Realism, for Searle, is not an empirical argument but rather a "transcendental" deduction that must be assumed for human communication and understanding to operate and that is required as a basis for positing the existence of social facts. A "socially constructed reality presupposes a reality independent of all social constructions, because there has to be something for the construction to be constructed out of," and thus there is "a class of speech acts that presuppose for their intelligibility a reality beyond *all* representations" (190–91).

One might ask why, in a work devoted to exploring the nature of conventional social phenomena, Searle devotes so much attention to what he contends is not socially constructed. But his most fundamental concern is to undercut what he believes is the dangers of irrationalism in our age, which he maintains are being exacerbated by intellectuals such as Jacques Derrida. Realism is not, he argues, just one of so many metaphysical "battle cries" but a faith that is required in our time. It is part of his conception of what he calls our "Background." While Searle rejects attempts by neo-Cartesians to ground social facts in unconscious structures, he opts for a basis of explanation that stands outside convention. This "background," according to Searle, consists of non- or preintentional skills and "capacities" or "abilities, dispositions, tendencies" that cannot be exactly specified but amount to a system of universal neurophysical *"causal structures"* (1995:129) that order experience and "enable" semantics, the determination of truth-conditions, and perception. This "background" assumption is, he claims, an alternative to both mental causation theory and behaviorism, and although it cannot be reduced to a deeper set of rules than the constitutive ones of language and other social practices, it is "causally sensitive" to such rules (141).

Finally, although Searle does not embrace the notion of mental causation, that is, the view that mind as such causes behavior, he does seek to ground conventional or social facts on mental predicates. Conventionality is, he claims, an expression of mentality. He argues that mental states are intrinsic features of the world and tied to the physiology of the brain and that collective intentionality is in the end a sharing of mental states such as beliefs, desires, and intentions. These thoughts that are constitutive of social facts are language-dependent for their expression, and thus even though animals can be said to think, they cannot be said to have thoughts in the sense that humans possess them. But, Searle holds, language requires thoughts, and in his ontology, brute facts and mental facts occupy an equally primitive status. While brute facts are what he terms "nongenerative," mental facts constitute a complex system ranging from individual pain experience to various types of collective social behavior.

My most fundamental disagreement with Searle revolves around both his ultimate theoretical reluctance to accept conventionality as ontologically autonomous and the manner in which his arguments appear to be framed, limited, and even overshadowed by a broader set of philosophical and ideological concerns that lead him to attempt to assure us that ephemeral conventional accounts of reality do not float free of more permanent and universal grounds. Despite his useful and challenging theoretical explorations of conventional objects, his concern about philosophically underwriting reality diverts him from a thorough account of conventional objects.

II

The philosophical literature on the theory of action is indeed vast, and much of what I am presenting in the following paragraphs is a highly distilled residue of a confrontation with a variety of specific arguments in the philosophies of action, language, and mind. Although I will briefly recapitulate the principal contours of recent discussions of the theory of action, as well as situate my particular claims within this realm, my concern is neither to retrace that path in detail nor to engage fully various alternative formulations. What I am offering is a systematic set of basic theoretical claims. Most of the points deserve further development and defense, but it is difficult to determine in advance of challenge and interpretation (and misinterpretation) what requires elaboration. With respect to most of the main issues in the theory of action such as the criteria of individuation, the place of the concept of intention and the meaning of various other mental predicates, and the relationship of bodily movements to actions, my position, and the arguments and assumptions with which it implicitly and explicitly contends, should be clear.

In some respects, the theory of action is a relatively recent subject of study. Although it is possible to suggest that such a theory is as old as philosophy itself, distinct attention to the phenomenon of action belongs largely to twentieth-century philosophy, and even in the early part of this century, many of the issues were primarily defined and informed by concerns about such matters as moral responsibility and freedom of the will. These concerns are still very much part of the field, but the work of Wittgenstein, Austin, Gilbert Ryle, and others contributed to shifting the focus more to action itself as a particular kind of phenomenon and as something different from the subject of empirical psychology. For two decades, beginning in the 1950s, a variety of philosophical works was devoted to attempting either to affirm or deny the autonomy of action vis-à-vis physical events and to determining whether historical explanations could be subsumed under the deductive nomothetic model (e.g., Dray 1957) or in some other manner the explanation of human action could be conceived as deterministic (e.g., Nordernfelt 1974). Much of this discussion turned on the issue of the extent to which it was possible to identify action as a manifestation of intention, purpose, and human agency and describe, or redescribe, and explain it teleologically or in terms of choices, intentions, and rules and conventions as opposed to bodily movements (Anscombe 1957; Winch 1958; Peters 1958; Hampshire 1960; Melden 1961; von Wright 1971; Kenny 1963; Taylor 1964, 1970a, 1970b; Taylor 1966; Brown 1968). This literature was in some respects a vindication of the commonsense notion of action as a consequence and representation of mental states, and it was conducted against the background of positivist and behaviorist claims about reductionism and deductive nomological explanation (e.g., Hempel 1965). Much of this material, often labeled contextualism, attempted to distinguish the explanation of action from causal explanation and thereby to extricate it from the positivist image of the unity of science. Some positivists, however, such as A. J. Ayer, were willing to admit mentalistic as well as physicalist explanations of action but insisted that they could be construed as causal and thereby sustain the idea of "man as a subject of science" (1967), and there were attempts to find complementarity between conceptual explanations and empirical psychology (e.g., Mischel 1969).

By the 1970s, the theory of action was approached in a yet more specific and systematic manner (Care and Landesman 1958; D'Arcy 1963; Powell 1967; White 1968; Brand 1970; Goldman 1970; Thalberg 1972; Aune 1977; Binkley, Bronaugh, and Marras 1971; Danto 1973; Castaneda 1975; Brand and Walton 1976; Thalberg 1977; Thomson 1977; Tuomela 1977; Davis 1979; Whittemore 1979; Hornsby 1980; Cranach and Harré 1982; Donagan 1987; Ginet 1990). In many instances, the focus continued to be on distinguishing actions from other "doings" and happenings and on the issue of causality and on whether mentalistic concepts were essential for the explanation of action. The traditional volitional theory of action, which was prevalent in the nineteenth century, construed action as a sequence combining a mental event and a bodily effect. In a somewhat similar vein, mental action theory held that a prior mental event causes a subsequent bodily movement or behavior. Both of these positions had been severely challenged by arguments, such as those of Wittgenstein and Ryle, that called into question the traditional concept of mind. New, or functionally similar, versions of these theories, however, have dominated the field for the past three decades. Davidson's influential articles (1963) resurrected, or put a new spin on, the idea of intentions as causal, and despite some pointed dissent (e.g., Wilson 1989), his work initiated a trend in the direction of defending both some version of the thesis of causal explanations of action and the priority of mental states. Much of the recent work in the theory of action has pivoted on Davidson's analysis (e.g., Schick 1991); a range of theories of this kind posit a mind/body duality and distinguish actions as doings or bodily movements explained by mental events or states such as beliefs, desires, choices, motives, reasons, wants, and so on. Although some have approached the issue of causality in terms of a theory of agency whereby the agent is taken as the cause of an action (Taylor 1966; Chisholm 1976), the principal focus, particularly in the wake of Davidson's work, has been on prior mental phenomenon, or what, following Bertrand Russell, has been called propositional attitudes (mental states defined in terms of semantic content). These have been construed as causes, and this claim has suggested a détente between intentionalism and causalism.

Individuals such as Norman Malcolm (1963), A. I. Melden, Charles Taylor, and von Wright (1971), influenced by Wittgenstein, were concerned about distinguishing action from natural phenomena and about situating it in a social context. They argued that intentions, reasons, and the like could not be viewed as causes of behavior. They claimed that social behavior expressed conventions and norms and that mental predicates were logically, rather than contingently, related to descriptions of bodily movements in a manner that did not allow them to be conceived in causal terms. This formulation was, however, increasingly viewed as based on too narrow a concept of cause and as failing to distinguish between intention as a mental event and intention as manifest in action. The search for a causal theory of action was persistent (e.g., Dretske 1988; Bishop 1989), and one major issue has continued to be whether mentalistic causes can be construed in a naturalistic and/or nomological manner, as Myles Brand (1984), Jerry Fodor (1983), and others (Bratman 1987; Mele 1992; Audi 1993) have contended. Philosophers such as Davidson and Raimo Tuomela maintain that it is possible to develop a non-nomic theory of intentional or purposive causation, and there have been several attempts to reconcile the everyday notion of explaining actions in terms of reasons with some version of causal explanation (e.g., Lennon 1990). In one way or another, volitional or mental cause theory is deeply embedded in the theoretical assumptions and explanatory practices of social science and history and in assumptions about how ideas, attitudes, ideology, and so on affect behavior. Although these notions are seldom examined and defended within these disciplines, philosophers have struggled to make sense of this picture.

   In addition to the issue of the place of mental states in accounting for
actions, the principal theoretical problem in the philosophy of action has
been that of specifying and individuating actions, that is, how to recognize
an action and differentiate it from another action and from the category
of behavior. Some (such as Alvin Goldman) hold that the performance of
an action or actions is the instantiation, or a token, of a type of action by
an agent at a specific time. According to this position, walking and moving
one's legs, for example, would be viewed as different actions performed
simultaneously. Such a formulation entails issues about how actions are
related and whether there are some actions, such as moving one's legs,
that, as Arthur Danto (1965), Goldman, and others argue, are more basic
or primitive and that causally "generate" others on a different "level." The
more currently dominant view, however, defended by Davidson, Robert
Audi, and others, is that while bodily movements or physical behavior can
be construed in some sense as a kind of basic action, actions are particulars or events that can be described in various ways. Thus, for example,
walking and moving one's legs constitute one event or action that is open
to two descriptions.

   Closely related to this issue, and of special relevance for social science,
are the problems of what can be the subject of action—individuals, institutions, and so on—and of whether social reality is ultimately individualistic or holistic, that is, whether social facts can be reduced to matters of
individual action (e.g., Quinton 1974–1975) or whether there can be a
"plural subject." Anglo-American philosophy and social theory have largely
assumed, as did John Stuart Mill, that when individuals are brought together into a collectivity, they are not converted into another kind of thing.
Even when a contemporary philosopher such as Margaret Gilbert (1989)
elaborates, and defends at length the thesis of a plural subject and the
ability of collectivities to perform actions and ascribes "reality" to them,
she still, in the end, views these wholes as primarily individuals in a particular "state" and maintains that individuals are the constituent elements
of society. Gilbert also views thought and language as presocial. Arguments about the priority of the mind and of the priority of the individual
tend to coincide. Similarly, Tuomela has extended his theory of social action (1984) to an analysis of collective action and the manner in which
groups can be said to act, but he insists "that no supraindividual social
entities exist" (1995:5).

   Since the time of Weber and Durkheim, holism versus individualism
has been a pivotal and much debated, but often inadequately explored,
issue in social theory. Even in areas such as the new institutionalism and
rational choice analysis, where assumptions about this matter are crucial,
there has been little in the way of an extended examination. In political

theory as well as the broader literature on the theory of action in philosophy, "ontological individualism" (Tuomela 1984) has dominated. Collectivities have characteristically been accounted for functionally or treated as compound entities. While it may be admitted that collectivities can and do perform actions, such actions are often viewed as secondary and ultimately constituted by, and explained in terms of, the actions of individual persons. Since social science is only occasionally or derivatively concerned with actions of particular individuals, it is something of a paradox that its theoretical assumptions are often based on the model of a single agent. But this is simply another indication of the close connection, sometimes explicit but often implicit, between ideology and social theory, that is, between, for example, liberalism or Marxism and a particular vision of social reality.

I will engage the issues of the individuation of action, the status of mental states, and the units of social reality as I proceed with an elaboration of the theory of conventional objects. It is not so much that we lack, either in everyday life or social science, a theory or ontology of such objects. It is rather that what we have in both cases is a confused and incoherent, and often indefensible, image or congeries of images. Social scientists and historians talk, and often with a sense of some confidence, both in general and in their particular explanatory endeavors, about the explanation of social behavior and of such matters as the relationship of ideas to behavior, but most of this talk cannot withstand much analytical scrutiny or be extended very far without running out of theoretical grounding. Part of my concern is not only to broaden the theoretical scope in order to include more than actions, and actions performed by individuals, but to focus on conventional objects as such and to devalue theoretically a number of issues such as the question of what can be the source and bearer of action.

There is, for example, often an assumption that action, linguistic competence, and conventional activity in general are distinctly, and maybe defining, *human* attributes. Although this may, as an empirical generalization, be quite defensible, it is not, I maintain, a matter that is central to understanding the theoretical character of conventional objects. We are still, as Daniel Dennett has suggested, obsessed with extricating ourselves from the confines of "Darwin's dangerous idea" and finding a way to distinguish ultimately between natural and artificial intelligence (1995). If we should, in all functional respects, successfully teach an ape to use language and a computer to "think," would we then say that they are human or would we seek another basis for the demarcation of human being? Many philosophers, such as Alasdair MacIntyre, are "hung up" on the issue of what can manifest an action, and they are intent on demonstrating that, for example, machines "are incapable of action," since they lack such things as moral properties, reasons, and social history (1986:80). For MacIntyre it finally comes down to the quality of "intelligibility," which ultimately is a kind of ineffable sense of connectedness. But here again, the theory of action is secondary to some ideological agenda or to arguments about such issues as the epistemological difference between natural and social science, overcoming relativism, or legitimating metapractical inquiry.

My concern is to reverse this distribution of emphasis, to confront the theoretical issues involving action, and then worry about the implications for other matters such as whether machines or animals can act or whether social theory possesses cognitive superiority. We probably will not find it necessary to deal with the latter issue in the near future, since neither Koko and Washoe nor artificial intelligence seem capable of achieving what some advocates believed possible. But why should we care? Will we feel constrained to extend the protections of the Fourteenth Amendment to our computers? I do not want to contend with those who insist that animals reason, have beliefs, manifest intentions, and the like, but I assume that conventional behavior requires linguistic and conceptual capacities that most creatures and mechanisms do not appear to possess. The attribution of conventional activity to nonhuman animals by sociobiologists and others, as well as explaining conventions in biological terms, often seems largely to involve interpreting animal behavior in anthropomorphic terms or positing functional equivalence between such behavior and that of humans. Although I will not attempt to settle the question of what can be the bearer of a conventional object and although I do not worry about conventions being attributed to other than humans and other than individuals, I will insist that such objects are not theoretically reducible to something else such as biological states or phylogenetically determined adaptions. Again, the issue is, in the first instance, the theoretical character of conventional action and its products and not what makes it ultimately possible or where it is manifest—even though these matters are not easily disjoined.

Such matters as whether language and convention are in some way predicated on something deeper or more fundamental—whether, for example, as Chomsky and others believe, the variety of natural languages is structured by "the simple computational design of Universal Grammar" (Pinker 1994:411)—and whether there are underlying "human universals" behind cultural differences (Brown 1991) are questions that I would be inclined to answer in the negative, but they have little immediate bearing on the theory of conventional objects. What ultimately makes conventional objects possible, that is, what the biological grounds may be of the phenomena associated with human consciousness (Dennett 1991), and what would in that respect constitute an explanation are issues that I will not address. My concern is with description and explanation within the theoretical domain of conventionality. The theory of conventional objects also sidesteps, or rejects the relevance of, the perennial and often metatheoretical issue of identity and difference with respect to behavior and action. Although behavior, as posited in behaviorism, is a theoretical concept, I employ the concept of behavior generically to encompass both action and other things that people (and animals and physical objects) do. The concept of behavior, in my discussion, has no theoretical status, and although many theorists have attempted to discriminate actions as things that people "do" as opposed to other more biologically induced behavior or what happens to them, this, I think, is too constrained a use of "doing."

As I noted earlier, many theories of action, as well as numerous metatheoretical spinoffs, in both philosophy and social science, that are devoted to talking about the explanation of action have been framed by a set of problems that have tended to place prior restraints on the discussion. These include the relationship between thought and action, or ideas and behavior; whether action can be construed as a form of speech or vice versa; and the question of agency. My arguments seek less to resolve some of these issues than to dissolve them. In his treatise *On Interpretation,* Aristotle stated that "spoken words are the symbols of mental experience and written words are the symbols of spoken words." This image continues to govern much of philosophy as well as common sense, but it must be confronted and examined, if not discarded. The theory of conventional objects jettisons the notions of agency as lodged in the subjectivity of an actor and as giving rise to action as well as volitional or mental action theories in general, and it eliminates the problem of whether speech is more fundamental than action.

Central to my formulation is the thesis of conventional realism that entails the primacy of conventions and a rejection of views that would construe them as instruments of, or predicated on, something else. Conventions include norms and customs, both what Weber called *Convention* and *Sitte* and what Winch refers to as rules. The root question, however, which has been insufficiently addressed in the literature of both philosophy and social theory, is what are these things, what kinds of entities are we talking about? Despite all the attention that has been devoted to the subject of conventions in recent years, there has been little direct and extended examination.

III

The most detailed philosophical account of conventions as such is that of David Lewis (1969), but it is a narrow analysis. He stresses behavioral regularity as both a precursor and attribute of conventions that may be explicit or implicit. Lewis views conventions as primarily instrumental or functional and as ultimately a product of individual agreement. His Quine-inspired approach is based on game theory and construes conventions as a response to coordination problems and as a way of reconciling individual preferences and interests. In one sense, everyone seems to know what conventions are, that is, the forms of action and speech that constitute social relations, but it also seems to be difficult, even for philosophers, to go beyond such general claims. We might say that conventions are shared practices, but we might also say that practices are shared conventions. It is apparent in two symposiums on the subject of convention in literary and philosophical analysis (*New Literary History* 1981, 1983) that extended discussions of convention rarely escape such tautologies. Cavell notes that we can say of conventions that they are "those forms of life which are normal to any group of creatures we call human, any group about which we will say, for example, they *have* a past to which they respond, or a geographical environment which they manipulate or exploit in certain ways for certainly humanly comprehendible motives" (1979:111). But such statements still leave us with little criteria for thinking specifically about the matter. Probably the best work on conventions has been that of individuals such as Cavell who have, through deep analysis of exemplars, brought many of the essential features to the surface, but there is still reason, I believe, to start at the other end and seek a more general theory of conventionality.

We start from the wrong vantage point if we attempt to think of conventional phenomena as rooted in some kind of subjective individual like-mindedness. Conventions are grounded in practices and language games or, to use Wittgenstein's own words, "not agreement in opinions but forms of life" (1953:241). My core claim is that *action, thought,* and *speech* are theoretically identical *modes* of conventional objects. All three modes have a common theoretical structure. As modes, they are, it might be argued, related to one another like water, steam, and ice are related to H_2O. The apparent, and intriguing, parallels between thought, speech, and action have led to arguments about social science as hermeneutical and to claims about textual interpretation as a model for social inquiry (Ricoeur 1971; Taylor 1971) as well as to puzzles about how intentions are expressed in language. The parallels, however, are a function of the theoretical identity of the modes. Similarly, much attention has been devoted to the question of which dimension is the most fundamental, but this problem dissolves if the modes are theoretically identical. An *instance* of one mode may give rise to an instance of another, but one mode, as such, is not the cause or explanation of the other any more or less than steam is the explanation of condensation. No mode, as such, has priority or constitutes an explanatory ground. Thought, for example, cannot be construed, generically, as the source of action or speech, and neither action nor speech can be construed, generically, as derived from the other. And determining agency is a contextual matter of deciding and designating what, at a particular time and place, is the instantiator or bearer of a conventional object rather than a matter of explaining where actions, either as such or as particulars, come from.

In rejecting behaviorism and materialist reductionism, much of the theory of action and contemporary philosophy in general, as well as common sense, has been mortgaged to various forms of ontological intentionalism or an intention-based semantics. Much of this has derived from the influential Gricean argument (Grice 1957) that meaning can be defined in psychological terms that are independent of language and convention in general—that a speaker's meaning or mental intention informs language and action (Bennett 1976). It is my contention that such a notion of meaning is theoretically sterile. Although I will not attempt to base this claim in any specific manner on the work of Austin and Wittgenstein, I am assuming that it is implied in their accounts of action (Schiffer 1987; Bilgrami 1992) even though many (e.g., Searle, and see the discussion of Quentin Skinner in chapter 5) continue to interpret them as embracing mental intentionalism. Wittgenstein, for example, stated that "now it is becoming clear to me why I thought that thinking and language were the same. For thinking is a kind of language" (1961:82) and "language is itself the vehicle of thought" (1953:329). Although this particular phrasing, if literally construed, might still seem to suggest a reduction of thought to language in one instance and the subservience of language to thought in the other, what is basically implied, I believe, is the theoretical identity of thought and speech and their subsumption under the category of convention. I would subscribe to Nietzsche's view that "thinking, as epistemologists conceive it, simply does not occur: it is a quite arbitrary fiction" (1967:477). Or as Wittgenstein put it, "Thinking is not an incorporeal which lends life and sense to speaking, and which it would be possible to detach from speaking. . . . Speech with and without thought is to be compared with the playing of a piece of music with and without thought" (1953:339).

Davidson also insists that there is a kind of theoretical identity between thought and speech—"beliefs and intentions are like silent utterances." We know beliefs only through language, and "if we understand what a speaker says, we can know what he believes" (1984:144, 153). Yet despite Davidsons's claims that thought requires participation in a "speech community" and that we usually get access to thoughts only through speech, he still claims that in the end, "to speak is to express thoughts" (1984:155, 170) and that action is the manifestation of mental events that are hidden from view. Although he disagrees with individuals such as Fodor who believe that it is possible, at least in principle, to formulate causal laws relating mental states to actions, he nevertheless holds that mental states or propositional attitudes (reasons in the form of beliefs and desires) can be inferred from behavior and then treated, in a weak or non-nomological sense, as causes of action. He holds, as a basic assumption, that mental states are supervenient and manifestations of physical or brain states, but he argues that the "mental" is nevertheless anomalous and not reducible to physical states. Davidson wishes to keep actions within the realm of causal events while accepting the claim that reasons or mental predicates are explanatory factors. In his view, the "primary reason" for an action both causes the action and *"rationalizes"* it. For Davidson, a theory of action becomes, in part, a scheme for redescribing behavior teleologically, and thus it is, and has been, attractive to a variety of social theorists who seek a philosophically credible and "scientific" basis for viewing human action purposively.

While I would agree that it is possible to construe *a* thought as the cause of *an* action, I reject, as I have already stressed, the claim that thought, as such, is the cause of action. My approach to the concepts of thought and thinking is Rylean in that it does not treat thought as a special activity requiring some special apparatus and theater of operation (Ryle 1949, 1968a, 1968b). Coming to grips with the concept of thought requires that we begin by disabusing ourselves of the notion that thinking is a function of some nonbiological organ called mind that resides in an inner space as well as of the notion that thinking is reducible to whatever physiological processes make it possible. The mind is either the brain (if we are looking for an organ and location), or it is a concept representing a certain range of dispositions and capacities, maybe not always adequately exercised— such as the ability to "keep one's mouth shut." I construe thoughts as, in effect, empirically distinguishable episodes defined by intentionality, but that is only to say that they are not reducible to overt behavior.

Like Wilfrid Sellars, I embrace a "modified form of the view that thoughts are *linguistic episodes*" (1963:178) whereby intentionality is conceived semantically. Thought, we might say, is silent speech in the same sense that steam is evaporated water, and in that manner, we could take action to be overt thought; but the problem with such descriptions is that they tend to be misleading. Instances of thought sometimes precede instances of speech and action, just as they precede other instances of thought, but they also are sometimes subsequent to them. The first may be called premeditation, and the latter may be designated reflection. In our society, and in the company of philosophers, there is a tendency to lapse into the intellectualist fallacy that thought is, in general, the precondition of speech and action, but if we had lived all our life at the edge of a glacier, we might have come to believe that ice was always prior to water. There is some logical and anthropological evidence to suggest that in terms of both cultural and individual development, thought is actually a derivative capacity; that is, the ability to keep our speech and action to ourselves is, like reading without moving our lips, something that took practice to acquire.

One might argue that what we call mind is socially or conventionally constituted, but that still implies that the mind, in general or singularly, is some kind of "thing." The theory of conventional objects rejects theories of action predicated upon the existence of some universal subject. As Wittgenstein put it, "There is no such thing as the subject that thinks and entertains ideas" (1933: 5.631), and the notion of an individual mind as something other than corporeal is best conceived as a repertoire of conventions. The concept of mind refers to a range of capacities. Thinking, to the extent that it is a distinct performance or activity, as Ryle suggests (1968a) in the case of *le Penseur,* belongs in a category of its own, but the category is not theoretical any more than the image of John Wayne as the "man of action." These are simply cultural paradigms attached to a certain mode of conventional objects. A particular thought may sometimes precede action or speech and be construed as an explanation, even, if we wish, a causal one, but as Ryle suggested, it precedes in the manner in which a rehearsal in the theatre precedes a public performance. Thought preceding action, and viewed causally, is, theoretically speaking, no different from one action preceding another and understood as its explanatory antecedent. This is not to deny, for example, intentionality but rather to claim that individual intentions are instances of conventions. Language is not simply a tool for expressing prior intentions. Intentionality is a function of conventions of which thought is one mode (Savigny 1988). It is, then, important not to construe any mode of convention as a generic explanatory factor.

Another persistent issue in the philosophy and practice of social science has revolved around the explanatory priority of thought vis-à-vis social and institutional contexts, but once we view thought and institutions as, respectively, modes and artifacts of conventional phenomena, this metatheoretical dilemma, like that revolving around thought and action, dissolves. Thoughts, for example, might in some situation be construed as causing or giving rise to a configuration of activity, or particular institutions might be viewed as regularizing certain thoughts; but thoughts, as such, do not cause or explain institutions, and institutions and general social contexts are not, as such, the origin of "ideas." A consideration of this issue leads directly to the perennial question of whether institutions are, or can be, construed as actors or agents. To pose this question is often to assume already that actions are somehow tied principally to individuals, but if action is a mode of conventional objects, this problem loses its theoretical significance, as does that of the whole conflict between ontological individualism and ontological holism, that is, the issue of whether it is the individual or society that is prior.

If conventions are theoretically autonomous and action is a mode of conventionality, the question is really one of what things can instantiate an action and not whether institutions are individuals or whether collectivities are agents. Institutions may assume, in the conventions of law, for example, the status of persons, but this does not tell us anything about their theoretical status. They are, like all social practices, historical configurations of conventions. This also brings us to the issue of whether there can be nondiscursive practices. If we construe "discursive" narrowly as referring to linguistic performances and activities or, as in the case of Foucault, to highly organized practices of knowledge, there are, of course, nondiscursive practices. If we understand the concept of discursive more broadly, as I do here, as theoretically identical with conventions, it does not make any sense to speak of any practice as nondiscursive. The point is not to give priority to language in the narrow sense but to stress the theoretical identity of conventional objects.

Another issue that the theory of conventional objects eliminates is the tension in social theory among ideological, agential, and structural explanations. The concept of structure as employed here does not signal a particular kind of explanation that can, for example, be discussed in terms of whether it is more fundamental than explanations in terms of individual action or ideational factors but rather signals a particular class of things to be explained. Structures are configurations of conventions and are not theoretically distinct from other conventional objects. Action and structure do not refer either to different theoretical entities or to different basic types of explanation but rather to different aspects of convention. And they are not logically comparable concepts. Action is a mode of conventional objects, and structure is a category of particulars whether institutional or behavioral. The relationship between an actor and a structure is a historically specific one that cannot be theoretically generalized.

There has been much discussion of rules and conventions and the relationship between them (Emmett 1966), but in my usage, rules, like institutions, are a species of convention. We can think of instantiations of conventional objects as "rule-governed" (Winch 1958) or "conformative behavior" (Shwayder 1965), but this terminology should not, as I have already stressed, be construed as indicating conformist or conventional in the sense of normal or inhospitable to change. On the contrary, conventional implies variability and the possibility of, and susceptibility to, transformation, even though sedimentation, in rules and institutions, for example, is a characteristic of conventionality. Conventional objects themselves, however, have structure, and that structure is theoretically significant.

IV

There are three necessary and integral, but analytically distinct, dimensions of any conventional object. This basic formulation reflects Austin's analysis of speech acts, but I do not want to stake my claim specifically upon his analysis or, particularly, upon interpretations of his work, which seems to mean very different things to different people. The first dimension is physical *extension* or manifestation in terms of bodily movement, vocal sounds, inscriptions, and so on. By "first," I mean necessary but not sufficient, or most elemental rather than most fundamental. The sequence chosen in discussing the dimensions of a conventional object is not indicative of one being most essential. This has been a persistent mistake, for example, in attempting to define linguistic meaning, that is, to define it in terms of one dimension such as reference or illocutionary force. It might be asked how thought can be understood as having extension, but we could not talk about thought without extensional or physical criteria, whether firsthand reports or extrapolations from contexts of speech or action. Thought must be treated, like many theoretical entities, as only secondarily observable.

Extension, however, must, to support the concept of convention, have *significance*. This is a function of its location in some context that enables its identification as an instance of a certain type. In the case of speech, this would be conventions of sense and reference, which involve discriminations of kind and denotation of particulars, and conformance with rules of grammar and syntax. Actions and thoughts also have a logically comparable "grammar" and "syntax" and rules of "reference." Significance, however, still does not make a conventional object fully intelligible. As I have already suggested, maybe the central problem in the theory of action is that of individuation. While extension and significance are necessary and collateral dimensions, they do not fully establish the *identity* of a conventional object. There has been a persistent temptation in the literature on the theory of action to seek a criterion of individuation that is extraconventional, just as in the theory of language there persists an urge to posit at least a core of linguistic signifiers that correspond, in some relatively unproblematical way, to the "world." I have already discussed those who claim that actions can be reduced to bodily movements or that, if bodily movements as such are not conceived as basic actions, there is some a priori category of primitive actions that cause or generate more complex actions. Even antireductionists often suggest that identifying actions is a matter of redescribing such putatively basic forms. Often what is involved in this type of argument is a confusion between an action as such and the extensional dimension of an action, but individuation, like significance, is a conventional and contextual matter.

Individuation is ultimately a function of intentional force that gives rise to *meaning*. Meaning is the defining dimension of a conventional object, and it, in turn, although integrally related to extension and significance and supported by them, is the basis of resolving, at least in principle, the ambiguities of identity inherent in those dimensions. A particular meaning could be conveyed by a number of significations, just as a particular signification could be expressed by various extensions. In the wake of Austin's account of illocutionary forces, there was a great deal of debate about whether they were an aspect of meaning or something additional, but often the issue reflected assumptions about the duality of intention, that is, nonnatural and natural meaning as well as more extended notions of intention such as what a speaker was seeking to communicate and what the speaker intended to produce by the communication. By the concept of intention, and meaning, I am referring neither to a representation in the mind, to some intentional object of consciousness in the tradition of philosophers such as Edmund Husserl, nor to some other notion of a mental state such as that advanced by Searle.

Intention is not, any more than significance, nonconventional. Intentions are a property of the conventions that are available for invocation and evocation. As Wittgenstein noted, "An intention is embedded in its situation, in human customs and institutions. If the technique of the game of chess did not exist, I could not intend to play a game of chess. Insofar as I do intend the construction of a sentence in advance, that is made possible by the fact that I can speak the language in question" (1953:par. 337). As in the case of language and speech, it is fruitless to seek some priority between intention and convention. There could be no intention without conventions, but conventions emerge and evolve as the product of intentional performances. Seeking either temporal or logical priority in these cases is simply posing an inappropriate issue. Like most chicken-and-egg questions, there is a failure to recognize that we are not talking about two different things but about aspects or instances of the same theoretical entity.

Intention is not specific to thought but rather a basic property of conventional objects. Every intention is the instantiation of a convention from a public stock of conventions. The criteria of intention are public, and while we might speak of keeping one's intentions private, in the sense of thoughts not expressed, or of an intention (thought) preceding actions, there can, in principle, no more be private intentions than private languages. The notion of an intention as a mental event and antecedent of a physical action cannot be satisfactorily theoretically sustained. This is, again, not to say that there could not be an unconventional intention or that new conventions of intention could not be created. Conventions are, after all, conventional. This analysis of intention extends to other mental predicates. Whatever brain-states or psychological states might ultimately underlie concepts such as intention, purpose, desire, belief, and the like, this has no more, or less, to do with individuating, describing, and explaining conventional objects than physics does with baseball. Understanding a sacrifice bunt is not, usually, to inquire into either a psychological or a physical event.

There has, then, been a tendency to seek priority among modes of convention, or to reduce one to the other, and a persistent move in the theory of action has been to identify an action with, or reduce it to, one of its dimensions, such as bodily movement or intentionality, and thereby mistake a part for the whole. It is also important to distinguish between, for example, an action and its relationship, causal or otherwise, to other objects and events. Although not, strictly speaking, a logical or integral component of the structure of a conventional object, a kind of fourth dimension, roughly what Austin called "perlocutionary," involves the contingent *relation* of a conventional object to a wider ambient world of conventions and other things. Some conventional objects are so characteristically, either "conventionally" or causally, involved in certain relations to other objects, conventional and otherwise, that they become—like fire and smoke or movies and popcorn—virtually part of the identity of those objects. But any instantiation of a conventional object may cause, or otherwise lead to the generation of, other events and have outcomes—that is, effects, consequences, and results—of both a conventional and nonconventional character. And these may be *purposive* or accidental, or, as sometimes designated, intended and unintended. The concepts of intention and purpose are often used interchangeably, or sometimes philosophers speak of two kinds of intention (one that defines an act and one that refers to why the act was performed). The concept of intention, however, is reserved in the context of this discussion for identifying a conventional object, while purpose is construed as involving the practical vector of speech, thought, or action.

A crucial proposition in my theory of conventional objects is that like all theoretical entities, they are, despite the historicity of their particular manifestations, *universals.* While action events are particulars and unique, the same action may be performed in various times and places and instantiated by different agents. Actions or speech acts, for example, are not tokens of a type. Promising, for example, is not a category of particulars but rather a universal that is instantiated in particular events. The performance of an action is an *act* and an event situated in space and time, but like a quality such as color, actions are repeatable (Landesman 1969, 1972). In the case of speech, for example, the uttering, and understanding, of a sentence is a unique event, but the meaning of the sentence, what one is doing with words, is not a particular. This distinction between particular and universal is crucial in a number of respects, but first and foremost, it makes it possible to differentiate clearly between the *specification* of a conventional object, on the one hand, and its description, categorization, explanation, and evaluation, on the other hand. This is, for at least two reasons, an especially important distinction in the case of the social sciences. First, it points up the status of the social sciences as metapractices as well as the preconstituted discursive character of their subject matter. Although social science may talk about a conventional object in exogenous or social scientific terms, the object already possesses an endogenous identity upon which the language, categories, and theoretizations of social science are imposed. Second, it is the failure, within social science, to distinguish categorization, description, and the like from theoretical specification, that is, an explication of the kind of thing that is talked about, that is at the root of many perennial problems in social scientific inquiry. The various analytical schemes utilized in social science are not theoretical claims but presuppose theoretical claims.

At this point, it may be helpful to provide examples, one of speech and one of action, that concretely and schematically, even if hypothetically, both illustrate some of the principal features of my analysis and serve to distinguish it from alternative formulations (see figure 2.1).

The first thing to be noted about these (admittedly stipulated and stilted) examples and the general scheme is that the dividing line distinguishes first- and second-order spheres. The second point to be stressed is that an action is manifest in an act, and that meaning arises from intending, and understanding, an act as an action. The criteria of what counts as the meaning, significance, and extension of the act in which the action is manifest depends on the exact context, in this case a hypothetical one that would sustain the particular example just described. We would not want to say that what constitutes an action is a function of its context or is determined by the context if that would imply that the action is somehow derivative or something secondary to other elements. It would be more pre-

THEORETICAL DESIGNATION OF MODE

speech   action

PRECONSTITUTED CONVENTIONAL ACTIVITY

politics   politics

SOCIAL SCIENTIFIC CATEGORIZATION

radicalism   rational choice

SOCIAL SCIENTIFIC DESCRIPTION

dissident activity   citizen participation

- -

PRACTICE

politics   politics

ACT/MEANING/ACTION

prescribing revolution   voting for Clinton

SIGNIFICANCE

saying "down with the system"   using voting machine

EXTENSION

uttering words   moving arm

RELATION

causing riot   affecting election

Figure 2.1

cise to say that an action is a move in the holistic setting of an activity or practice or that it is a strand in a web of meanings. In some circumstances, using a voting machine or moving an arm could itself be construed as an action rather than as a component of an action. The centrality of context is why it is necessary to reject both the reductionist position that there are certain basic actions and the antireductionist claim that certain bodily movements can be redescribed as actions.

The notion that some element of a conventional object is perceptually or logically primitive is simply the equivalent of the logical positivist account of factual observation. What we perceive is conventional objects, and only in retrospect can we analyze them into components such as bodily movements, sounds, inscriptions, and the like. We do not first apprehend the latter and then extrapolate and infer the former any more than in the case of the natural world we grasp immediate experience sense-data and then interpret them as physical objects. It may be reasonable to suggest that there are situationally primitive or basic actions within a particular conventional context, such as kicking the ball in soccer, but the idea of a class of basic actions in a more general sense—as the cause or condition of a class of derivative actions, that is, simple as opposed to complex and involving the expression of a certain fundamental repertoire of human capacities—is futile. Such an idea usually involves confusing the specification of an action with a component of an action, with a conventional relationship to another action, or with a description of an action.

Conventional objects are, so to speak, given. They are "natural" in the sense that we speak of natural languages such as English, French, and so on. There is no non-natural (pace Grice) or nonconventional meaning. As I argued in chapter 1, this claim entails a certain positivity in that in principle, the specification of such objects is not, in the first instance, relative to a metapractical account of them. Endogenous specification may be contested by metapractical discourse just as the anthropologist may respecify the internally defined actions of an alien culture, and there may be an empirical issue of what action has been instantiated; but actions and other conventional objects are prior to and independent of their interpretation. This issue will be addressed more fully in chapter 5, but it is the source of much confusion regarding the explanation of conventional phenomena. Some hold that meaning is relative to interpretation, or at least relative to the interaction between the object and interpreter, while others hold that there is an objective meaning to be recovered. There is no metatheoretical solution to this problem because it is a conflict between the ghosts of two contending but often dimly explicated theories. The answer that flows from the theory presented here is that interpretation is always a claim, and therefore potentially corrigible, but what is being interpreted is not a discursive artifact of interpretation but a preconstituted meaning. What is often involved in this controversy is the issue of the relationship between a mental event and its public manifestation. One party holds that we can objectively recover the intention while the other maintains that it is inaccessible and thus meaning is ultimately a function of interpretation. But if the theory that tacitly underlies both positions is jettisoned, that is, the theory that actions, texts, and the like are, generically, the overt dimension of prior internal mental meanings, the issue disappears.

Since so many of the problems attending an analysis of conventional objects arise from a failure to distinguish among these objects and their structural components, it is worthwhile examining this matter even more closely. The relationship between, for example, a component of an action, such as a person moving an arm, cannot be said to be the cause of another component, such as its meaning (for example, waving good-bye) any more or less than one might say that a part is the cause of a whole. Nor can we really even say that the former gives rise to the latter. If, however, moving the arm was itself determined to be an action, and the action at issue, one could claim that it was the cause, for example, of another action by someone else as well as certain other events (e.g., the inadvertent breaking of a glass). Not everything that one could, analytically, be said to do in the course of performing an action is itself an action. All actions are basic or simple in that they are not made up of other actions, and all actions are complex in that they have constituent elements and are composed of analytically distinguishable "doings" and in that they are situated in a web of other actions. What is best referred to in terms of such adjectives as *simple* and *complex* or *thick* and *thin,* however, is not actions themselves but talk about actions, that is, description, explanation, evaluation, and the like.

The notion that the identity of conventional objects such as actions or sentences is relative to descriptions or categorizations of them usually involves, once again, the assumption that there is something fundamental and given to us in immediate experience, such as bodily movement or words, which is the bearer of these descriptions; otherwise the question of what has been variously described would be begged. It would, however, be a mistake to analyze the previous illustration as a situation in which a person, by moving an arm, performed several actions—pulled the lever on the voting machine, voted, helped elect Clinton, acted as a citizen, and so on. Specifying or identifying an action is prior to and different from analyzing, describing, and categorizing it. But what is also often involved in arguments about the equivalence of identity and description is a certain form of nominalism or the assumption that conventional objects are particulars.

If conventional objects were themselves particulars, such as events, descriptions of them could be taken as referring to and emphasizing various properties, and thus the specification of the object would be relative to the description offered. But conventional objects such as actions and speech are identified in terms of their intentional force or meaning, which is a universal predicate, that is, universal within the parameters of a conventional domain. Particular words, for example, may have a certain historical residue of meaning attached to them because of their characteristic uses, that is, what we find in dictionaries, but in most instances, it is sentences and propositions, and not particular words, that are the primary bearers of meaning. There often seems to be no end to the meanings that we attribute to many words, because words are not intrinsically meaningful. And the meaning of sentences is, following Wittgenstein and Austin, essentially a matter of what is done with them, that is, what conventions of intention are being invoked or instantiated and in what practices. There can be many potentially correct descriptions of an action or an utterance, since description is supervenient with respect to specification or identity and can be based on various possible criteria, but there can, logically speaking, be only one correct specification. This is not to say, however, that the correct specification is obvious or that it cannot be contested. The old story of the elephant being interpreted as different things by several unsighted persons touching various parts of the beast is, in an unintended sense, apposite. The moral of the story is usually taken to be that what is posited as reality is relative to the perspective of the observer, but the story presupposes the specification of the elephant and the supervenient character of the variable descriptions that come to be identified with it. If the audience of the story was not told that an elephant was the entity at issue, the point would be lost. The very concept of description implies the prior identity of what is described.

Even though my goal here is not to undertake the almost infinite task of confronting in any systematic way alternative theories of action and their variations, I will, for explicative reasons, contrast elements of my account with that of Davidson. From its first elementary formulation, in 1963, Davidson's analysis has been philosophically influential, and it has, in various derivative ways, left its mark on the literature of social science. It has served both as a justification or rationalization for what social scientists and philosophers of social science already tended, in some sense, to believe and as a basis of new renditions of the nature of social scientific explanation and the role of social theory.

By interpreting mentalities as causal, Davidson was in effect, as he later explicitly stated (1994), bringing together, or mediating, positivist and postpositivist accounts of action, that is, giving explanatory weight to both causation and teleology. In doing so, he advanced some very specific arguments and made some distinct assumptions that touch on the main themes of the theory of action. Davidson argued, hypothetically, that by flipping a switch, turning on a light, illuminating a room, and alerting a prowler, a person would have performed one action and that one event would have taken place that could be described in at least four different ways. He claimed that first and foremost, there was a primitive or basic event consisting of one "doing," but this could sustain more than one action-type description. Many, such as Goldman, would in this case posit four actions, but my analysis of this situation would entail the claim that only one action has been performed. Both Davidson and Goldman assume that there is some fundamental datum on which these actions or descriptions of actions are predicated, and it is this proposition that I contest.

Although, assuming a few initial contextual facts and conditions, it is plausible to say that only one action has been performed, it is incorrect to say that only one thing has been done. *The* action performed was turning on the light. This was done, and signified, by flipping the switch and by the collateral bodily movement or movements required to do so. Illuminating the room and alerting the prowler were, respectively, the purposive and nonpurposive relational effects and consequences that the action caused or produced or to which it was linked in some empirically specifiable manner. The action could be described (or evaluated) in an infinite number of ways that would be compatible with this specification—as an event that, let us say, took place in New York City late one night, as a fortunate set of circumstances, and so on. Actions as such cannot be described. It is action-events that are the subjects of description. Since describing something presupposes the possibility of specifying what is being described, Davidson assumed that a "bodily movement," that is, a "primitive action," was the bearer of these descriptions and that all descriptions of an action could ultimately be reduced to a more basic description of that movement. Following Joel Feinberg's (1965) image of the "accordion effect" that is involved as an action is expanded by multiple descriptions, Davidson claimed that "our primitive actions, the ones we do not by doing something else, mere movements of the body—these are all the actions there are. We never do more than move our bodies: the rest is up to nature" (1980:59).

One central difficulty in this formulation is the failure to distinguish between specification, or individuation, and description. Even if the reference in each case was to the same thing, what Davidson offered was actually multiple specifications rather than alternate descriptions. But what leads to the conflation of specification and description and to his version of reductionism is in part the assumption that actions are events or particulars and ontologically primitive (1980:165). Although the act that constitutes the performance of an action or the instantiation of a conventional object is a particular event that can be described in such terms as how, when, and where, Davidson treats each description as representing an action. It is not, however, conventional objects that are like accordions and that expand or contract as we talk about them. It is descriptions and accounts of them that are either compressed or inflated.

Another indication of Davidson's assumptions is evident in a distinction that he makes between eating and playing tarot. He claims that the latter is conventional, wheras the former is not. "In explaining what it is to eat, no mention of rules or conventions needs to be made" (1984:265). This claim could be analyzed in various ways. One might be talking about the functions of the digestive system, and in this case, Davidson *might* conceivably be correct. But in such a case, probably the concept of eating would not be central to the discussion. Eating, however, on its face, refers to a highly conventional sort of doing. What seems obvious here is that Davidson has quite arbitrarily equated eating with the physical movements involved while identifying tarot with its conventional dimension. Both eating and tarot are actions that are constituted by all dimensions of a conventional object and that, as a whole, can be described in various ways depending on the event in which they are instantiated.

Another problem that emerges in Davidson's analysis is that of sorting out the relationship between intentions and purposes as well as the status of other mental predicates. I would again urge construing purpose as what actors wish to achieve by doing what they do while reserving intention to specify what one does or means. It would be possible to speak, for example, of the purpose of an institution in that the institution was either an artifact that was created in order to effect certain results or that it came to function in such a manner. Purpose, no more than intention, need be understood as strictly reflective. Other mentalistic language (such as ideas, reasons, beliefs, attitudes, desires, and motives) that attaches to conventional objects also requires some discrimination. While it might be possible to speak of some of these concepts as causes of action and other conventional objects, cause is better employed in talking about the relationship of conventional objects to one another and to other things and events. The principal problem with referring to these concepts in terms of cause is the retention of the image of prior mental states as the generic antecedents of action. Most of what we do, or do well, does not require the silent rehearsal of thought. Actions might in various senses at times be evaluated as unthoughtful, but this need not imply that they are not intentional. Although there might be a theoretical psychological meaning for many mental terms, they are best understood, in terms of an analysis of action, as categorical concepts. I do not employ the concept of idea as a theoretical term but as a generic category for certain mental predicates. Sometimes beliefs and desires are spoken of as reasons, but this transforms reasons into a label for mental states. Reasons are best understood as claims made in support of an action or statement—either before or after the fact. Beliefs and desires are either self-ascribed or imputed statements about, respectively, what one takes to be the case, or the truth of a matter, and what one wants. And attitudes are basically dispositional attributions—not mental states. Much of this mentalistic terminology has uses, but it is often a mistake to take these words as referring to something or the occurrence of something. They refer, instead, to *kinds* of things.

V

One purpose of the theoretical arguments that I have advanced about conventional objects is to provide a foundation for epistemological claims about the nature of social scientific explanation and interpretation. My aim is also to bring to the surface the submerged or latent theories in such formulations and exorcise some of the ghosts of old theories that haunt these formulations. More specifically, I am concerned with providing a coherent theoretical infrastructure for a long-standing genre of third-order accounts about the nature of social scientific inquiry. Despite its diverse philosophical heritage, this genre has been around from Weber to Winch and is still reflected in a variety of contemporary claims about an interpretive, or interpretive/critical, social science. The basic problem with all these formulations is that they lack an explicit and developed theoretical ground, and they have become part of a surrogate metatheoretical conversation. Although the theory of conventional objects underlies much of the analysis in chapters 3 and 4, it is only in chapter 5 that I systematically confront metatheories of interpretive analysis and attempt to seek theoretical answers to the issues that surface in these accounts.

An answer to the question of what constitutes, or should constitute, social scientific explanation is bound to be elusive unless it is addressed at the theoretical level, but at the same time, it cannot be divorced from concrete issues connected with particular forms of second-order practice. It is when the question is posed, and answered, simply in metatheoretical terms that it loses identity and significance. A metatheoretical answer can never be the foundation, or provide the procedures, of the actual practice of inquiry. The philosophy of natural science, for example, is not, and cannot logically be, the basis of the practice of natural science. When an activity such as social science attempts to proceed on such a basis, it is inevitably distorted. Although there may be some reasonable way in which one could offer a general philosophical answer to how science explains things, it could at best be some abstract and partial characterization that would not convey a great deal. The concept of explaining makes sense primarily with reference to either the theories that inform inquiry or the particular problems posed. The problem of what it is, in general, to explain nature or explain social phenomena is not genuine. It is a pseudoproblem. Theories provide certain limits and possibilities with respect to the definition of what can be an explanatory move, but explanation is, in the end, a pragmatic problem-specific affair. In the case of a conventional object, it might entail clarifying meaning, reconstructing purpose, examining the manner in which action generates or causes something to happen, providing a history of a practice, and so on. Outside of a context of specific explanatory problems, theory can do little apart from confronting other theories and subverting certain parasitic metatheoretical constructions.

It is in part because of the characteristic one-dimensional metatheoretical construals of the nature of social inquiry that epistemological compromises are always being floated. Thus we find many (futile and sterile) attempts, in both social science and the philosophy of social science, to reconcile rival metatheories such as those associated with positivism and postpositivism. Since some believe that looking for the meaning of social action is too narrow, "understanding," it is sometimes argued, must be supplemented by, or synthesized with, "explanation" or something that is more like the treatment of natural objects (von Wright 1971). More specifically, it is sometimes suggested that while focusing on the hermeneutical dimension of social inquiry is important, it is also necessary to account causally for such things as why actors possess the beliefs that they do (e.g., MacIntyre 1970). Thus, it is argued, what is required is, for example, an equal concern with structure and its relation to human agency. As I have already noted, it would be a mistake to assume that social inquiry can be reduced to the domain of one theory, but the kind of dualism represented in these arguments is distinctly metatheoretical. Structures are not, in most instances, theoretical objects but rather a category of particulars. Second, in terms of what I have been arguing, they are artifacts of action and therefore the instantiation of conventional objects. There is much to be explained by structures, but there can be no *theory* of structures any more than there can be a theory of institutions.

Individuals such as Anthony Giddens have devoted much attention to matters such as reconciling the explanatory poles of agency and structure and stressing, through an emphasis on process, the reflexivity of structure, that is, how it is both a product and cause of action. He, like Habermas, focuses on notions such as the double-hermeneutic or the manner in which an observer must both interpret the actions of actors and grasp the actors' interpretations of each other. One difficulty with Giddens's arguments, however, is that they yield largely metatheoretical generalizations that have a limited theoretical import and backing. And they represent the typical but futile attempt, when confronted with such dichotomies, to resolve the issue by seeking a metatheoretical middle ground that ultimately retains the contradiction (Holmwood and Stewart 1991). At best, they provide an analytical framework for thinking about and approaching social phenomena. I do not want to speak to the question of the research utility of such a framework, which seems to be a large part of Giddens's concern, but ideas of agency and action, for example, are thinly portrayed. Much of Giddens's efforts are devoted to synthesizing conflicting third-order epistemologies of social inquiry that were characteristic of debates in the philosophy of social science. He also attempts to amalgamate (vertically) the concepts of theory, epistemology, and method, and it is difficult to determine exactly how Giddens understands the status of his "theory" of "structuration." The impetus for his claim was the growing proliferation, during the 1960s and 1970s, of critiques of and alternatives to functionalism and positivistic naturalistic accounts of social scientific explanation. This turn toward alternative metatheories and attempts to deploy them as approaches to research amounted, in large measure, to a repetition of the same kind of mistake that had characterized mainstream social science's embrace of positivism. Although Giddens largely rejects the positivistically inspired idea of social scientific explanation as the development of law-like generalizations, explanation, however (as in the case of Winch, Taylor, and others), that he seems to believe is an adequate account of natural science, he embraces the instrumentalist image of theory in his account of social scientific inquiry. He understands what he offers as primarily a logical alternative to schemes such as functionalism.

Giddens claims that "conceptual schemes that order and inform processes of inquiry into social life are in large part what 'theory' is and what it is for." His structuration construct is presented as a scheme for the "understanding of human agency and of social institutions" (1984:xvii). The problem is that neither agency nor institutions are theoretically elaborated in any extensive manner. Giddens claims that he wishes to turn away from "epistemological issues" and to "the more 'ontological' concerns of social theory" and that functionalism, interpretive approaches to social science, and the like are "often taken to be epistemological, whereas they are in fact also ontological" (xx). He is not very clear about what this means, but it would seem that he is saying that he wants to downplay questions of how we can know social phenomena in favor of talking about ontological or theoretical concepts such as agency and structure. I would

endorse this general agenda, but constructing a metatheoretical framework of analysis consisting of implicitly ontological terms in many ways
only exacerbates the problem—particularly when Giddens draws on and
attempts to synthesize such a diverse variety of literatures dealing with the
nature of social inquiry.

Giddens definitely understates the matter when he says that he has "not
been reluctant to draw upon ideas from quite different sources" (1984:xxii).
Much like Habermas, he consistently expands the frontiers of his framework to capture each insurgent philosophical idea that might be construed
as touching the territory of social theory, and he appropriates and fuses
constructs from every discipline from philosophy to psychology. And despite his wish to eschew epistemology, he largely defines his project as an
attempt to reconcile objectivism and subjectivism, naturalistic and hermeneutical claims about explanation—all of which are the essence of theoretically alienated epistemological discussions. The issue here is, again, not
the utility or instrumental research value of such a framework but rather
its status as theory. Disparate theoretical claims and concepts are melded
in this enterprise without any real attention to their commensurability or
to whether they are defensible in their own right. One way to test the
theoretical significance of this framework is to imagine whether, in principle, it would be possible to say that it is in some fundamental sense either
true or untrue. I am not suggesting here either a positivist philosophical
argument about truth as correspondence with facts or a Popperian notion
of falsifiability but only that this framework is not a claim about social
reality but rather a claim about how we can fruitfully *think* about social
reality and that it still carries the vestiges of the old dichotomy. It is assumed that social reality is in some gross manner presented to us and that
the problem is how we can conceptually sort it out, understand it, and
explain it. But this brings us back to the issue, and claim, broached in
chapter 1, that is, that there cannot be a theory of politics.

This claim might be taken as merely a somewhat counterintuitive turn
of phrase sustained only by my legislation of the concept of theory. Certainly there can, in many senses of the word *theory,* be a theory of politics,
but if politics is a historical conventional configuration and theory is understood as referring to empirical ontology establishing a domain of
facticity, there can no more, or less, be a second-order theory of politics
than there can be a theory of chess, despite the less determinate and more
expansive character of the "game" of politics. While this might seem from
some perspectives to be an innocuous proposition, much of the enterprise of political theory, and even political science more generally, has
involved attempts to ontologize politics and to find criteria for specifying
its autonomy in a manner that goes beyond conventions. While I have

argued that the frameworks and approaches in social science that have often been called theories are not *theoretical* in the sense that I have employed the term, they do reflect an urge to establish "the political" in a transcontextual manner. The extent to which the search for the identity of politics has been tied to concrete professional concerns is often forgotten. In the history of political science, for example, there has been a constant struggle to distinguish politics from society, and even elevate the former over the latter, and consequently to make a case for the distinctiveness and importance of political science vis-à-vis sociology. And when political theory in turn sought a measure of independence from the mainstream of political science in the 1960s, its autonomy was often predicated on the latter's submission to interdisciplinary authority and concepts derived from economics and sociology and its failure to maintain the integrity of a vision of politics. Such professional concerns are still also very much alive in the discourse of political science and the attempt to find some theoretical unity behind the plurality of approaches and methods that characterize the field. But the search for the autonomy of politics is also tied to a variety of normative and ideological claims.

These arguments have oscillated between idolizing and seeking to abolish, both cognitively and practically, their subject matter. Seldom has what might be understood as everyday politics been an object of approbation. Politics as an actual social practice has been depreciated in favor of more epic and heroic images or, at least, understood as in need of significant purification. Yet politics has been characteristically viewed as more than an ephemeral historical phenomenon and as possessing or manifesting some essential nature and, in turn, as both reflecting human nature and being necessary for human realization. Even for Marx, the state, despite its pending demise, was an ontological entity. When political scientists and political theorists have talked about a theory of politics, they have meant one of two things. They have embraced either instrumentalism or essentialism, which despite their opposition both involve a similar kind of mistake. These positions assume, albeit in a different manner, that politics possesses a certain kind of transconventionality, and they lead to a neglect of both actual political practices and the theoretical datum that underlies those practices.

A problem with the concept of politics (and science or religion, for that matter), at least in the English language, is an inherent prismatic ambiguity that leads to, and allows, confusion. As I noted in chapter 1, "politics," in one sense of the term, refers to a preconstituted historical conventional practice or configuration of human activity, and in this sense, it is neither necessary nor universal. It has a career and a genealogy, and thus any attempt to define it in terms of its properties or attributes is necessarily either very partial or very abstract. And if we are not quite certain about the units and boundaries of politics, definitions are of little use. They only codify vagueness. There is, however, a characteristic second sense of "politics" that seems to lend itself more easily to definition. We might say, for example, that science is an attempt systematically to make sense of the world around us or that religion is a belief in the supernatural—or that politics is the clash and compromise among interests. In the end, such definitions nearly always appear both too broad and narrow, but it is important to see exactly what is involved in this use of the concept of politics and how it differs from, and relates to, the first.

In this second sense, the concept is employed analytically or functionally to designate and demarcate an aspect or structural component of human practices and institutions. As such, it is quite arbitrary and could, in principle, be replaced with "X." While there is nothing inherently wrong with such apparently abstract definitions, they tend to reflect and be abstracted from historical political forms and carry cognitive and ideological bias in discriminating what is political. Thus what is called, by anthropologists, a political system in a culture such as highland Burma becomes more than merely a heuristic analytical category, and it may both obscure indigenous aspects of a society and prejudice the understanding of a second-order analyst. When David Easton defined politics as "the authoritative allocation of values," he was attempting to distinguish the "political system" as a distinct object of inquiry and, in part, thereby vouchsafe the identity of political science, but this definition also attributed to politics a certain theoretical or scientific universality that transcended the particularity of its historical forms. This kind of universality may not have satisfied those who sought a deeper sense of political, but as I have already suggested, the two positions are more closely related than might be assumed.

Functional or analytical characterizations of politics tend to slide over into a third concept of politics that I will call essentialist or ontological. There is often the tacit assumption that we are not simply extrapolating from familiar uses of "politics" and applying them functionally or metaphorically to other phenomenon in the way that we might talk about corporate mergers in the language of chess. What is often assumed is a certain universality and givenness to politics that makes possible such extensions—that the application is more than merely analytical. What is assumed is a sense of theoretical or ontological sameness, something more than historical family resemblance, and this is closely related to arguments that pursue a more self-conscious strategy for distinguishing "the political" as a deeper and necessary element of the human condition. Attempts to ontologize, or reontologize, "the political," however, often really amount to little more than isolating properties of social relationships or functional characteristics that we tend conventionally to regard as political. Carl Schmitt, seeking to halt what he believed was liberalism's depreciation of political authority, sought the universality, objectivity, and autonomy of "the political" in human nature, in the necessity of a sovereign power that could decide in exceptional cases, and in the inevitability of distinctions between friends and enemies. Similar claims were advanced by Leo Strauss. Hannah Arendt, also lamenting the modern inversion of the priority between public and private or society and politics, revived the Aristotelian notion of the political as grounded in, and demanded by, the human condition—a space in which the human capacities for speech and action could be manifest and realized (1958). And Habermas has made somewhat similar arguments about the modern loss and recovery of the political realm and its grounding in the basic structures of human life. Sheldon Wolin, while softening the ontological claim, nevertheless found in the idea of the political the basis of a tradition of thought and action that despite the dangers of its modern "sublimation" was nothing less than part of the identity of Western civilization and the key to its salvation (1960). None of these claims celebrated contemporary conventional political practices. On the contrary, they represented such practice as a deformed instance of a deeper unrealized value. But what is called political in all these cases seems, in the end, to lack any distinct theoretical status. It is little more than the discrimination of a functional or analytical entity that is designated as political because it possesses attributes that we associate with the concept as either a practice or an ideal. Other writers have attempted to distinguish the political on more processional grounds.

Ernesto Laclau and Chantal Mouffe, in pursuit of a revision of socialist thought and democratic theory that would reverse Marx's emphasis on civil society as the locus of social transformation, argue for the distinctiveness of politics on the basis that it is the activity or practice, in a world of inevitable social antagonisms, in which the always fluid, porous, and incomplete social hegemony is constantly articulated and rearticulated. Politics is defined as "a practice of creation, reproduction, and transformation of social relations" that both institutes and desituates institutional forms (Laclau and Mouffe 1986:111, 122). Laclau, drawing on postmodernist and poststructural imagery, develops this notion of the autonomy and "primacy of the political over the social" even further (1990: 33). The social, he claims, is the realm of conservatism and "sedimented forms of 'objectivity,' " but since it can never fully achieve coherence and eliminate contingency, power and antagonism are always immanent even if temporarily hidden and suppressed. Politics is this manifestation of temporality, contingency, ultimate undecidability, power, and conflict.

Drawing on Plato and Hobbes as archetypal imagists of the elimination of the political and enemies of plurality, Laclau suggests the impossibility of this dream. "The moment of antagonism where the undecidable nature of the alternatives and their resolution through power relations becomes fully visible constitutes the field of the 'political' " (69). Laclau argues that like Heidegger's and Arendt's accounts of the structures of human existence, "the distinction between the social and the political is thus ontologically constitutive of social relations" (35). He even suggests that nominal politics or "political victory" momentarily achieved in the state or particular forms of political "space" is only the "elimination of the specifically political nature of the victorious practice," that is, that conventional politics is epiphenomenal.

Viewed in its context as an attempt to deal with the frustrations of traditional Marxism and to move beyond to a socialist theory consonant with pluralism and democracy that is legitimated by drawing loosely upon a variety of contemporary philosophical authorities from Wittgenstein to Derrida, the argument makes rhetorical sense. Viewed outside that context, it has little to sustain it. Very conventional images of politics as characterized by conflict, power, and plural interests and as a source of social transformation are abstracted and reified and offered up as ontological structures. There is at best a kind of conceptual sleight of hand that is played out here or at worst a conceptual confusion among functional, historical, and ontological notions of politics. Claims about the "autonomy of politics" (Clarke 1988) based on concepts such as conflict or "cooperation" tell us little. They make it easy to say that in some instance politics either does or does not exist. Even someone such as Clifford Geertz, who has pressed for "thicker" interpretations of unfamiliar cultures and sensitivity to the autonomy of "local" concepts, seems to find no difficulty in transferring the category "political." He describes the culture of Bali as having an "indigenous political system" and as involving a "political game" with players such as "kings," "lords," "gentry," and "commons" (Geertz 1975:23).

Although my analysis of the orders of discourse and the theory of conventions that I am urging may carry a distinct prejudice in favor of the first formulation of politics as a conventional and historical entity, the issue is less a matter of the correct way to define it than one of clarity about the differences. But if what could appropriately be called theory in natural science approximates the kind of claim that I have described, that is, claims that talk about what kind of things exist and the manner of their existence and that constitute a domain of facticity, there could, as I have argued in chapter 1, no more be a theory of politics than theories, for example, of the things recounted in natural history. If we take natural history to be a study of the behavior of specific natural objects, that is, an account of temporally and spatially bound manifestations of natural facts, theories are inherent in the specification of those facts, but the account is not a theory. An account of politics is in many respects like a natural history account, only it is even more situationally and historically circumscribed. It is an account of a configuration of human convention. To the extent that there can be a theory of politics, it must be a theory of human action or conventional objects just as theories of natural phenomena underlie natural history. Frameworks, models, and approaches may be useful, but they must, in the end, be theoretically predicated.

The idea that "the political" has an essential character that is in some way demanded for human realization, that *le politique* is manifest and in varying degrees realized in *la politique,* need not be dismissed out of hand, but there has been little in the way of a focused attempt to elaborate and defend arguments of this type, which have usually appeared in relatively rhetorical and ideological contexts. I would submit that *the* political, either as ontology or an instrumental category, is little more than an abstraction from historically situated first-order political forms. Both instrumental and ontological images of politics fail, in their respective ways, to recognize the conventional character of political life. To say that politics is merely conventional is not, however, to deny its importance, autonomy, or even, in some sense, its naturalness. Ontology is not necessarily the basis of autonomy. There may be any number of reasons, from those of Aristotle to those of Arendt, for defending the autonomy, and priority, of politics, but there are no theoretical reasons. Searching for the essence of politics, however, has been closely involved with the search for cognitive and practical second-order authority over politics, and it is here that we encounter the issue of relativism that, at least since the work of Karl Mannheim, has permeated second- and third-order discussions of the nature of social scientific inquiry in both Europe and the United States (Gunnell 1993).

Relativism

A spectre haunts human thought: relativism.
—Ernest Gellner

The profuseness of attestations to supreme devotion to truth on the part of philosophy is a matter to arouse suspicion.
—John Dewey

Why are so many academicians, across the ideological and disciplinary spectrum, disturbed about the issue of relativism? What, for example, moves a prominent philosopher of psycholinguistics to exclaim, "I *hate* relativism. I hate relativism more than anything else, excepting, maybe, fiberglass powerboats" (Fodor 1985:5)? What is the source of this agitation, and what, exactly, is the position that precipitates such a response? There is often, as this quotation may indicate, a kind of cultural elitism reflected in a range of antirelativist positions, but the problem of relativism is primarily both an entailment of certain philosophical persuasions and a manifestation of a structural problem inherent in the relationship between metapractices and their object. Relativism, I will argue, is indeed an apparition, but it is the shade of philosophical foundationalism as well as the phantom that foundationalism seeks to escape. When we attempt to confront it concretely, it, like most ghosts, dematerializes, but there are many philosophers who take it seriously and have adopted the vocation of "relativism busters." What relativism haunts, however, is less human thought in general than the philosophical account of thought. At some level, both the search for certainty and the presence of skeptical doubt may be construed as elements of the human condition, but it is a mistake to assume that these issues in philosophy are simply a reflection of this natural propensity. The pervasive concern with relativism in political theory, the philosophy of science, literary criticism, anthropology, and various other metapractical enterprises is less a reaction to Cole Porter's observation that "the world has gone bad today, and good's bad today" and so "anything goes" than a displacement and sublimation of the problem of the relationship between second- and first-order practices. Relativism is the return of the repressed. What is involved in each case is the issue of the authority of metaanalyses and their search for some form of epistemic privilege. The issue of relativism is the philosophical residue of the practical problem of the relationship of metapractices to their object, and to the extent that it is a real issue or the aura of such an issue, it is rooted in the historical situation of these practices. Its transformation into an epistemological problem has created what is actually a pseudoproblem that is sustained by the fears and aspirations of philosophical rationalism. Relativism is the ghost of rationalisms past. Only when the metatheoretical search for transcontextual certainty is abandoned and the problem of relativism is dissolved can social science confront in an authentic manner the issue of its cognitive and practical relationship to politics.

I

Although not always explicit, the problem of relativism and the search for a solution structures, in many fundamental respects, the language of political and social theory and constitutes a "grammar" common to many of the dispersed conversations that compose these fields. A few familiar and salient contemporary examples would include the Straussian persuasion and adherents to other varieties of natural law; the tradition of Critical Theory represented by Max Horkheimer and Theodor Adorno; the immanent transcendentalism of Habermas and related and derivative attempts to derive standards of judgment from the structures of communicative action (e.g., Apel 1985); neo-Kantian formulations of individual rights such as those associated with the work of John Rawls and Ronald Dworkin (Rawls 1971; Dworkin 1977); Alasdair MacIntyre's return to virtue and tradition (1982); the latent rationalism in images of a critical/interpretive social science and political theory such as that advanced by Charles Taylor (1971, 1982); biopolitics (Masters 1989); and certain forms of neo-Marxism, especially those associated with scientific realism (Bhaskar 1986).

Although those who have been designated, or charged with being, relativists have sometimes themselves subscribed to the label, relativism has, for the most part, represented less a distinct philosophical position than a critical attribution pointing to the putative implications of a particular position such as that of Kuhn, Winch, or some school of thought such as postmodernism or poststructuralism. It is then construed as a general problem to be philosophically encountered. There are two basic issues that are usually involved in formulating the problem of relativism. The first is how we can escape perspectivity and confidently access the "world," including the meaning of what others say and do, and the second is how we can assess the truth or rightness of the words and actions of others. Both of these problems, however, are inappropriately posed as generic transcontextual epistemological issues. There cannot be a credible general metapractical answer to questions about how we can understand others

and ascertain truth and rightness. This conclusion, however, does not entail the philosophical position that claims to truth are vacuous but only
that second-order practices are not necessarily the arbiters or underwrit-
ers of first-order claims. It is not exactly, as individuals such as Richard
Rorty sometimes say or are construed as saying, that truth and falsity are
matters of solidarity but rather, in Wittgenstein's words, "It is what human
beings *say* that is true or false; and they agree in the *language* they use"
(1953:241). There is a subtle but important difference. The concept of
solidarity makes it appear as if truth were somehow a matter of sentiment
or commitment. Although this may be part of the history, sociology, or
psychology of truth claims, it does not tell us what they are as such or
address the question of criteria.

The contemporary period of debates about relativism, which has persisted for a generation without any apparent loss of momentum, is, in
general structural terms, similar to earlier twentieth-century discussions in
history, philosophy, and social science, and there are distinct discursive
and contextual continuities. It is interesting that in his extended study of
the discipline and profession of history in the United States from the perspective of the search for objectivity and the controversy over relativism,
Peter Novick (1988) never seems to quite grasp, or maybe fully articulate,
the extent to which "that noble dream" reflected the search for second-
order authority. The underlying issue has been, and remains, the authority
of metapractices. A variety of second-order discourses, often as disparate
as the philosophy of science and literary criticism, are hardly distinguishable with respect to how they conceive and address this problem. The
issue posed is whether there is some way to privilege an idea of reason
that can serve as a basis for a critique of common sense and various more
circumscribed first-order practices. Although the underlying problem may
be a practical one, the immediate concern is largely, either directly or indirectly, prompted by a fear that antifoundationalism in philosophy, as well
as various forms of contextualism, hermeneutics, and poststructuralism,
have threatened to level all discourses. Although this fear is sometimes
expressed by those who are worried about social stability and the mainte-
nance of authority and community, relativism is equally an anathema for
others who believe that it, implicitly if not explicitly, engenders a conservative or at least quiescent attitude. The latter see it as raising the issue of
how second-order enterprises can retain a "radical edge" (Norris 1985:10)
and the ability to demystify texts or everyday assumptions in a philosophical climate that engenders skepticism about epistemology. Individuals such
as Christopher Norris argue, much like those who blamed the rise of National Socialism on relativism and liberalism, that postmodernism and other
such academic attitudes do "more to promote than counter the drift

toward an ethos of cynical acquiescence" in contemporary British politics—and that different academic postures such as a "causal-realist approach" would have an opposite effect (1996:ix). Debates such as that
between Habermas and Gadamer, that is, between neo-Enlightenment
rationalism and neo-Romantic aestheticism, are viewed as only a manifestation of the wider crisis of reason precipitated by Richard Rorty, Lyotard,
Derrida, and others. While the discussion is characteristically cast in terms
of whether theoretical reason can be grounded, that is, whether there can
be a philosophical warrant for critical theory, the underlying issue of the
practical relationship between metapractices and their object is rarely directly confronted. Even if there should be a philosophical consensus asserting the right and power of reason embodied in second-order discourses
to engage in critical assessments of the practices that constitute their object, this would hardly solve the historically situated problem.

Often relativism is represented as a danger to the business of practical
judgment. It is suggested that relativism, as a philosophical attitude, is
subversive of political order or the search for truth in science. Leo Strauss,
as well as individuals such as Herbert Marcuse, warned about the vulnerability of liberalism and its relativistic attitude of pure tolerance and indicated that it was linked to the rise of Nazism. Allan Bloom suggests that
this philosophical persuasion has insinuated itself into modern culture
and that relativism is both the cause and the harbinger of social chaos.
MacIntyre focuses on the atrophication of communal virtue, and Habermas
suggests that we are losing the basis of democratic deliberation and social
criticism. Philosophers such as Karl Popper claim that relativism inhibits
the objectivity and progress of science, and Charles Taylor suggests that
the relativism implied in poststructuralism threatens the very ideas of truth
and rationality. This family of arguments claims, or suggests, that practical, for example, political, problems are the manifestation or reflections of
philosophical problems. Somehow relativistic doctrines have crept into or
invaded general social practices as well as the practices of knowledge. But
the implication is also that practical problems potentially have philosophical solutions, that solving the metatheoretical problem of relativism would
be to solve the problem of practical judgment and provide purchase for
critical reason. If this were the case, if political problems and solutions
could be reduced to philosophical ones, then, of course, the great dilemma
revolving around the role of metapractices would be solved. It is, however, precisely this problem that is actually at the root of the issue of
relativism.

Despite allusions to connections, analogous or real, between philosophical relativism and problems of practical life, the actual locus of relativism
is philosophy. It is a philosophical and, more generally, metapractical

dilemma that has no real first-order counterpart. It is the logical mirror image of foundationalism, and outside the discursive context of philosophical foundationalism, the problem has little meaning. Although it is tempting to suggest a parallel, or even a connection, between the breakdown or absence of grounds of practical judgment and the attitudes associated with philosophical relativism, this attempt fails on both logical and empirical grounds. One reason that the parallel is inappropriate is that in most instances what is understood as the relativist rejection of cognitive or ethical universalism is not actually a claim to the effect that knowledge or standards of normative judgment are impossible, in philosophy or elsewhere, but rather an argument that involves a rejection of philosophy as the adjudicator of practical judgment. And the idea that, historically, philosophical relativism leads to a failure of political and moral nerve is, at best, dubious. Despite, for example, the common claim of émigré scholars such as Strauss that philosophical relativism seeped into the Weimar culture and undermined resistance to Nazism or the criticism directed toward Karl Mannheim by members of the Frankfurt School, the fact of the matter was that, in general, the liberal "relativists" were more engaged and effective than transcendentalists on either the left or right (Gunnell 1993). It is a peculiar leap in logic to suggest that a rejection of rationalism and foundationalism in philosophy either leads one to give up the capacity for moral judgment or makes such judgment impossible.

It is sometimes difficult to isolate exactly what is at issue in discussions of relativism. As a position or claim, relativism, both self-ascribed and imputed, overt and latent, can be broken down into various, often overlapping, species (cognitive, moral, ontological, epistemological, conceptual, etc.), and some of the confusion attaching to the issue involves a failure to differentiate between species (Sankey 1997) as well as between their counterparts (Harré and Krausz 1996). One kind of argument is that there are alternative but incomparable accounts of the world. Another claim that is often considered relativist is that the criteria of rationality are context-dependent. A related, but stronger, claim is that truth, and what we mean by knowledge, is relative to theoretical contexts. Finally, there is ontological relativism holding that the "world" is dependent upon our conceptual constructions. I would defend all of these arguments. There are no transcontextual metapractically specifiable truth-conditions or criteria for specifying the "world." The criteria of valid judgment in any practice or activity are necessarily indigenous in both a de facto and de jure sense. While concepts such as knowledge, truth, and right may have a certain universal force or connotation, they have no substantive universal meaning or criteria of application. Many of the critiques of relativism, however, are directed either toward crude images that cannot be easily identified with any actual argument and individual or toward what is believed, and feared, to be the implications of particular philosophical claims.

Although there may be a tendency to associate concerns about relativism with arguments such as those of Strauss and Allan Bloom, in which relativism is selected as a distinct target of criticism (Strauss 1961; Bloom 1988), the basic concern is much more ideologically and philosophically widespread (e.g., Raven, Tijssen, and de Wolf 1992). Habermas, for example, claims that "the context-dependence of the criteria by which the members of different cultures at different times judge differently the validity of expressions does not, however, mean that the ideas of truth, of normative rightness, of sincerity and authenticity that underlie . . . the choice of criteria are context-dependent in the same degree" (1984:60). Given the contemporary attacks on subject-centered reason, Habermas seeks a path that would lead to the immanence of reason in the communicative practices of life but to a certain transcendental status for the kind of validity claims that are represented. For Habermas, however, as well as for someone such as Strauss, post-structuralism, postmodernism, and other forms of antifoundationalism are simply the heritage of the Nietzchean/ Heideggerian attack on reason that, they believe, reduces philosophy to literature and undermines the critical authority of metapractices by adopting a radical, and ultimately self-denying, historicism (Habermas 1987). Social and political theory remains wedded to the rationalist dream. Although it does not require a great deal of scrutiny to discern that the underlying issue, although maybe in some cases quite vestigial, is that of the status and role of metapractices, what is less transparent is how questions about the rise and fall of reason in the world (that is, in science, political life, morality, etc.) can be reduced to matters of academic philosophy, how the dilemmas of philosophy can be equated with the dilemmas of humankind writ large. Philosophy not only wishes to assimilate itself to the practices that it talks about and addresses but comes to believe in its ultimate identity with these practices; yet at the same time, paradoxically, it is obsessed with establishing its distinctiveness.

The philosophical turn against foundationalism was initially looked upon favorably by many because of the characteristic link between foundationalism and conservative ideology, but it was soon apparent that the attractions of the former were ecumenical and transcended ideology. Maybe the greatest concern about relativism today is not among those who fear change but among those who wish to produce it. The most vocal are those who worry about "the possibilities for ideological criticism in a postmodern age" in which "every claim to truth is immediately placed under suspicion." They fear that the "flight from foundationalism" threatens to become a "flight from politics" (Simons and Billig 1994:1, 5) and that in

Strauss' point

persuasions such as postmodernism the critique of foundationalism has turned against itself (Bauman 1992). What has been created, it is claimed, is a "hermeneutics of suspicion" (Ricoeur 1986) that undercuts any claim to reason. So how, it is asked, can we "as scholars and citizens" in the face of contemporary relativism, posit "moral authority" and "recover the central role of old-fashioned social science in forming a democratic public space" (Brown 1994:17, 24–25). What is involved in such questions and answers, however, is the assumptions that the feasibility of academic social critique is a matter of its philosophical posture and that from the ruins of foundationalism can spring a functional surrogate. Despite concerns about the contemporary crisis of reason, it is not unusual for political theorists to seek to derive something like an ethic of democracy, as well as second-order critical authority, from what appear as such unlikely sites as poststructuralism and postmodernism (e.g., Connolly 1991).

No ground

Since modern academic philosophy has characteristically been rationalist in character, much of political theory has become a rationalist enterprise. A change in philosophical fashion, such as that initiated by Kuhn's work or signaled by postmodernism, almost always, despite some cultural lag, entails a crisis of identity in political theory or a recasting of its foundationalist agenda (Rosenau 1992). And in one way or another much of what is considered to be contemporary manifestations of relativism can be traced to the implications of Wittgenstein's work (Barry 1996) and the manner in which it suggests that there are no truth-conditions outside particular practices (e.g., Kripke 1982). While individuals such as Martin Jay (1989) and Charles Taylor (1982) worry about whether we can rescue order, reason, truth, and objectivity in the face of poststructuralism, others (e.g., White 1991) seek new grounds of authority in such schools of thought and attempt to make relativism a virtue. Norris believes that while many strains of postmodernism imply relativism and threaten the critical enterprise, deconstructionism, via Derrida, offers a basis for a new form of socialist political criticism (1985, 1990). What characterizes many of the contemporary arguments against relativism, as Joseph Margolis has emphasized (1986), is what might seem to be a paradoxical attempt to find some way to reconcile historicism and universalism, to find a middle road or to admit, and even embrace, the fact of relativism and stress the manner in which it may support values of diversity and democracy and yet claim that it is possible to achieve some form of transcendentalism grounded in immanent criteria such as conditions of human communication or the very path of history itself.

Social scientist want a claim to both rule and

There is a great deal of florid imagery attached to the characterizations and criticisms of relativism as a philosophical claim, and it would be very difficult to find a person fitting the straw person or scarecrow that is often conjured up. We are told that the "extreme" relativist holds that "each belief is as good as another" (Krausz 1989:1), but it would be difficult to identify anyone who takes such a position. It is, again, largely a position attributed to individuals such as Richard Rorty who have attacked foundationalism and philosophy's traditional self-image. It is also often characterized as a position holding, or amounting to, the view that the concept of truth is meaningless and entails a descent down a slippery slope toward the dissolution of scientific objectivity and moral and intellectual quiescence, if not nihilism and political fanaticism. In political theory, the dangers touted include the loss of a critical attitude and a fall into an inert and ultimately self-destructive liberalism. It is, however, indeed difficult to miss the fact that the defense of "rationality" against "relativism" is often in one way or another a defense of contemporary Western science, common sense, and culture against alien images (Wilson 1970; Hollis and Lukes 1982). This is as true of neo-Marxist Critical Theory and its variations as it is of Popper and his disciples. It would be a mistake to assume that valorizing Western "theoretical understanding" and the progress toward "truth" exemplified in its "technological control" of the world necessarily represents a politically conservative posture (Taylor 1982). The motives behind the attachment to rationalism in social theory are in fact probably more often critical than legitimating, just as conservatism often finds comfort in antirationalism. The real issue is less one of general ideological attitudes, or even philosophical positions, than of the role of philosophy and other metapractices.

Amelie Rorty argues that the contemporary polarized controversy between relativism and rationalism in philosophy is an exaggerated confrontation between abstract positions alienated from common sense and any practical context. It is, she claims, "the kind of dispute that gives intellectuals a bad name among sensible people," and she suggests that "the hidden agenda is the horror of being judged or evaluated, mixed with the pleasure of judging and evaluating" (1989:18, 22). Richard Rorty argues that the fear of relativism is really "a fear for our culture," a fear that accepting truth as "solidarity" or a function of communal agreement means that our "liberal habits and hopes will not survive the reduction" (1989:42). Geertz suggests that it is a "fear of diversity" and that "if we wanted home truth, we should have stayed at home" (1989:32). These fears, I would agree, are indeed in various ways involved, but most essentially, the concern about relativism springs from the problem of the identity and authority of second-order discourses. This is the most fundamental "hidden agenda" even though in the many, and often highly specialized, discussions of relativism in philosophy, the roots of the issue have become obscured.

Almost without exception those, such as Kuhn or Winch, who are attacked as relativists have actually not questioned the substantive grounds of truth and judgment in any concrete historical practice but rather have challenged, either explicitly or in effect, the possibility of philosophy specifying some universal and transcontextual standard of validity regarding those grounds. The danger that is sensed is neither to the practice of science nor to critical reason in some generic sense but to metapractical authority regarding the grounds of science and reason. In nearly every case, those who defend philosophical foundationalism are less concerned either with truth in some abstract sense or with the integrity of some first-order practice than with professional identity and authority. This is not to say that one could not find various underlying agendas attached to antifoundationalism. Many have been quick to see connections, for example, between Richard Rorty's antifoundationalism and his brand of liberalism, but it is probably fair to say that he was drawn into debates about liberalism and political theory as a consequence of critiques, from both the philosophical (and ideological) left and right, regarding the implications of his position. There are few instances in which a defense of rationalism and an attack on relativism are not quite distinctly in the service of some ideological program and philosophy's role in carrying it out, but again, more important than any academic expression of ideology is the general problem of the status of metapractices. Even Rorty cannot, in the end, resist positing a didactic, albeit somewhat muted, role for philosophy as an "edifying" enterprise—with all the practical and semantic ambiguities that the word *edify* carries (1979). He may demand that philosophy "join the conversation of mankind," but it still appears to enter with a privileged therapeutic role. And Rorty never really confronts the concrete historical issue of the articulation between philosophy and first-order practices. The contemporary critique of foundationalism and transcendentalism has, unfortunately, for the most part been singularly silent with respect to examining the implications for reassessing philosophy's practical relationship to its object of inquiry (Nielsen 1991).

When relativism is defined, as it typically is, as a position holding that "cognitive, moral, or aesthetic claims involving such values as truth, meaningfulness, rightness, reasonableness, appropriateness, aptness or the like are relative to the contexts in which they appear" (Krausz 1989:1), there is considerable ambiguity. If this putative claim is understood as a factual assertion, it is, of course, correct and could conceivably be countered only in terms of, for example, some sociological account of the *jus gentium,* a Levi-Straussian brand of structuralism, or a historical demonstration of the constancy of certain beliefs in an enterprise such as natural science. But the sociological fact of the spatial and temporal diversity of truth-claims and their criteria is not really what is at issue. What is at stake is the possibility of some discourse rising above such diversity and making comparative judgments. Maurice Mandelbaum, for example, characterizes cognitive relativism as the view that the truth or falsity of an assertion is to be judged by reference to the properties or situation of the person making the assertion rather in terms of a correspondence between the assertion and the world (1982). And Mandelbaum also raises the argument, common to nearly every critic of relativism, that the relativist position logically deconstructs itself. The argument is that relativism involves something like the liar's paradox and that there is "an incoherence at the heart of relativism" whereby it "tends to undermine its own cognitive status" (Norris 1985:28, 194). This is an old idea, long advanced by Strauss and others, but the idea of relativism as self-refuting is persistent (e.g., Harris 1992) even among those who are sympathetic to much of what might be "the truth about relativism" (Margolis 1991). W. V. O. Quine also presents a classic statement of the view that relativism is neither correct nor possible. He claims that the relativist "cannot proclaim cultural relativism without rising above it, and he cannot rise above it without giving it up" (1975:328). Sometimes this type of criticism is lamely countered (Barnes and Bloor 1982) with the defense that every position, including that of relativism, should be tentative, but the claim that relativism is contradictory involves a typical misconstrual of what is usually asserted in actual arguments as well as a failure to sort out differences between orders of discourse.

It would be difficult to find anyone who would defend a position such as that characterized, or caricaturized, by Mandelbaum and others, but neither relativism nor what may be construed as its antithesis, that is, rationalism or foundationalism, refers so much to specific arguments as to *kinds* of arguments that are abstractly opposed. Most of the arguments that might fall under the category of relativism do not involve claims that undercut their own criteria by holding that no claims are rationally defensible or that there could not, in principle, be agreement across cultures. What is common to most of the arguments designated as relativist is the claim that there is no neutral or transcendental position from which to arbitrate differences and that philosophy cannot adduce universal criteria of judgment. While Mandelbaum's account implies that relativism is a denial of the practical meaning of the concept of truth, it is, in most instances, in fact, only a denial of the ability of philosophy to provide substantive transcontextual meaning for that concept. There are, however, some claims that rhetorically come close to slipping over into a formulation that resembles Mandelbaum's image.

When, for example, Nietzsche attacked the idea of truth, he was, for

the most part, challenging the philosophical pretensions of traditional rationalism, but his aphoristic claims could be construed as asserting that
the concept of truth is meaningless. Part of the difficulty was that he
tended to hold on to the language of those he attacked and speak of truth
as if it were an object rather a category for designating what is taken to be
justified belief in some substantive realm of discourse. Similarly, despite
the rhetorical context and playfulness that characterizes Derrida's work,
his claim that there is "no such thing as truth" or that "truth is plural" has
a kind of nonsensical character if it is literally construed. What, one may
ask, is it that does not exist or is plural? Such claims perpetuate the idea
that somehow conventionality is a swamp even if one might claim to be a
relatively happy denizen. It is one thing to attack the traditional epistemological project, which is the essence of most arguments that are characterized as relativist, but it is quite another thing to adopt a kind of negative
foundationalism that is really only another form of philosophy's will to
power. Philosophical founding and philosophical destruction are ultimately
the same kind of project. Attacking the rationalist notion of truth may too
quickly lead to the assumption that the concept of truth does not have
practical meaning and criteria of application, but the loss of transcendental criteria does not entail the loss of regional criteria. Certain strands of
antirationalism represent another philosophical strategy for dealing with
the problem of first- and second-order discourses. While rationalism claims
the authority of transcendental knowledge, some postmodernists, for example, attempt to extend the attack on the rationalist version of truth to
substantive practices of knowledge and thereby give philosophy as much
to say as any other discipline, if not a special status as the keeper of critical
wisdom. Again, the real concern about relativism is not about the lack, or
dissolution, of the grounds of validity within the universe of first-order
practices but about the ability of philosophy to command a metatheoretical
basis of judgment with respect to such practices. The nervousness is distinctly philosophical no matter how much that anxiety is projected onto
the practical world.

Ultimately what makes political theory beholden to philosophy is the
same thing that drives the epistemological quest in philosophy—the search
for the authority to underwrite or undermine judgments in the activities
that constitute their object of inquiry. Since there is often no institutional
basis of such authority, it must, it seems, be predicated on the authority of
knowledge, on deeper and more ahistorical criteria than those manifest in
the substantive practices of knowledge and activities of life. For much of
formal philosophy, however, the problem of its relationship to its subject
matter has lost a sense of immediacy, and probably the reaction against
relativism is largely a matter of defending past professional investment. It

would be a mistake to neglect the extent to which political theory is also governed by a search for professional identity, but in political theory, sensitivity to the practical underlying issue of "theory and practice" remains more acute despite the tendency to drift off into epistemological diversions. The problem of relativism, then, is a philosophical surrogate for the practical problem of the relationship between second- and first-order discourses, and in the case of political theory in the contemporary context, it is the ghost of the problem of the relationship between the academy and politics. It is the metatheoretical reflection of the dilemma of an enterprise devoted in principle to political criticism and evaluation but both institutionally estranged from political life and genetically limited to some form of the idea of theoretical intervention. In few instances have political theorists contemplated practical intervention or direct political advocacy and action. The issue is nearly always one of how to make theory practical. If, however, the problem of relativism is really a practical problem, or the manifestation of a practical problem, then it is only a pseudophilosophical problem.

The perpetuation of the search for a philosophical solution derives in part from an unwillingness to face the practical issue, but equally important is the latent hope, and the original inspiration, that such a solution might carry practical purchase, that the claim to epistemic authority will be heard and heeded in the world of politics. But while there may be a practical issue of relativism construed in this light, as a problem arising out of the historical tension between second- and first-order practice, between the authority of knowledge and political authority, relativism, conceived as a practical issue within an activity such as politics or science, is also a pseudoproblem conjured up by philosophy—the evil twin of rationalism. Although what is presented as the dilemma of relativism might be construed, like Hobbes's state of nature, as pointing toward certain conceivable practical problems, such as the conditions under which criteria of judgment break down in a particular practice or realm of discourse, or the absence of such criteria, and although it may, in part, be the philosophical memory or residue of such problems, it has no genuine practical counterpart. In the natural sciences, the question of the foundations of knowledge, as an issue extending beyond the validity of particular factual and theoretical claims, is neither posed nor confronted. There are a number of reasons relativism and other philosophical anxieties are not a problem *in* the discourse of natural science. These include its security about its social status and its internal theoretical hegemony, but the most important reason, as I emphasized in chapter 2, is that it has no practical relationship to its subject matter. There is no issue of the authority of its knowledge vis-à-vis that subject matter. This is part of the explanation for the limited impact of Kuhn's work on natural science, whereas it had a great impact on second-order discourses in philosophy and social science.

II

Kuhn's work precipitated much of the recent concern about relativism, but there are two, often obscured, characteristics of his argument that should be noted. First, it is easy to overlook the fact that as much as Kuhn may have been a philosophical dissident, his work was still in the final analysis, like previous philosophies of science, a vindication of science. As much as critics worried about his destroying the epistemic grounds for assessing scientific progress, his theory of paradigmatic transformation was still an account of how science developed and succeeded. Second, despite all the attention that his image of the history of science evoked, his historical account, like early postivistically informed histories, was designed, or served, to validate a particular epistemology and methodology. It was an account of the nature of scientific knowledge and its acquisition that exceeded science's understanding of itself. What, then, one might ask, was all the fuss about Kuhn and relativism that emanated from so many disparate philosophical quarters? The basic answer is that Kuhn's argument undercut, in several respects, latent but discursively persistent hopes about the authority of philosophy. As I will explain more fully in chapter 4, it collapsed both the theory/fact and the logic/pragmatics distinction. Positivism rested on a claim of special philosophical access to the general epistemic and logical foundations of science, but Kuhn's analysis rendered the logic and factual domain of science relative to the theoretical contexts or paradigms of scientific practice and made the meaning of "science" the province of that practice. A typical criticism of Kuhn was that he called into question the ideas of truth and objectivity in science and rendered scientific knowledge subjective and relativistic, but he did no such thing. He only challenged a particular philosophical account of the epistemology of science. But it was not simply *an* account. It was, first, one that was so entrenched that both proponents and opponents had come to identify it with the practice of science. Second, and more significant, he called into question the competence of philosophy to do more than understand science. The real problem of relativism raised by Kuhn's work was not one involving the practice of science but rather one involving *philosophy's relationship to that practice.*

While in the case of logical positivism the actual practice of science was depreciated as an object of inquiry, because of philosophy's putative grasp of rational foundations that scientific practice could at best approximate, philosophy was, in Kuhn's work, cast in a role where its claims became little more than historical and analytical generalizations about past practice. As Nelson Goodman notes, even the concept of similarity was taken out of the "philosopher's dwindling kit" (1992:22). The implication of Kuhn's work was that the degree to which philosophy was meaningful with respect to scientific practice was itself a practical rather than an epistemological issue. Although for the most part, professional academic philosophy no longer had much real concern about its influence on scientific practice, its discourse remained structured by this issue. For other second-order activities, however, such as social science and political theory, whose practical aspirations were much more vivid, Kuhn's arguments were, to say the least, worrisome. Although his historization of science provided ammunition for distinguishing epistemically between natural science and social science, it seemed at the same time to undercut any basis of epistemic privilege—and practical authority—for second-order activities.

Kuhn could be construed as one of the first to embrace arguments that are now associated with postmodernism. Postmodernism can, of course, be defined in a number of ways depending on what attributes are stressed, but most essentially it represents a crisis in the traditional understanding of the relationship between second- and first-order discourses, that is, suspicion about the authority of metanarratives. The controversy surrounding Richard Rorty's work is largely a broader replay of the dialogue attending the debate about Kuhn. Political theorists, for example, face a serious paradox in their relationship to such arguments. They are drawn toward these claims because they characteristically feel constrained to filter their concerns and claims through the reigning philosophical persuasion, but postmodernism and other alleged harbingers of relativism also tend to deny what political theorists sought from philosophy—the authority of knowledge. Before we turn directly to this matter, however, a brief examination of the case of Winch is instructive, since it is more directly apposite to the problem of political theory and social science.

Although Winch's *The Idea of a Social Science* (1958) was essentially an argument about the logical asymmetry of explanation in natural and social science—based on a particular construal of Wittgenstein's remarks about rule-following behavior—and despite the fact that it occasioned considerable controversy in those terms, its more persistently contentious implications, exacerbated by his essay "Understanding Primitive Society" (1964), involved the issue of relativism (e.g., Wilson 1970; Hollis and Lukes 1982). Notwithstanding the fact that Winch could be construed as implying that there might be a modest therapeutic role for second-order enterprises, his account of the epistemological autonomy of linguistically defined first-order communities raised the issue of the degree to which philosophy and social science could make apodictic judgments about the validity of truth-claims within those activities. He was unrepentant, maintaining that there was no philosophically specifiable "reality" that made language meaningful and that "reality" was, in the end, in effect, a discursive artifact. Winch argued that it was impossible to say from some neutral perspective that, for example, the "magical" beliefs of the Zande were false and that Western science was true. Although, he acknowledged, we must initially approach understanding an alien society in terms of our own categories, criteria of rationality and truth and falsity are ultimately internal to a language or realm of discourse. Understanding such a society is like learning a new scientific theory.

It would require a separate and extensive essay to recapitulate the variety of criticisms that were heaped upon Winch's arguments—ranging from Popperians such as I. C. Jarvie to critical theorists such as K.-O. Apel and that, in slightly altered form, often appeared in several published contexts and were adopted in numerous derivative claims. Like Kuhn after him, Winch became a whipping boy for a variety of people with diverse philosophical fixations and often for those whose real concern was fear of Wittgenstein. Many of these criticisms involved patent distortions of Winch's position—such as the claim that it did not allow for translation between cultural paradigms, that it entailed the impossibility of external criticism of social norms, that it rendered social scientific inquiry a matter of empathy. Others, such as Alasdair MacIntyre, wanted, after the fashion of the day, to view reasons and mental states as causes and to maintain that there was a difference between explaining (or understanding) rational beliefs and irrational beliefs, and that understanding actions in terms of things such as rules must be supplemented by structural explanations. They construed Winch as arguing against, or at least inhibiting, such claims, but all of this had very little to do with what Winch actually said. The "get-Winch" phenomenon, despite the philosophical diversity among those who joined the attack, was a consequence of the perceived threat to the enterprise of philosophy and second-order analysis in general, which was, in turn, couched in various arguments about the existence of universal formal and substantive rationality and the superiority, in principle and practice, of Western science and its grasp of reality. Probably Jarvie was one of the more candid critics. He made no bones about saying these things outright, that the Azande should simply give up their view of the world and join the progress of the West (1970).

Although the main thrust of Winch's work was hardly in the direction of a full-blown challenge to traditional philosophy, he insisted on defining rationality, both procedurally and substantively, as internal to a conventional practice, and he stressed the philosophical incommensurability of such practices. Despite what some critics claimed, he did not argue that practices could not be compared and judged or that one is imprisoned within one's own language. On the contrary, he stressed the public character and, in principle, accessibility of language. His principal concern was to press the point that understanding an alien society required grasping its internal view of reality and rationality, but his dicta certainly implied that second-order accounts had no automatically privileged basis of judgment. And his reliance, as in the case of Kuhn, on Wittgenstein brought into relief the profound antifoundationalist implications of the latter's work and the threat to the identity and authority of second-order discourses that was involved in such a position.

Winch, like many other "relativists" who sometimes are even themselves prone to a certain nervousness about their conclusions, did not disallow the possibility of functional limiting conditions and commonalities in the human condition (sustenance, sex, death, etc.) that ultimately bind all societies together. And he explicitly argued against those who hold that truth, integrity, justice, and the like are merely conventional (1959–1960). Winch's analysis of ethics clearly moved in the direction of suggesting that normative judgment was something that could not be detached from particular situations, but he rejected decisionist accounts of ethics as well as other positions that are often construed as relativist (Winch 1972; Gaita 1990). But he stressed the radically different manner in which what he took to be basic human values could be conceptually manifest. Philosophers (e.g., Jarvie 1972, 1984) and critical theorists (Apel 1985) worry about the implications of Winch's work for a critical philosophy and an appraising social science because they cling to the idea that the basis of a critical enterprise is epistemology and that epistemology can reveal transcontextual standards of truth and logic. Winch's arguments have nothing to do, necessarily, with whether social science is critical, since the extent to which social science is critical is a matter of its actions and historical context and not a matter of what abstract epistemology it embraces. What called so much attention to Winch was not that he was a defender of moral relativism but that his argument implicitly challenged two things that are behind most of the concern about relativism. Even a cursory reading of the debates that have followed Winch's work and of the criticisms of Winch by individuals such as I. C. Jarvie and Ernest Gellner (e.g., 1973, 1985), who have devoted so much time to refuting an (almost always less than accurate) account of his position, starkly reveal an anxiety about the status of second-order discourses and a fear of not being able to underwrite philosophically the beliefs of Western science and culture. To extrapolate from Winch's argument the view that there are no grounds for saying that science is better than witchcraft is simply a distortion. His claim was that there are no metatheoretical grounds. If one is not satisfied that science, on its own terms, is better than witchcraft, or religion for that matter, then philosophy is not likely to provide any decisive weight. And the charge that Winch's argument entailed a profound relativism was presented against a background of faith that philosophy could in some way accomplish what science had historically failed to achieve—a conception of reality that was beyond corrigibility.

In the case of Richard Rorty, it is easy to see why philosophers are agitated by his work, since his argument both calls into question the intellectual significance, and even integrity, of the traditional enterprise of academic philosophy and implicitly challenges the authority of second-order practices in general. Both concerns, however, reverberate in the world of political theory. Although the worry is in part about Rorty's defense of liberalism in a climate where much of political theory is, in one way or another, defined by a critique of liberalism, the essential concern is that his attack on philosophical epistemology somehow disempowers social and political theory. Richard Wolin's response to Rorty is typical. He suggests that Rorty falls into the relativist trap of claiming an absolutist basis for his relativism and that "by entirely ceding the power of 'right' or 'normativity' to context, he studiously ignores the context-transcendent powers of reason and critique, and thereby ends up with a *de facto* endorsement of an essentially neoconservative position" (1992:155). Part of the difficulty is that Rorty's phrasing of his own argument is not always felicitous. At times he does seem to suggest that by attacking traditional epistemology, he has destroyed the idea of truth in general and reduced it to social solidarity. But like Winch and Kuhn, what Rorty really challenged was the idea of metatheoretical claims to transcendental truth. While solidarity may be the social prerequisite of the application of the concept of truth, truth-claims in social practices are neither logically vouchsafed nor undermined by philosophy. Wolin's claim, however, that the attack on foundationalism in philosophy is just another "foundationalist argument" is simply based on a confusion.

To argue, as Rorty, Winch, and others do, that the criteria of truth are context-dependent is not logically equivalent to claiming that substantive truth-claims are in some way inherently debilitated. The critique of foundationalism, in the case of someone such as Rorty, is not simply another epistemological claim even though it participates in epistemological discourse. It is a rejection of traditional epistemology as a metapractical enterprise. If the claim involved was the transcendental one that there are no grounds of knowledge, there would indeed be, as is so often charged, an inherent contradiction, but antifoundationalism is, in its cogent form, a rejection of philosophical privilege rather than a denial that the concept of truth has meaning and criteria in practices such as science. The very metaphor of foundation may not be appropriate when applied to discussions of knowledge, but if we retain it, we might say that there are, for example, scientific (and commonsense) foundations of knowledge (theories) but no philosophical (epistemological) foundation of knowledge. All houses have foundations, but there is no general foundation on which they all rest. Many political theorists, however, continue to see the attack on epistemology as a threat both to political judgment and to the authority of political theory. The critique of philosophical rationalism and the attack on the epistemological project has put the identity of philosophy into question, but it has also thrown political theory into crisis. Yet rather than confront the underlying practical issues of the criteria of judgment that are operative in political life and the relationship between academic and public discourse, political theory has too often retreated into the rear guard of rationalism and sought an answer to relativism. The historical path through which Critical Theory, as practiced by the Frankfurt School, devolved into a rationalist project during and after Weimar is an interesting and complicated case, but the perpetuation of this syndrome in the contemporary academic community of political theory seems to rest on little more than academic convention and professional solipsism. This is epitomized in the work of Habermas, which has now become part of the resurrected debate about universalism in ethics (Dallmayr and Benhabib 1991), but it is also characteristic of the more general literature. Although there are few attempts to stonewall the forces of antifoundationalism, in part because political theory finds it very difficult to resist the weight of popular philosophical authority, there is a reluctance to let go of the idea that "ontological praxis" is a kind of political action and that "critical bite" in political theory is an epistemological problem (Dallmayr 1987; Shapiro 1990).

When one is faced with the poles of rationalism and relativism, a popular recourse is to construct a philosophical compromise and seek a middle ground between "objectivism" and "relativism" (Bernstein 1983). Or if one flags in the face of antirationalism, there is sometimes a lapse into a kind of neo-Mannheimian stance suggesting that it is less *the* "truth" that theorists possess than a position outside the constraints of practical life that allows them to participate in a community of reflective discourse. MacIntyre suggests that the existence of such a tradition provides a kind of historical answer to historicism (1984, 1989), and Taylor argues that what separates Western society from primitive societies and privileges modern science is that "we have this activity of theoretical understanding which seems to have no counterpart among them" (1982:89). Taylor does not argue for the truth of any particular scientific belief but for what he claims is the payoff of the "disengaged perspective" and mental discipline of academia and the superiority of "theoretical culture" over atheoretical ones (89, 104). He argues that in the end "there is an inner connection between understanding the world and achieving technological control which rightly commands everyone's attention, and doesn't just justify our practices in our own eyes" (101). And he also claims that there is something immanent or "original" in the history of practices that can be recovered as a basis of judging competing claims in the present (1984).

The notion that the success of natural science solves the problem of relativism is, as I will argue more fully in chapter 4, hardly confined to one philosophical and ideological persuasion. Gellner, who is distant from Taylor on both fronts, argues,

> The philosophical significance of the scientific-industrial "form of life," whose rapid global diffusion is the main event of our time, is that for all practical purposes it does provide us with a solution of the problem of relativism. . . . The cognitive and technical superiority of one form of life is so manifest that . . . it simply cannot be questioned. (1968:405)

What is more significant than any matter of philosophical or political partisanship is the threat to the authority of philosophy. This is why people as diverse as followers of Popper, critical theorists such as Habermas, and interpretive theorists such as Taylor feel constrained to do battle with what they take to be relativist arguments.

Since a focus on language tends to dominate contemporary philosophy, many of those who have recently taken up arms against the windmill of relativism have turned for support to some form of linguistic rationalism such as that advanced by Donald Davidson. At a time when many of the old philosophical authorities seem to be collapsing and when there is a stress on language as constitutive of reality, but floating free of representation, Davidson's work has emerged as one of the great philosophical hopes, and it deserves careful scrutiny. The following more detailed discussion of Davidson's work is important, however, for at least two other reasons. First, it further clarifies his assumptions regarding the theory of action discussed in chapter 2, and second, it relates to recent work dealing with philosophical realism in the philosophy of science that I discuss in chapter 4.

III

Despite recent trends in postempiricist philosophy that reject other than a conventional connection between words and things, or even see language as the only avenue of access to the "world," there are many who still wish to find some philosophical basis for resurrecting representationalism, or a surrogate, and believing that "there really are things and kinds of things and actions out there in the world, and our mind is designed to find them and label them with words" (Pinker 1994:154). Davidson has led the way in developing a postpositivist account of how words and the world go together. His arguments are complex and the subject of extensive discussion, and I cannot pretend to do full justice to them here (see LePore and McLaughlin 1985, 1986; Vermagen and Hintikki 1985; Ramberg 1989; Evnine 1991; Malpas 1992; Farrell 1994). But Davidson has attempted to defend, albeit in a distinctive manner, what many might construe as basic tenets of rationalism while rejecting empiricism in its traditional form. Although individuals like Richard Rorty (1979) are drawn to Davidson because of his attack on traditional theories of knowledge, the fit between these two philosophers is not an easy one. Davidson is, for example, adamant in his rejection of pragmatic theories of truth and linguistic reductionism. In the literature of social science, there has been an increasing frequency of references to Davidson's work. This is particularly the case in areas such as social choice theory, which has drawn upon his account of decision, but his work has appealed to those in search of the foundations of a critical social science and a transcontextual image of truth. There is, however, a need to look carefully at Davidson's position, since his arguments, or dubious versions of them, are often simply appropriated and deployed to bolster rationalist positions in the philosophy of social science, literary theory, and other second-order activities (Macdonald and Pettit 1981; Norris 1985).

While it might seem that Davidson is still deeply rooted in the assumptions and concerns of positivist/empiricist philosophy, persuasive cases can be made for his break with traditional epistemology. Some even suggest that there is an affinity between his work and individuals who would normally be considered quite estranged from the analytic tradition, such as Heidegger (Malpas 1992) and Derrida (Farrell 1994), but such comparisons tend to distract from a careful analysis of his basic claims. Davidson, for example, believes, like Plato, that in texts "the interaction between perceiving creatures that is the foundation of communication is lost" (1993:610), and this could not be further from the position of someone such as Derrida. As Davidson himself has so frequently acknowledged, understanding his work requires beginning, historically and conceptually, with Quine as well as with the issue of the extent to which Quine broke away from positivism and traditional empiricism (e.g., Davidson 1994). Since Quine is himself a party to disputes about the meaning of Davidson's work, it would be regressive to attempt fully to recapitulate the controversy surrounding Quine's work (see Gibson 1982), but Quine's arguments are essential as a starting point in interpreting Davidson.

Despite Quine's early attachment to logical positivism, he was eventually instrumental in undermining "two dogmas of empiricism" that were central to the positivist program. The first was the verificationist theory of meaning, which assumed an ontologically distinct and primitive observation language. The second was the synthetic/analytic dichotomy that supported the basic distinction between theory and fact (1953). He then complemented these arguments with dual theses about the necessary underdetermination of theories by evidence and the indeterminacy of translation (1960). The former involved the claim that in principle there can be empirically equivalent but incommensurable and logically incompatible scientific theories. The latter involved the contention that for a natural language, there can be incommensurable but viable hypotheses about meaning that cannot be externally adjudicated. Even though these claims seemed to have relevance for the philosophy of social science and particularly the reaction against positivism as well as a metatheory of interpretation (e.g., Hookway and Pettit 1978; Roth 1987), there were other aspects of Quine's work that were less congenial.

Central to Quine's formulation was a thoroughly holistic view of language and theories as conceptual schemes consisting of a web or network of interdependent sentences. This was a distinctly postempiricist, or at least postpositivist, position, since it entailed that the criteria of truth and reality are internal to a theory. This might suggest an endorsement of some form of relativism, but Quine had, at least from his perspective, a significant caveat that stood in a somewhat anomalous relation to his other claims. People in the same circumstances, he argued, have basically the same sensory experience, and any conceptual scheme is tangentially tied to experience through stimulus-prompted observation sentences within the general web of sentences and corresponding beliefs. Although traditional epistemology and the suprascientific search for philosophical certainty and extrascientific grounds of knowledge were unacceptable to Quine, something like the old empiricist notion of correspondence or representation was retained. Epistemology could, he suggested, be naturalized and resurrected as a scientific investigation into how we gain knowledge of the world as well as learn and acquire language through intersubjective exposure to a shared physical environment (1969). There was, then, after all, according to Quine, a nonconventional naturalistic connection between words and things, since language is ultimately rooted in nonverbal stimulation (1995). Early on Quine had been involved with the ideas of B. F. Skinner. This correlation of meaning with behavior was part of Quine's argument about indeterminacy, since different hypotheses about meaning could in principle fit the same data, but it was also the basis of his analysis of translation. He conceived of translation as radical, that is, in terms of an idealized situation in which an alien language is encountered without prior knowledge of its elements of meaning and in which the translator must start with the behavior of the speakers. Radical translation, however, was more than a matter of studying behavior. It involved extrapolating or projecting the interpreter's substantive truth-conditions and logic. While indeterminacy entailed the possibility of not gaining a full and determinant account of meaning, parity between some elements of behavior and language, along with the universality of logical structure, provided initial access.

Davidson ultimately rejected what could be construed as Quine's residual dualism and emphasis on sensory experience while accentuating holism and intersubjectivity, but at the same time, he sought to bring language and the world yet closer together. His well-known article "The Very Idea of a Conceptual Scheme" attacked conceptual relativism and called into question the kind of indeterminacy suggested by Quine, with a new twist that aimed at collapsing further the subjective/objective dichotomy in a nonidealist direction. His argument was against what he construed as the residue of neo-Kantian relativism, that is, the idea that the constitution of reality is in some way relative to a conceptual scheme. Davidson labeled this idea the "third dogma of empiricism." (1984: 189). This, he argued, was the last vestige of empiricism and the myth of the given, since it implied an uninterpreted reality, something universal and fixed on which concepts provide a perspective. Exactly who was the principal target of Davidson's criticism is difficult to say, since he did not directly challenge any particular argument. Certainly traditional empiricism, and probably Quine, were lurking behind his generic critique, but Davidson, on weak grounds, attributed scheme/content dualism, that is, the idea that there is one ineffable world but different and incommensurable, and potentially untranslatable, conceptions of it, to Kuhn's position. As I will argue in chapter 4, this is an incorrect rendering of Kuhn's argument—and indeed a surprising one given Kuhn's explicit rejection of the theory/fact dichotomy and his emphasis on theoretical incommensurability.

For Davidson, there is no exiting the universe of belief and behavior, but he is not content to follow the pragmatist argument, from C. S. Peirce to Rorty, that truth is a function of communicative consensus. He argues, much like Quine, that at least a central core of words does have what might be characterized as a kind of given and indubitable meaning. Utterances, and beliefs, are, he claims, causally linked to objects and to the circumstances in which language is learned, and thus, he claims, we cannot have cogent doubts about the independent existence of the world and its correspondence with language. Davidson comments that he has "dropped the idea that philosophers are in charge of a special sort of truth" (1994:44), but he still wants to go beyond the pragmatist image of truth. As in the case of Quine, meaning and belief are viewed as holistic interdependent realms, but while Quine focused on the connection between words and world (1981), Davidson embraces a broader holism that rejects the issue of finding and defining such a connection. This might seem to lead even further in the direction of indeterminacy and suggest the impossibility of breaking out of the circle of meaning and belief. But although Davidson holds that criteria of truth and falsehood are relative to a language, or, as someone such as Ian Hacking would have it, a "style of reasoning," certain words and sentences are, Davidson argues, simply "true," so to speak, in that they reflect what people are disposed to say in particular circumstances. Both Hacking and Davidson would agree that the possibility of interpretation also rests on a "common core of verbal performances connected with what people tend to notice around them" (Hacking 1982:61), even though Hacking allows the possibility of incommensurability between styles or schemes.

Relinquishing the idea of an uninterpreted reality does not, according to Davidson, require surrendering a philosophical rendering of objectivity and truth and submitting to the idea that "two schemes might be equally plausible to believe." In doing away with "dualism of scheme and world, we do not give up the world, but reestablish immediate touch with the familiar objects whose antics make our opinions and sentences true or false" (1984:198). He maintains that beliefs are true or false, but they represent nothing; we have "reality without reference" (1984:215). Their meaning comes from the objects and circumstances that give rise to or cause them. One characteristic difficulty in Davidson's work, however, is the problem of how to square his holism with this apparent privileging of certain kinds of familiar objects. What, and whose, objects one might ask.

Davidson's somewhat oblique answer is that the traditional correspondence theory of truth must be dispensed with in favor of a form of coherence coupled with a semantic theory such as that advanced by Alfred Tarski. This is in part why Davidson has moved from the issue of translation, in the narrow sense of establishing linguistic correlations, to that of interpretation and the problem of creating theories of meaning for natural languages. Interpretation, he argues, is a matter of developing a theory based on how and when speakers hold sentences to be true, and this, in turn, warrants assumptions about belief and, consequently, meaning. Such interpretive intervention, however, requires a foothold achieved by the application of the principle of "charity," or the assumption that most of a speaker's beliefs are both true and like those of the interpreter and that both individuals share a similar and universal form of reasoning. Charity plays a large role for Davidson because, unlike for Quine, there are no semantic anchors. In addition to the principle of charity, Davidson relies heavily on his revision and redeployment of Tarski's theory.

Tarski's theory of truth (1949, 1956) was directed toward defining truth in a formal language. It was neither a general theory of truth nor a theory for dealing with natural languages. It claimed that the truth of a sentence is a function of the truth of the components of the sentence, and it was a recursive theory in that the truth of complex expressions was viewed as based on the truth of more primitive ones. Tarski introduced the concept of a T-sentence, which held that a sentence in a particular language is true if and only if certain conditions are satisfied, for example, "snow is white" is true if, and only if, snow is white. Each T-sentence pairs a sentence in an object language with one in a metalanguage that provides a translation in terms of the truth-conditions of the sentence. Although Tarski's concern was with the concept of truth rather than with meaning or translation, Davidson, in effect, inverted this relationship and defined meaning in terms of truth and applied it as a way of achieving equivalence between sentences in different natural languages. Despite his holistic view of language, whereby only in sentences do words have meaning and only in a language do sentences have meaning, he maintains that any learnable or natural language has a "finite number of semantical primitives" on which the meaning of sentences depend (1984:9). He reconciles these two ideas through adopting Tarski's theory of truth and then adapting it (a kind of move about which Tarski and many after him were dubious) as a theory of meaning, relativized to a particular language. Such a theory would give the meaning, that is, the truth-conditions, of a sentence by analyzing it as composed of elements derived from the "finite stock" of semantical primitives and by relating each singular term to some object. In short, Davidson argues that it is possible to interpret Tarski's formal system as an empirical theory about languages. Despite the reliance on Tarski and "convention-T" and the emphasis on the relationship between language and the world, this is, again, not a traditional correspondence theory of truth, since Davidson rejects the idea of truth as representation. Although it appears that he once construed it as a version of such a theory, he no longer wishes to identify it in that manner (1990). He does not, however, subscribe in any way to theories of truth that take truth as an epistemic concept internal to a theory.

For Davidson, "the methodological problem of interpretation" is "how, given the sentences a man accepts as true under given conditions, to work out what his beliefs are and what his words mean" (1980:162). This is not, he claims, a matter of having a prior theory or sharing some aspect of a common language. Meaning is dependent on belief, and beliefs are ex-pressed in utterances. Interpretation would involve constructing an em-pirical theory about the linguistic behavior of speakers. Truth-conditions, or what speakers (by their behavior) take to be true or false, and coherence with other statements are substituted for meaning in the more traditional senses of intention and reference. What Davidson argues, in effect, is that while in one sense meaning is public and depends on at least a minimal social situation, truth comes before language and meaning, that is, that truth is not fundamentally a matter of linguistic convention but rather the basis of both learning and understanding language. What ultimately makes language public is less conventions than the fact that all communicators share the same world.

This brand of nominalism even leads Davidson, when pressed, to deny the reality of language, and meaning, as such. He claims that actually "there are no such things in the world; there are only speakers and their various written and acoustical products" (1992:256). An utterance does not be-long to any unique language even though an interpreter in effect assigns a language or theory to a person in order to understand behavior. The con-cept of language becomes, then, at best a heuristic and at worst an in-stance of misplaced concreteness or reification. Certain sentences in ev-ery "language" have the same truth-conditions, and the principle of "charity" allows us to find equivalence. This dictates that in order to un-derstand others, we must assume that we are dealing with language users, or rational creatures, and that most people are right about most empirical matters. Beneath apparent differences in language, Davidson argues, is a great deal of fundamental conceptual agreement, and the adoption of the principle of charity both allows entrance to the object of interpretation and constrains the process of assigning meaning. This is not, however, quite the same as the claim that there is a common human nature or even what some (Gandy 1973) have referred to as the principle of "humanity," which assumes more specific substantive and moral agreement than Davidson implies.

Davidson's position is difficult to locate among traditional notions of linguistic meaning. He not only rejects any equation of meaning and refer-ence but, despite his view that thoughts cause actions and that the mental world has a certain autonomy even though ultimately "the mind is nothing more than the brain" (1994:50), he certainly is not in the tradition of those who see thought or a speaker's intention as independent of language and prior to it. For Davidson, the meaning of language is not thought, even though language and belief are entwined. He also rejects the notion (e.g., Wittgenstein, Austin) that meaning is a matter of conventional or linguis-tic usage. His semantics, in the tradition of Gottlob Frege, Alfred Tarski, and Rudolf Carnap, assumes that meaning is a function of particular words that have extensional significance. It is, again, basically a nominalistic position. Yet his work, like Quine's, is a distinct challenge to empiricism and the view that language is learned by moving upward from ostensive reference and conditioning and that words are tied down to bits of experience that allow meaning to be equated with reference. There is, Davidson maintains, no logical connection between words and things, no general theory of reference. Reference, strictly speaking, is yet another reification and "drops out. It plays no essential role in explaining the relation between language and reality" (1994:225).

For Davidson, intersubjectivity, that is, "thought itself," is something that "absolutely depends on a three-way relationship between at least two people and a series of events that are shared in the world" (1994:49). This would seem to be a pointed rejection of Quine's privatized construction of the mind and its relation to the world, but it is not an acceptance of the identity of language and the world. "The ultimate source of both objectivity and communication is the triangle that by relating speaker, interpreter, and the world, determines the contents of thought and speech. Given this source, there is no room for a relativized concept of truth" (1990:325; also 1992). Unlike empiricist arguments, his claim is that there is a relation between words and the ostensive world rather than the world expressed in propositions or statements of fact. He sees the problem of relativism as engendered by traditional theories of truth that attempt to find a connection between ideas and the world. Although Davidson was once willing to categorize himself as a philosophical realist, he now rejects as ultimately unintelligible the realist claim that truth is independent of our beliefs, since it implies the possibility of skepticism or the idea that our beliefs might as a whole be false. Yet despite his claim that there cannot be any fundamental break between our beliefs and the world, he is distinctly against various forms of antirealism. He describes his theory as a "theory of truth for describing, explaining, understanding, and predicting a basic aspect of verbal behavior" (1990:313). Since he takes meaning and truth to be matters of observable behavior, he believes that something like Bayesian decision theory offers a scheme for systematizing his account even if it contains too thin a notion of rationality. Whether speakers are deemed to be in touch with the world is judged by how well they are equipped to observe their environment and how well their sentences hang together. But again, Davidson assumes basic agreement and common modes of rationality. "The possibility of understanding the speech or actions of an agent depends on the existence of a fundamentally rational pattern, a pattern that must, in general outline, be shared by all rational creatures. We have no choice, then, but to project our own logic on to the language and beliefs of another" (1990:328).

Davidson argues that there cannot, in effect, be a general theory of interpretation or meaning but only a theory, or code, for a particular language that is developed from "facts about the behavior and attitudes of the speaker in relation to sentences uttered" (1990:133). There is not, as opposed to Quine, a translation manual or metalanguage. "All understanding of the speech of another involves radical interpretation" (126), that is, the mapping of truth-conditions for the alien language and finding a parallel in one's own language. Meaning is a theoretical construct, and this is where the principle of "charity" becomes operative, that is, the assumption that despite the possibility of some indeterminacy, a good theory is one that would maximize agreement and consistency. In fact, translation and interpretation could not take place without general "massive agreement" on truth-conditions (137). "What makes interpretation possible, then, is the fact that we can dismiss a priori the chance of massive error" (168–69). Davidson holds that "in sharing a language . . . we share a picture of the world that must, in its large features, be true," since "massive error about the world is simply unintelligible." And "successful communication proves the existence of a shared, and largely true, view of the world" (201). Thus, the argument goes, communication proves the existence of a shared world, and a shared world makes communication possible. "To see too much unreason on the part of others is simply to undermine our ability to understand what it is they are so unreasonable about" (153).

This account of Davidson is admittedly truncated, but if existing discussions of his work are any indication, a longer version would not necessarily be clearer. The purpose of this excursus, however, is less to render any definitive account of this complex corpus than to demonstrate both how it differs from the position I am advancing and how shallowly it has been plumbed by social theorists who seek support for various second-order claims about empirical and normative judgment. Exactly what Davidson is arguing in a positive sense is less evident than what he rejects, but social scientists sense something hopeful in their limited and often secondary grasp of his philosophy. It is easy to see why Davidson's position is appealing, since it seems to provide a basis for claiming both how understanding takes place and how claims to truth can be adjudicated, but it also presents the perennial difficulties of both comparing and assessing contending philosophical positions and moving from philosophy to social science. Those who believe, for example, that postmodernism, deconstructionism, and "the belief in an exclusively linguistic universe leaves humanity more or less vulnerable to the forces of political tyranny" (Lehman 1991:99) find hope in Davidson's arguments, but it is interesting that Davidson himself, as opposed to those who wish to either enlist or demob his ideas, notes that his approach is not "meant to throw any direct light on how in real life we come to understand each other, nor how we master our first concepts and our first language" (1990:325). He is simply addressing the abstract philosophically delimited issue of what makes it all possible. And when it comes to the question of the social sciences and their object, he sees this as a suspended relationship between other minds that lacks the "yardstick" of a shared "outside world" (1994:52).

IV

Arguments such as those of Quine, Davidson, or others (e.g., Dennett 1987) that assume some universal logic and structure of belief represent a return to the spirit of a priori philosophy and a rejection of what might be called "cognitive pluralism" (Stitch 1990) or the idea that people really do think in quite fundamentally different ways at different times and places. The worry seems to be that if the latter were the case, both communication and criticism would be impossible, that epistemic relativism not only fails to explain how the world is intelligible but places the very idea of human judgment on a slippery slope. Much of the material in the philosophy of social science that relies on something like Davidson's thesis grew out of an attempt to find a way to counter claims such as those of Winch, Kuhn, and, more fundamentally, Wittgenstein suggesting that rationality and reality are the legitimate property of first-order discourses and that second-order discourses do not have a mortgage that allows them to foreclose by fiat.

There is a certain kind of argument that has been advanced, in slightly varying form, against Winch as well as against proponents of the "strong program" in the sociology of knowledge who claim that all beliefs are equal in terms of the "causes of their credibility" (Barnes and Bloor 1982; Barnes 1977; Bloor 1976). Its proponents include, among others, MacIntyre, Larry Laudan, Imre Lakatos, Stephen Lukes, and Martin Hollis. They all claim that understanding someone's, or a society's, beliefs and actions calls for two modes of explanation—one for rational beliefs, which are immediately intelligible and validated because they are logical and correspond to reality, and another, causal, form of explanation in the case of beliefs that are logically and substantively irrational. The "strong program," or the "symmetry thesis," which holds that both "true" and "false" knowledge must be contextually explained, actually has little to do with Winch's primary concerns, but it embraces a discursive conception of knowledge and rejects the idea that there are universally valid criteria of truth and rationality. It maintains that understanding and judging are two different things, while antisymmetrists maintain that the two are inextricably linked.

The latter claim that there can be metatheoretical discrimination between true and false beliefs because all cultures share a common core of true belief and patterns of inference that philosophy or a second-order discourse such as social science can extract and use as a standard of judgment.

What all this amounts to is the assumption, very much like that of Taylor, that the beliefs of Western science and its culture are basically correct and that social science can use these as a standard for both interpreting and judging various social practices. What is propounded by Hollis, Lukes, and others is that there is, fortunately, a "bridgehead of true and rational beliefs" that, although maybe minimal, "consists of what a rational man cannot fail to believe in simple perceptual situations." They argue that if it were not for the existence of such a "bridgehead" that is "universal among mankind," we could neither understand (translate) nor critically analyze alien beliefs and practices. Quine, Davidson, and other cognitive monists offer little evidence for their claims that human evolution has somehow provided this common ground, and borrowers of some form of this thesis provide even less in the way of an account of the exact content of this bridgehead. They tend to assert simply that "there has to be an epistemological unity of mankind" and "a massive central core of human thinking that has no history." Since, they claim, the very idea of human communication presupposes this, one can "simply enter a plea for metaphysics" and posit these "transcendental grounds" (Hollis 1982:74–75, 83–84).

Lukes, explicitly drawing on Davidson, claims that "we must presuppose commonly shared standards of truth and inference" (1982:262), and William Newton-Smith argues that it is simply "massively implausible to suppose . . . that there is no common observational core of perception and belief." He claims that the very fact of translation dictates that we relinquish the idea of relativism (1982:113) and that natural science, in effect, contradicts relativism (1981). The basic issue may be less whether this position is philosophically and empirically defensible, which seems, to many, dubious (e.g., Cherniak 1986), than whether it is defended. The idea of language learning and translation assumed here is at best contentious, and the advocates never work through the complex arguments, such as those of Davidson, on which they rely for authority. The claim, for example, that translation is predicated on commensurability or that incommensurability is equivalent to untranslatability are dubious empirical and philosophical claims. And whether arguments such as those of Davidson really support this kind of extrapolation is difficult to say. Even if the bridgehead notion were credible, it is far from evident what this would imply with respect to assessing matters of moral and scientific belief. Even if one accepted the idea that throughout time and space people, in some important respect, share a common cognitive world, it does not follow that this is sufficient, whether in principle or practice, to mediate differences or to provide second-order discourses with critical authority. When someone such as Lukes does actually attempt to defend this position, rather than merely asserting it, the argument sounds much like a reversion to some notion of positivist phenomenalism—the idea that we can have different perspectives but not a different sensory experience. He suggests that "Wittgenstein's duck-rabbit can be neutrally described as a set of lines drawn in a certain manner" (1982:271), but this would seem to contradict the very point that Wittgenstein was making and his account of "seeing-as." It would be like saying that words can be reduced to a basic, and common, meaning by describing them as marks on paper. We do not, in the everyday process of seeing, dismantle things into their component parts and reconstruct them. As I will stress in chapter 5, we do not interpret them but rather see or understand them as we participate in various practices and activities.

There are, appropriately, many ways to look at the significance of postmodernism, but J.-F. Lyotard's notion of "incredulity toward metanarratives" (1984) is both widely noted and persuasive. Postmodernism and the problematic that attaches to it present yet another example of the manifestation in philosophical form of what is really a practical problem, that is, the authority of knowledge and the relationship of metapractices to their subject matter. My concern has been to emphasize just how dubious the epistemological project is and how doubly dubious it becomes when appropriated by social theory as a basis of either cognitive or practical authority. And when traditional epistemology is challenged by skeptical positions, a surreal dialogue between "unnatural doubts" (Williams 1991) and unnatural certainty arises. Skepticism is the inevitable reaction to the epistemological quest (Stroud 1984; Nagel 1986), and even those, such as Cavell, who have raised severe doubts about that quest have difficulty rejecting the significance of a generalized skeptical attitude. Cavell believes that for both Wittgenstein and Austin, "skepticism and metaphysics are forms of intellectual tragedy" (1995:61), while he sees skepticism more deeply rooted in the human condition. My position is closer to Wittgenstein and Austin. While both certainty and doubt have meaning within a practical context, neither have meaning as universalized philosophical attitudes. What emerges is a dialogue grounded in the common but erroneous assumption that epistemological objects such as knowledge of the external world are really intelligible entities. All this, however, is really rooted in the problematic of the relationship between the orders of discourse and their historical manifestations.

In the end, it is necessary to ask, once again, what the purpose of these efforts to overcome relativism may be. What exactly are we supposed to fear when we are told that we are in danger of losing the world, that it has thinned and contracted, that pragmatism has gone too far, and that someone such as Davidson can deliver us from the increasing subjectivity that has characterized modern thought and culminated in postmodernism (Farrell 1994; Prado 1987). We are warned apocalyptically that "the chill winds of relativism and even nihilism are blowing ever more strongly" in the work of Kuhn, Feyerabend, Winch, Rorty, Goodman, and others. The point is supposed to be that "reality" is "at risk," but it is not credible to assume that these philosophers have in any way undermined anyone's belief in reality or "the status of the parts of human knowledge, which have seemed most firmly established" (Trigg 1989:ix). Nor is it credible that if some dimension of human knowledge has been undermined, philosophy can reinstate it. There may be grounds for arguing that modern science has threatened the unity of our conventional world through technological proliferation or even that the vision of the universe in modern science appears to be a much less certain one than that provided by Newton. And there are all sorts of social, political, and cultural diversity with which we must cope and, maybe, eventually overcome. But it is far-fetched indeed to believe that philosophical arguments about the cognitive unity of humankind can solve these problems. Philosophy can neither put reality at risk nor save it, because its concept of reality is too generic to be counted as either a gain or a loss. It seems that philosophy is being asked to do what religion does or has done, to assure us that we are at home in the world and that the world is not merely a projection of ourselves. But who is the "us" that is given reassurance?

Why is it, for example, that Hollis, for one, is so worried about preserving what he calls the "autonomy of reason" and, like so many others such as Habermas, finds something transconventional at the very heart of conventionality (1977)? Is the fear really that philosophical claims like those of Winch are likely to undermine the practices of life? The real fear is for the autonomy and authority of philosophy—or social science. What is really at stake is the status of metatheoretical practices. But there seems little hope for facing up to the real issue—the practical issue of the relationship between first- and second-order discourses—until the spirit of foundationalism is exorcised and the issue of relativism is dismissed. Without rationalism, there is no "problem" of relativism, but without relativism, the underlying practical problem cannot be concealed. All first-order discourses, as substantive theoretical practices, are, so to speak, by definition foundationalist and "rationalist." There is no place for a language of generalized skeptical doubt in practices such as natural science where constitutive criteria are operative. Within a theoretical context, truth *is*, after all, a matter of correspondence as well as coherence. And although we might, like Rorty, argue philosophically against the rationalist and claim that truth is a function of "solidarity," this is an argument about the concept of truth and logically has no significance as far as the substance of truth-claims in science. It does not undermine science, although it might be construed as undermining what some might conceive as philosophy's relationship to science. Second-order discourses are also properly understood as internally foundationalist in that they involve theoretical constructions of their subject matter. What is inappropriate and futile is *foundationalism as a second-order metatheoretical project.*

The question that must be faced, and that has not been squarely addressed by either individuals such as Rorty or those who are sympathetic to his position, is exactly how the role of philosophy can be conceived "after the demise of the tradition" (Nielsen 1991). There seems to be a general sense that philosophy must come into greater contact with the practices that it professes to understand and address (Kolenda 1990; Hull 1994; Nielsen 1995), but no more than social science has it really confronted the issue of what this would entail. The answer usually, in the end, tends to be unilateral, that is, some adjustment to the internal character and commitments of academic philosophy. But on the whole, rationalism is not dead. It continues to give us philosophical, that is, epistemological, answers to such questions as how language is possible, how we can have knowledge of the world, why Western science is truer than magic, why modern science has greater verisimilitude than older science, how we can enhance the growth of knowledge, and how we can judge truth and right in our social and political practices. It is this kind of concern that has always drawn social science to philosophy and particularly the philosophy of science. Although positivism seemed at one time to offer a basis for the epistemic and practical authority of social science, it has in more recent years been viewed as a constraint on both the latter's autonomy and on its capacity for critical judgment. This has not, however, deterred social theory from continuing to seek aid and comfort from the philosophy of science. The career of the philosophy of science tells us something about the nature and problematics of second-order practices in general, and the story of political theory's involvement with the philosophy of science tells us something about philosophy's relationship to other second-order practices.

Theoretical Realism

We may even say that what is regarded as "nature" at a particular time is our own product *in the sense that all the features ascribed to it have first been invented by us and then used for bringing order into our surroundings.*
—Thomas Kuhn

It is worthwhile emphasizing again that few of the most prominent and extended arguments, among both social scientists and philosophers of social science, about how social science can and should or cannot and should not emulate the methods of natural science have been based on any intimate acquaintance with the practices of natural science. The "myth of the scientific method" (Bauer 1992) has sprung from a number of sources, but among social scientists, images of natural science have been consistently drawn from the literature of the philosophy of science and, probably most often, from secondary and tertiary accounts of this literature. This fact is, in itself, justification for a critical examination of the philosophy of science and its uses, but there are other reasons. First, as I have already suggested, the history and character of the philosophy of science tell us something about the general nature and career path of many second-order practices and discourses, and second, they offer a concrete example of the problems involved in social science's tendency to turn to philosophy as a basis of identity and authority. The philosophy of science has been used to legitimize everything from positivism to Marxism. Although I will briefly consider earlier work in the philosophy of science as well as social science's attachment to its doctrines, my focus is primarily on postpositivist philosophies of science and their implications for social science. I will argue, first, that recent interest in the philosophy of science among social theorists is yet another example of the tendency to substitute metatheory for theory and to adopt unreflectively philosophical arguments that are themselves contentious. Second, it is my contention that the contemporary emphasis on varieties of realism in the philosophy of science, as well as uses of this philosophy in the social sciences, reflects the characteristic anxiety about relativism and the attending foundationalist propensities of these academic cultures. In the process of sorting through arguments in the philosophy of science, I will favor a position that I call *theoretical realism,* which is compatible with the image of theory that I have elaborated earlier.

I

Although there may be few social scientists who would still overtly subscribe to the tenets of logical positivism/empiricism (LP/E), the principal elements of this philosophy remain sedimented in the apologies and practices of these disciplines. The problem with the social scientific appropriation of LP/E as an account of scientific explanation was, however, less its rhetorical role in justifying certain research programs and techniques than the extent to which it actually came to structure theoretical and empirical practices in the social sciences. Nowhere is this more evident than in the persistence, in thought and deed, of various forms of the instrumentalist account of scientific theory, which has dominated not only political science and sociology but psychology and economics. Traditional empiricism, with its emphasis on the ontological primacy of facts, inevitably created the "theoretician's dilemma" (Hempel 1965) and the "paradox of theorizing" (Tuomela 1973), that is, the issue of why theoretical concepts, if they accomplished their job of establishing the relationship between observables, need be retained. The problem was engendered by the instrumentalist image of theory, that is, the assumption that theories are conceptual constructs, inherently neither true nor false, for economically describing and explaining a distinct and, in some form, experientially given and epistemically privileged realm of facts. This image of theory was closely allied with the deductive, or covering-law, model of explanation and the notion that theoretical explanation can be equated with the subsumption of singular statements under generalizations. These doctrines were, together, the epistemological and logical linchpins of LP/E's image of scientific theory and scientific explanation. One might have supposed that during the last generation, after the point at which this "received view" (Suppe 1977) of theory had been thoroughly challenged (if not discredited) in philosophy, social scientific assumptions about the character and demands of science would have been substantially transformed. But for several reasons, this has not been the case even though in many areas of social and political theory, LP/E has been significantly undermined as an account of science.

There tends to be a significant cultural lag between philosophy and social science; it takes time for changes in philosophy to affect these disciplines. Furthermore, among those who had adopted the vision of LP/E, or some mediated version of it, there was a great intellectual and material investment that continued to bind the conduct of inquiry and the practice of "theory construction" to these philosophical images. And it was not simply the particular philosophical reconstructions of LP/E that were accepted but also the ancillary background claim about the unity and hierarchy of science that suggested there was an essential core to scientific endeavor, a method, that could be isolated, appropriated, and, in varying degrees, applied—that "science" was less a class concept than a term that referred to a universal form of knowledge of which specific activities were in varying degrees manifestations. Even many of those social scientists who rejected LP/E were, in various ways, as I have already argued, often as much the prisoner of that philosophy as those who embraced it, since what they understood themselves as rejecting was nothing less than the logic of natural science. It continues to be common to identify the practice of natural science with this philosophical reconstruction and then assume that objecting to its premises constitutes rejecting natural scientific explanation. For both opponents and proponents of L P/E, science and positivism were, in many instances, viewed as identical, and they continued to attach themselves to the dogmas that there was *a* method of natural science, that it was possible to distinguish a class of facts peculiar to these sciences, and that there was something special about the nomothetic form of natural scientific explanation that differentiated it from the idiographic mode demanded by the phenomena of the social and human sciences.

Although by the mid-1970s, the philosophical critique of LP/E had begun to seep into the social sciences and provide a basis for challenging the dominant criteria of scientific identity, as well as facile dichotomies between natural and social science, the result was more a reconstitution of a scientific image through the incorporation of dissident ideas such as those of Kuhn than either a transformation in scientific practice or a reevaluation of the relationship between social science and philosophy. Even among the critics of LP/E, there was a tendency more to turn to postpositivist metatheoretical arguments and offer them as an alternative or complementary way of "doing" science or approaching social phenomena (Bernstein 1976) than to examine the crucial nexus. Social science continues to accede to the authority of the philosophy of science in a wide range of matters, and transformations in the philosophy of science continue to produce crises of social scientific identity. Why this is the case is a complicated matter rooted both in the peculiar history of the social sciences and in a more general connection in our academic culture betweeen philosophy and other specialized fields. Thus even though political theory, by the 1970s, had begun to break away from the intellectual bondage of LP/E, it remained hostage to both the historical career of that philosophy and to the general belief that there were philosophical answers to social scientific problems. By the 1980s, however, pointed discussion of issues in the philosophy of science dramatically receded from the literature of social science. Although there may be a number of factors that contributed to this trend, the principal cause was the waning of the debate about the possibility and appropriateness of cloning the methods of natural science.

Ideas from the philosophy of science entered the discourse of social science at a relatively late date. This is, in one respect, not surprising, since it was not until the 1930s with the emigration of logical positivism to the United States that the philosophy of science became a clearly differentiated academic enterprise. What had functioned as a model of science prior to that point was references to a somewhat random collection of authorities such as John Stuart Mill, Auguste Comte, or John Dewey. Apart from an occasional rhetorically motivated borrowing, social science remained, until the 1950s, relatively innocent of any systematic involvement with the philosophy of science. But prior to that time, there were few sustained challenges to the very idea of a social science, even one modeled on the natural sciences, despite variations in claims about the concrete character and purpose of such a science. In the case of political science, the frontal assault on science as a value and a goal began with the rise of the influence of the European émigrés in political theory and with the reaction of American political scientists (Gunnell 1993), but the scenario that structured debates in political science was very similar to that in fields such as sociology.

Post–World War II political science was seeking, for a variety of reasons that included both being accepted as a science and not being designated as political, to reassert and solidify its scientific identity. It found, however, that for the first time, such an identity was being fundamentally called into question. By the early 1950s, political scientists embracing behavioralism, which at its core was predicated upon a commitment to emulating the methods of natural science, as well as other social scientists with a similar intellectual disposition were turning in a much more direct, although often unsystematic, manner to the philosophy of science as a source of validation. As it turned out, this was an academic field now defined by the intellectual hegemony of LP/E. What was sought was an identity that would both withstand the new antiscientific challenge and finally legitimate political science as an authentic science that could command social and professional authority. The issue of behavioralism was largely the focus of a dialogue between political theorists, between what came to be called "traditional" and "scientific" theory. One group was largely influenced by the émigré literature, and the other consisted of representatives of mainstream behavioral political science. The LP/E reconstruction of the logic and epistemology of science was, however, initially taken by both parties as definitive and representative of the practice and demands of science. The issue was viewed as one of whether political science should be scientific.

By the late 1960s, as postpositivist influences in the philosophy of science and philosophy of social science began to enter the discourse of political science, the central issue was no longer one of simply choosing between science and some more humanistic image of inquiry but rather the adequacy of positivist claims about the nature of science. While the critics of behavioralism deployed revolutionary doctrines in the philosophy of science, behavioralists called upon counterrevolutionary arguments in philosophy. By the mid-1970s, the controversy about behavioralism was in large measure transformed into a debate among contending surrogate philosophical images of science that mirrored the battle over LP/E in the literature of the philosophy of science. Although the theomachy in the philosophy of science continued to be reflected, in various ways and places, in the sublunar world of political science through the late 1970s, both the particular evolutionary path of the discipline and the changing character of the philosophy of science served to dissipate controversy.

Postbehavioralism, as it emerged in the 1970s, was characterized by the policy turn in political science and a falling away from the rhetoric of scientism, but in many respects, it also signaled the victory of behavioralism in the internal disciplinary practices of inquiry. The victors, however, allowed and even propagated a new pluralism in the field that mitigated the polarization that had characterized the 1960s. At the same time, the subfield of political theory, the seat of the most intensive criticism of behavioralism and LP/E, became an increasingly autonomous and diverse realm that, while institutionally linked to political science, tended to disengage from the discourse of the discipline. The 1980s were, then, marked by the dissolution of the parties in the controversy that had brought issues in the philosophy of science to the forefront of discussion. Although interest in these issues continued in certain enclaves both within and outside mainstream political science, they lost their former salience. This situation was complemented by developments in the philosophy of science. Although the arguments that would eventually lead to the decline, if not the demise, of LP/E in philosophy were clearly manifest in the 1960s, it was not until the 1970s that something on the order of an epitaph could safely be written. LP/E's death, however, was slow and incremental, and even though its most essential doctrines were gradually repudiated or severely modified, its spirit continued to structure the conversation about such matters as the nature of scientific theory. But despite the persistence of certain basic issues, the discussions have become increasingly specialized and technical and, consequently, to a large extent inaccessible to outsiders. Gone were the days of wholesale arguments about the nature of scientific explanation that could be packaged and retailed to social scientists. Less prominent were works such as those of Kuhn, Popper, and Lakatos that could be easily absorbed by a social scientific audience and that seemed to hold some relevance for the social scientific enterprise.

One might reasonably take the position that the present situation is salutary and that it is best if social science and the philosophy of science go their separate ways. After all, it could be argued, natural science does quite well in its relative ignorance of academic philosophy. The recession of philosophical discussion could also be construed as a sign of scientific maturity. The situation, however, is too complex to move simply in the direction of a no-fault divorce. As I have already suggested, elements of the old philosophy of science remain deeply embedded in the practices and apologies of political and social science and have at times been pointedly rearticulated in various quarters. The problem goes far beyond merely the intellectual residue of an obsolescent philosophy of science. It is not a situation where, as in the case of natural science, naive and philosophically antiquated images of science sit rather harmlessly in the introductory chapters of textbooks and have little to do with the substance of scientific education and practice. Unlike in the case of natural science, these images continue to govern how social scientists both theorize and conceive of theory, and now new explorations into the terrain of the philosophy of science are gaining attention. But there is yet a more general and fundamental problem. The assimilation of the philosophy of science in the discourse and practice of political science, and the retreat of explicit discussion of these issues, have served not only to obscure operative ideas but to repress the basic problem of the relationship between social science and philosophy as well as a consideration of such matters as the nature of theory in social science.

Recent interest in the philosophy of science is still motivated by concerns about intellectual legitimation and practical authority, but it also derives from concerns about finding a rationale for the increasing methodological pluralism that characterizes the social sciences and about seeking some epistemological unity behind the cognitive diversity (Thomas 1979; Roth 1987). But whatever the concern, the questions that must be raised are these: Can the philosophy of science be taken as descriptive of scientific practice? To the extent, in principle, that it can, what is the degree of verisimilitude in some particular reconstruction? Even if a particular account of *natural science* is judged acceptable, in what degree is it relevant for understanding social scientific inquiry? Although the language of the philosophy of science is often either explicitly or implicitly normative, what bearing does it have on the practice of scientific inquiry? To what extent is it possible to move from a philosophical claim *about* science, even if deemed philosophically valid, to a conclusion with respect to *how* to conduct science? These questions cannot be answered adequately without some general understanding of the philosophy of science as a field, and this in turn entails the need to have some grasp of its genealogy.

II

The historical origins of the philosophy of science were in a project that can best be described as the justification of substantive scientific claims. Although this practical concern and role has receded, its discursive imprint has remained. The structure and content of the language of the field reflects the fact that most essentially the philosophy of science, and philosophical methodology, have been and continue to be devoted to the vindication of science, to a demonstration that scientific knowledge is possible, to explicating its foundations and the mode of its acquisition. While science, we might say, is concerned with knowing, the philosophy of science assumes the task of knowing that what is known is known. It is easy to lose sight of this congenital aspect in the array of technical issues that now dominate the field. And although epistemology, of which the philosophy of science has always been a part, has been the subject of some bad press in recent years, many of the critics such as Rorty seem strangely neglectful of what epistemology was historically all about. Rorty, for example, still situates the problem in the context of a generalized history of philosophy in which individuals as diverse as Plato and Descartes are assimilated as representatives of the epistemological vocation. Despite their recognition that this syndrome is somehow tied to professionalism in philosophy and philosophy's relationship to its subject matter, they do not indicate a very concrete historical grasp either of the origins of the problem or its external significance. First, the argument remains circumscribed by the boundaries of the contemporary practice of philosophy. Despite their skepticism about modern philosophy, the critics remain mesmerized by the idea of the integrity of the classic canon and tradition, and they project the problems of foundationalism backward upon putative ancestors who, in turn, become implicated in the ills of the present. I would suggest that the perspective, and problems, of contemporary philosophy can no more be attributed in any significant manner to these distant figures than academic political theory can be understood as the progeny of the classic canon. My account, because of its brevity, is somewhat mythologized, but it is, I think, essentially correct.

Although the common historical image of how the natural sciences slowly, after the Middle Ages, became differentiated from philosophy may not be entirely incorrect, it is too general, and in at least one important respect, it reverses the relationship that characterized the actual course of development. Much of what is today part of academic philosophy had its roots in what we would, in retrospect, designate as the practice of science. Before the discourses of natural sciences, both as particular disciplinary enterprises and as a socially recognized generic type of endeavor, were distinctly institutionalized and professionalized, there were prototypical discourses *about* nature. These, however, were hardly autonomous and secure from external rival authorities, such as those that we would now categorize as religion and politics, or from more narrowly competitive and less differentiated endeavors such as alchemy. Equally important was the fact that these discourses were seldom paradigmatic or internally theoretically hegemonic. In this context, the kind and level of discourses that we might analytically factor out as the functional equivalent of natural science were entwined with a rhetoric of inquiry devoted to justifying and legitimating substantive knowledge claims and to demarcating and defining science. Neither these discourses about nature nor the criteria of validity advanced within them were sufficiently authoritative without demonstrating that what was claimed as knowledge was truly worthy of that status, without referring to its foundation and defending the procedures through which it was acquired.

This kind of rhetorical defense of "scientific" claims was apparent in the work of Descartes, Galileo, Bacon, the Port Royal logicians, Newton, Darwin, and others. These legitimating accounts almost always, however, involved a distorted, or at least purified, image of actual scientific practice—often reducing it to some logical or psychological ground and operation. This meant that its relationship to the actual process and product of empirical inquiry was inherently problematical. Although today we tend to approach the works of these early "scientists" categorically, that is, in terms of our disciplinary distinctions between philosophy and science, such an anachoristic and anachronistic reading belies the actual character of their work. It was in an important sense both prephilosophic and prescientific while functionally an amalgam of both philosophy and science. We make a grave mistake when we look at Descartes's discussion of method in terms of abstract contemporary issues about philosophical skepticism and fail to examine the manner in which it was contextually related to his justification of certain substantive empirical claims. Similarly, if we construe Newton's or Darwin's claims to reject speculation as other than an element in the rhetoric of inquiry, we mistake the order of discourse to which they belong.

As the sciences became increasingly disciplinized and differentiated, and both paradigmatic and autonomous, the rhetoric of inquiry gradually, but eventually, floated free of the substantive discourse of science and became constitutive of an emerging mode of discourse that we would now recognize as epistemology. Although in some generic functional sense, we can project epistemology backward to the beginning of civilization and although there are certainly ties between the modern epistemological project and earlier philosophy, the discourse of contemporary epistemology is rooted in the beginnings of modern natural science. The emergence of epistemology as a separate discourse was tied in part to the development of the modern university and its curriculum and the attempt within it to elevate philosophy as the queen of the sciences. Philosophy, as in the case of Kant, was initially often to a large extent still a justification of science, but it eventually developed into a broader array of epistemological and foundational discourses that in turn differentiated into specialized areas and finally took the form of academic fields. Contemporary academic philosophical disciplines are, then, to a large extent, strictly speaking, postscientific phenomena. These disciplines, as modes of institutionalized reflexivity, have as a whole, however, never escaped their somewhat paradoxical origins, that is, attempting to say something authoritative *about* the nature and criteria of knowledge in an activity in which they do not participate and largely do not know *how* to practice—and with respect to which they often have no close relationship. Although each branch of philosophy has had its own history and particular relationship to its subject matter, there have been some common dilemmas peculiar to second-order discourses. These are well exemplified in the case of the philosophy of science, whose historical career also bears a strong resemblance to that of the history of the social sciences. The latter, as I will argue in chapter 6, were not merely creatures of the academy but derived in part from the practices that became their subject matter.

The growing autonomy of the natural sciences rendered the epistemology of science, as a normative rhetoric of inquiry, somewhat obsolescent. It was increasingly transformed into an academic—in all senses of that word—enterprise devoid of obvious practical import. While setting and defending the boundaries of science is a perennial, and inevitable, practical problem within science and between science and other activities (Taylor 1996), the philosophical project of demarcating science is more anomalous. As epistemology became a more general and abstract endeavor, only loosely tied to the validation of any scientific theory and substantive practice of knowledge, and directed against equally decontextualized skeptical doubts, its role became increasingly problematical. From Locke to Kant, philosophy was still concerned, quite expressly, with justifying the ways of science to the world, and this still often meant, as in the case of Locke, devising images that both intentionally and unintentionally deviated considerably from scientific practice. By the time of Kant, however, vindicating science had become inseparable from both vindicating philosophical rationalism and justifying the preeminence of "theory" vis-à-vis "practice." Philosophy attempted to validate itself, both intrinsically and in terms of its relationship to its subject matter and society at large, through its image as a foundational enterprise that underwrote the practices of authoritative knowledge. The vindication of science, in short, was transformed into a vindication of philosophy.

Kant wanted both to vindicate science and to limit its authority and scope. Although he offered a critique of speculative reason or metaphysics, his aim was to demonstrate that science rested on transcendental categories accessible to philosophy. Nineteenth-century naturalistic philosophy struck out against the idealist tradition, eventually associated with Hegel, but it continued to pursue the foundationalist agenda, only now seeking empirical grounds in experimental psychology. The philosophical tradition that began with Frege and carried through Russell and the early Wittgenstein was distinguished by the motif of resurrecting the authority of philosophy as the underwriter of mathematics and natural science. For Frege, the ground of science was logic, and Husserl presented an image of philosophy as a rigorous transcendental science that went beyond the naive realism of scientific practice. Wittgenstein's *Tractatus* still focused on the logical world that was prior to, but compatible with, science. He wanted to demonstrate that there were no specifically philosophical propositions and that logic differed from science only in that it was not factual and had no semantic content, but he also wanted to put philosophy beyond the reach of psychology.

Of all the practices of knowledge, the natural sciences were least in need of second-order underwriting, but it was the social authority of science that lent authority to philosophy. Although science became professionalized and disciplinized, and in many respects routinized, it did not really become simpler in terms of either discovery or justification. But philosophy's consistent interest was to reduce it to a formula to which it could claim to hold the key, and this entailed a continuing estrangement from the details of scientific practice. The philosophy and methodology of science as a distinct form of discourse is conventionally, and properly, understood as emerging in the nineteenth century with the work of individuals such as Auguste Comte, J. F. W. Herschel, William Whewell, and John Stuart Mill. Both Whewell and Herschel were scientists in their own right and sought to provide an inductive empiricist account of scientific knowledge. Mill, however, was notoriously ignorant of the practices of natural science and, like Comte, more concerned with putting social inquiry on a scientific foundation. While his *Logic* was supposed to distill the method of science, it was the first work in a genre that would continue to have a dubious relationship to the actual practice of natural science. The connection between the philosophy of science and social theory represented in Mill's work would, however, be a constant one.

While the general epistemological project in philosophy emerged from what we would today think of as science, the philosophy of science as a distinct discourse evolved, as strange as it may seem, as a specialized branch of epistemology. It was still located in the penumbral world between science and philosophy, but it took concrete shape essentially as a response to the breakdown of mechanistic physics as a "realistic" image of the world and the subsequent crisis in scientific theory. The crisis *in* scientific theory precipitated a philosophical crisis regarding the nature of theory. From the beginning, the philosophy of science was marked by its suspicion of theory. This was in part the heritage of nineteenth-century prejudice against speculative reason, but it was also a response to the apparent impermanence of theories. The philosophy of science sought to demonstrate that theories could come and go without undermining the authority of scientific claims as such. The empiricism of Ernst Mach, J. H. Poincaré, and Pierre Duhem focused, in various ways, on the elaboration of an instrumentalist or conventionalist account of scientific theories as heuristic economical calculational devices for explaining and describing experientially given phenomena. It "saved the phenomena," but, more important, it saved theory and explained its place in science—even while cognitively depreciating it. It also saved empiricism. One of the crucial issues was the status of those elements of science that were not observable and their relationship to what was observable. This problem became definitive for the philosophy of science, and it fitted into the framework of traditional empiricism, which had been dubious about theorizing and sought to ground knowledge in experience. Despite the ways in which the discussion of the nature of scientific theory continued to be related to substantive problems in science, such as those emanating from the theory of relativity and quantum mechanics, the problem of theory, and of empiricism in general, increasingly, with the disciplinization of the philosophy of science, became a philosophical problem with a tenuous relationship to the practice of science. The problem that structured the discourse was that of how scientific knowledge is possible, but exactly what this had to do with scientific problems was a submerged, even if crucial, issue—along with the more general structural issue of the relationship between philosophy and science.

The bridge from discourse to practice in the history of the philosophy of science was the school of logical positivism. The philosophy of science as a distinct philosophical discipline began with logical positivism, and the agenda that was set, as well as the language of that agenda, was one from which the field never escaped. Despite certain definite ties to scientific practice and the fact that the problems that engaged the Vienna Circle and the Berlin School were still in many ways cued to scientific issues, the project was primarily bound to the issue of the identity of philosophy. Although Moritz Schlick and Philipp Frank had been practicing scientists, most of the influential members, as well as the individuals who influenced their agenda (Wittgenstein, Popper, Frege, Russell, Hans Reichenbach, Tarski), were philosophers, logicians, and mathematicians. The dispersion of the interlocutors and the reconstitution of the conversation in philosophy departments in the United States during the 1930s created the philosophy of science as a distinct discipline and academic field, and during the 1940s and 1950s, LP/E came to define and occupy that field, which developed in proximity with social science disciplines in a manner that was quite unique.

Although Feyerabend's claim that from the beginning, this tradition "was barren, from a scientific point of view" may be overdrawn (1995:119), it would be difficult to document any distinct impact of this philosophy and the philosophy of science in general on a significant aspect of scientific practice. Although some scientists, such as Albert Einstein, Werner Heisenberg, Erwin Schrodinger, Percy Bridgman, A. S. Eddington, and N. R. Campbell, may have engaged in reflections that had some bearing and influence on philosophical issues, and in turn some impact on scientific inquiry, these exceptions did not prove the rule. At the same time, although it might be an exaggeration to suggest that the average philosopher of science knew little more about the substance of science than Mill, those most influential in defining the project of logical empiricism, such as Carl Hempel, were quite explicit that what they meant by "science" was a logical construct, an idealized philosophical model of the form and basis of rational judgment and linguistic meaning that had little to do with the practice of science apart from the presumption that successful scientific claims came close to exemplifying this logical and epistemological paradigm. Despite the degree to which the work of certain individuals such as Popper was informed by the hope of making the practice of science, as well as philosophy, a more rational enterprise and the extent to which the language of the philosophy of science remained cast in a descriptive and normative mode, the paths of the philosophy of science and scientific practice diverged still further, and the issue of their relationship was increasingly displaced or repressed. The principal influence of the philosophy of science was, ironically, not on natural science but on other specialized fields that sought either, as in the case of the social sciences, a scientific identity and guide to practice or, as in the case of the humanities, a contrast-model. Since the natural sciences offered no systematic account of themselves and since LP/E provided such an exclusive and authoritative image of scientific explanation, the impact of the latter's philosophical doctrines is not surprising.

The revolution in the philosophy of science that led eventually to the defeat of the "received view" was prompted by the work of Kuhn, Paul Feyerabend, N. R. Hanson, Stephen Toulmin, Michael Scriven, and others. It tended in some ways, however, to obscure some of the endemic problems attaching to the philosophy of science. The new emphasis on the history and practice of science and the retreat from normative philosophical measures of scientific rationality may have served to reduce one dimension of the distance between philosophy and science. Yet it is a mistake to assume either that these claims to descriptive validity were adequately redeemed or that such redemption solved the problem of the relationship between philosophy and natural science—or between the philosophy of science and social science. The break between the revolutionaries and LP/E need not be minimized, but the continuities with the traditional project should not be forgotten. Despite the historical form of their arguments, the claims of the dissidents were still primarily logical and epistemological. Kuhn, for example, did not so much write a history of science that had certain philosophical implications as draw upon historical warrants to justify his philosophical account of such matters as the relationship between theory and fact. Much as his predecessors had done, he wrote a history of science that fitted his philosophical image. His project, particularly in its inception, was still that of explicating and underwriting scientific reason. His concern was to demonstrate how science worked and even "progressed." The fundamental problem, as well as language, that structured this work was the quite traditional one that had informed the institutionalization of the philosophy of science—the status of theoretical entities. Kuhn's work was still shaped by the discursive heritage of the turn-of-the-century crisis surrounding the idea of scientific theory. He was still bound to the problem of accounting for radical scientific change and explicating the role of theory in such changes.

Many social scientists may be correct in believing that the revolution in the philosophy of science gave rise to a literature that provides both a better account of the logic and epistemology of science and a more relevant way of thinking about issues in social science. But it is important not to allow this assumption to slip over into the belief that the new philosophy of science, any more than the old, offers some privileged image of science and that it can, in some direct way, be appropriated and applied in social scientific practice. What has happened is that one philosophical argument has been displaced by another, and the relationship, both cognitive and practical, between philosophy and science has not undergone any fundamental transformation. Kuhn's notion of a paradigm, for example, may arguably be more instructive than, for example, the covering-law model,

but there is no obvious basis for assuming that the concept has any significance for doing science or that it has changed the relationship of philosophy to science. It is an analytical concept for thinking *about* science that
has no particular logical connection to scientific practice.

As I suggested earlier, *theory* is largely a metatheoretical term. Much like
the word *observation,* it is not primarily a scientific word (such as *atom* or
mass) even though it occurs in the language of science. We can, without a
great deal of difficulty, trace the history of theory in the philosophy of
science, but to do the same for scientific practice would be a much more
difficult and dubious undertaking. It is, then, a mistake to assume that
scientific practice and discourse correspond to philosophical reconstructions; yet among social scientists there remains great difficulty in separating the two. All of the social scientific talk about what theories are, how
they relate to facts, how to construct them, how to test them, and the like
is largely the recycled residue of philosophical talk. Whewell suggested
that facts are confirmed theories, while theories are unconfirmed facts.
More recently, Nelson Goodman has noted that "facts are small theories,
and true theories are big facts" (1978:97). But as I argued earlier, we might
usefully think about the class of claims that is most often represented by
the use of the concept of theory if we are interested in the possibility of
"realizing theory" in social science. The persistent issue of the nature of
theory brings us to the postrevolutionary career of the philosophy of science. The conversation about theory has continued, but there have been
some important changes in its direction.

III

The discursive universe of the post-LP/E period is difficult to represent.
No new regime comparable to LP/E has emerged, and given the array of
specific and diverse issues, such a development is unlikely. Gone are the
titanic battles and dramatic polar arguments that characterized the debates
around Kuhn's work, and gone also, for the most part, are arguments such
as those of Kuhn and Lakatos that social scientists can either easily wrap
themselves within, for either critical or legitimating purposes, or deploy in
thinking about and practicing their own research. The problems that have
defined the contemporary period are, however, very much the legacy of
the revolution. Despite the complexity of the field, there are two fundamental and entwined problems that have structured the conversation: (1)
the problem of relativism and scientific truth and (2) the problem of the
character and status of scientific theories. These problems are also in part
rooted in the underlying, still unresolved, and seldom confronted dilemma
of the relationship between science and the philosophy of science.

What Kuhn's work, as well as similar and related arguments, most immediately precipitated were reactions among the orthodoxy to the effect that these claims, and the whole contextualist and neopragmatic movement in philosophy, threatened to undermine the objectivity of science and the idea of scientific truth. Again, what was actually undermined was a particular metatheoretical claim *about* scientific truth and objectivity. The failure to make this crucial distinction still haunts discussions in the philosophy of science as well as other fields influenced by it. To suggest that the revolution in the philosophy of science endangered scientific rationality is something on the order of suggesting that Wittgenstein's reformation of the concept of linguistic meaning endangers our ability to communicate. As I stressed in chapter 3, the fear involved in all these intimations of relativism is really a latent anxiety about the authority of philosophy with respect to the practices that constitute its subject matter. The traditional "dogmas of empiricism," including the determination of theory by facts and the logical and ontological distinction between theory and fact, may have fallen at the barricades of the revolution, but many of those who followed, as in the case of most revolutions, were uneasy with the vacuum of authority. Philosophy did not graciously surrender its perceived position as the arbiter of scientific judgment. Even many of those who more explicitly participated in, or accepted, the revolution were ultimately anxious about what they believed was its "relativist" direction. If there were not timeless philosophically accessible transcendental foundations of science that made the history of science meaningful as a story of the growth of knowledge, as the progressive revelation of the "facts" and their relationship to one another, was there not, after all, some meaning in history itself, something that, for example, made the succession of paradigms intelligible? Was there not some neo-Hegelian manner in which philosophy's passion for certainty could be reconciled with the record of changing scientific images of reality?

There may have been some misunderstanding regarding Kuhn's position, but the critics did sense the underlying and crucial claim that philosophy had little to add to the "truths" of science. To what extent Kuhn was historically correct about the exact manner in which scientific change took place was secondary to what both supporters such as Rorty and a great variety of critics accurately perceived as the conclusion that science as well as the world was a matter of scientific practice. One might quibble about what Kuhn meant by a concept such as paradigm, but his narrowing of focus to the "exemplars" around which scientific education and activity were organized left little doubt about Kuhn's commitment, from the beginning, to the idea of the philosophical "incommensurabilty" of scientific claims and to the notion that the "world" was a product of "language—or discourse-communities, sets of individuals bound together by the shared vocabulary which simultaneously makes professional communication possible and restricts that communication to the profession." Scientific visions of the world and the processes of change are a function of "primitive similarity differences and relations acquired during professional education," which supply "the taxonomy shared by a field's practitioners, their professional ontology" (Kuhn 1993a:xii–xiii). At the core of the identity of scientific practice and its theoretical products were what Kuhn finally came to call "kind-concepts," which in effect produce different and incommensurable worlds. Kuhn denied that "successive scientific beliefs become more and more probable or better and better approximations to the truth" and maintained that "the subject of truth claims cannot be a relation between beliefs and a putatively mind-independent or 'external' world." The "lexicon" of scientific practice is grounded only in "convention" and is "constitutive of *possible experience* of the world" (Kuhn 1993b:315–16, 330).

Even by the early 1970s, the emphasis had shifted from the LP/E focus on the logic and epistemology of justifying scientific claims to the issue of scientific change and to what positivists had viewed as the somewhat irrational context of discovery. Lakatos, like many others, had charged that Kuhn's account of science made the matter of judging scientific theories *"a matter of mob psychology"* (1970:178), but as with similar criticisms of Kuhn, it is important to understand what was actually being said—and not said. The real problem was not that scientific practice was lacking criteria but rather that Kuhn had left *philosophy* without a basis for assessing such criteria. Arguments such as that of Lakatos, however, tended to blur the line between science and philosophy and thereby begged the question of why or how philosophy could or should be in the business of assessing scientific knowledge and prescribing the criteria of its progress. Like his mentor, Popper, Lakatos assumed that philosophy had a critical role to play in the development of scientific knowledge, and he assumed that some kind of critical rationalism in philosophy could speak to the improvement of scientific practice and that there was "growth" in scientific knowledge when science was "rational." Lakatos was affected by Kuhn's argument and unable to subscribe fully to Popper's rendition of the theory of truth. He sought to locate scientific progress, and find criteria of theory assessment, in an explanatory and normative model of the evolution of scientific research programs that posited internal historical coherency in the process of scientific change. Where and when science is rational, Lakatos claimed, an internal historical account of its progress is its own explanation, and when it is not rational, external historical explanation is required. Similarly, rival logics can be tested in terms of their historical efficacy. There is, after all, Lakatos claimed, reason immanent in history.

Popper was an ambiguous figure and is likely to remain so. Those, such as the Frankfurt School, who treat him as a positivist cast too broad a net (Adorno et al. 1976). He was always at odds with the instrumentalist and conventionalist propensities of the Vienna Circle and its problematizing of theory and attachment to the correspondence theory of truth as set out by Carnap and others. He never embraced verificationism and the positivist theory of language. However, he was certainly too quick to play the sparrow to cock robin when he asked who killed logical positivism and answered, "I fear that I must admit responsibility" (Popper 1992:88). Popper strongly maintained that his position had remained consistent, and his followers have usually defended this image. But the ambiguity is not convincingly erasable. While he held strongly to the view that there can be no theoretically independent observation language or nonpropositional transconceptual knowledge, he at the same time spoke of theories as something out of which "we create a world: not the real world, but our nets in which we try to catch the real world" (1992:60). This sounds like instrumentalist language, but Popper must in the end, much like Kuhn, be understood as a theoretical realist as well as a metaphysical realist. Where he essentially differed from Kuhn, or what led him to berate Kuhn, was his view that science was not, and should not be, normal and hegemonic (1970; 1976:295) but a type of free-market discourse. Popper's vision of critical rationalism required constant competition between theories if progress was to be achieved (1965). Kuhn's suggestion, to the contrary, was that without entrenched dogmas and paradigmatic hegemony, there would be no regime to revolt against and, consequently, less impetus for change.

Popper also did not want to relinquish the idea that philosophy could say something authoritative about scientific truth. The concept of truth often seems quite empty in his work, and he even disclaimed any general theory of truth, but he held on to the idea of science moving progressively toward a greater approximation of truth and professed a faith that there is a world with regularities beyond language even if it cannot actually be articulated. Also, very early on, he embraced Tarski's semantic theory of truth, which Popper believed allowed the notion of truth as correspondence to be resurrected. Popper had always embraced an evolutionary account of scientific change, that is, the survival of the fittest theories in the face of the severest attempts at analytical and empirical falsification. Consequently, in response to what he perceived as the dangers of the Kuhnian formulation, he stresssd even further an evolutionary theory of scientific truth and posited a constantly evolving "third world" of reality consisting of statements, problems, and theories (Popper 1972). This third world he took to be real even if "not quite as real" as the physical objects in everyday experience (1992:183). The first world consists, he argued, of sensibly apprehended physical objects and events, while the second world is composed of thoughts and subjective experience. The third world "is a product of the human mind" (1992:186) but, according to Popper, not ultimately subjective. Although there is interaction between worlds one and three, it is only through the medium of world two. This would seem to constitute an ultimate breach between theory and fact, but it would still be difficult to construe Popper's position as positivist on any principal concrete issue.

Although Stephen Toulmin was a central actor in the revolution in the philosophy of science, he was uneasy with the implications of the retreat of philosophy from the enterprise of judging its subject matter and from an attempt to find criteria of rational progress. He had argued strongly against both the logic and the epistemology of LP/E, yet he was not content with what he believed was Kuhn's failure to sustain some sense of rational continuity in science. Drawing upon images of evolutionary biology, he argued that disciplinary matrices in science are like evolving species that provide a structure that maintains continuity between paradigmatic conceptual shifts. A study of both the context of a science and its internal dynamics would, he maintained, make it possible to explain how the selection of surviving ideas is incorporated into an evolving science (Toulmin 1972). Larry Laudan's arguments have followed a similar path. Laudan came closer to recognizing that the problem of rationality was a dilemma not so much of science as of philosophy, but his position was still framed in terms of the issues posed by individuals such as Popper and Lakatos and reflected a concern about the authority of philosophy. He suggested that the best way to explain the cognitive basis of science was to view it as a "problem-solving" activity. Conceptual and empirical problems, he claimed, give continuity to science across incommensurable paradigms. They also give rise to theories and research traditions that can be judged according to the degree to which they solve those problems and make the world intelligible (Laudan 1977; also Hesse 1980). The anxiety about relativism, however, remained.

The notion of science as "puzzle-solving" was a common one and one that had always been at the heart of Kuhn's arguments. But for Kuhn it was impossible to go any deeper. "Puzzle-solving is one of the families of practices" that emerged during the evolution of science, and for Kuhn, it was a rational activity. "Those who proclaim that no interest-driven pursuit can properly be identified as the rational pursuit of knowledge make a profound and consequential mistake" (Kuhn 1993b:339), but Laudan was not content to treat problem- or puzzle-solving at this level. Laudan confronted what he believed was the widespread notion that postpositivism, as represented in the work of individuals such as Winch, Kuhn, Quine, and Rorty, had culminated in a radical relativism that rendered problematical the very idea of knowledge as well as the assumption that the "natural world and such evidence as we have about that world do little or nothing to constrain our beliefs" (1990:viii). His wish was, particularly, to set misguided humanists and social scientists straight about these matters and to call to account those who attempted to use philosophical leverage in the pursuit of various ideological projects from feminism to religious apology. Since he believed the "relativist position to be profoundly wrongheaded," what, he claimed, was needed was a "purgative" for those who had succumbed to the "wiles of relativism" and a "prophylactic" for those who had not yet indulged (xi). Typically, Laudan evoked an image of the relativist position to which few would subscribe, and he presented it as a claim about the nature of scientific knowledge rather than about philosophy's capacity to underwrite such knowledge. Laudan's work indicates, once again, what is really at stake in much of this literature. In Laudan's work, however, another distinct thread in the forensic fabric of the dominant contemporary conversation in the philosophy of science was visible—antirealism. Laudan claimed, much along the lines of Kuhn, that no philosophical sense can be made of the general idea of scientific truth or the notion of science progressing in terms of an approximation of truth. The search for truth in some ideal sense could not be the goal of science. Theories, he argued, are to be judged not in terms of whether they are true, confirmable, falsifiable, or meet some other epistemological criterion but in terms of their pragmatic problem-solving ability. Since this claim, on its face, sounds a great deal like theoretical instrumentalism and its assumption that theories can be judged by how well they illuminate the world, it is necessary to make some distinctions and lay out the emerging positions more concretely.

Although I have stressed the manner in which what we take to be the natural world is a discursive product of the practice of natural science, this argument does not entail the philosophical claim that theories are merely conventional devices for explaining and predicting facts. The issue is what is understood to be the role and reference of theories. Although the instrumentalist perspective, or what is sometimes referred to as conventionalism, was, in its various forms, a central dimension of the tradition of LP/E, members of this school were never entirely of one mind with respect to the status of theory. Ernest Nagel, for example, claimed that the difference between theoretical instrumentalism and realism was simply a matter of a preferred mode of speech (1961). While the dominant image of LP/E has been defined in terms of the demand for explanation through the deductive subsumption of particulars under laws and generalizations, the core was always a nominalistic account of linguistic meaning and the attempt to privilege some set of propositions as grounded in immediate experience and as constituting the beginning and end of science; that is, science starts with observation statements, sense data, or some other basic datum and returns to explain them. In this construction, theories are presented as initially empirically empty calculi that, through correspondence rules or operational definitions, are given an empirical interpretation and become the basis of generating explanatory laws. As Sellars has noted, *"the positivistic conception of science"* always included the "myth of the given" and "the idea that the framework of theoretical objects . . . is, so to speak, an *auxiliary* framework of 'calculational devices,' the status and value of which consist in their systematizing and heuristic role with respect to confirmable generalizations formulated in the framework of terms which enjoy a direct ostensive link with the world" (1963:173). Although it sometimes seemed as if this account of theory contradicted, or at least conflicted with, the emphasis on verification and confirmation, it was not theories but derivative empirical claims that were understood as directly testable. Some in this tradition even toyed with the idea that in principle, and maybe practice, theories were eliminable or dispensable, but at least the instrumentalist image of theories as useful constructs tended to dominate. This conception was evident in the use of metaphors such as nets, lights, and maps to illustrate the nature of theory; the dichotomy between theory and observation and their respective languages; the distinction between the contexts of discovery and justification; and the theoretical agnosticism inherent in the "theoretician's dilemma," which, as already noted, posed the problem that if observational predicates are the foundation of science, why is a "detour" through theory necessary?

Although Kuhn's conception of theory has sometimes been characterized as idealist because of his apotheosization of theory, his position amounted to theoretical realism, that is, the idea that theoretical claims are existence claims. Any attribution of instrumentalism to Kuhn would be a severe distortion. Both he and Paul Feyerabend (1970) spoke, probably infelicitously, about facts as "theory-laden" and thereby remained bound to the binary language of LP/E while reversing its polarity, but what their claims amounted to was the abolition of anything more than a pragmatic distinction between theories and facts. Thus their arguments complemented more pointed accounts of theoretical realism such as that of Sellars as well as the critique of the "myth of the given" and other "dogmas of empiricism." Scientific theories, according to this perspective, must be interpreted as irreducible and putatively true and factual claims about the world and as entailing ontic commitments. When Kuhn, for example, is charged with relativism, it must be emphasized once more that to the extent that this label has relevance in his case, it is not because he is suggesting that there are no criteria of truth in the practice of science. He is a philosophical relativist who is claiming that philosophy cannot give metatheoretical meaning to the concept of scientific truth (see 1977). But it is precisely this issue of philosophical relativism, and the accompanying residue of the theory/fact issue, that continued to drive much of the conversation in the philosophy of science after the demise of LP/E (Moser 1993). The problem is, if the criteria of scientific truth and objectivity are a function of scientific theory, how can philosophy vindicate science and how does it claim any authority with respect to the issue of scientific judgment?

The conversation, broadly viewed, continues to be structured by the pragmatist challenges to traditional concepts of scientific truth (Pihlström 1996), but more complex is a narrower controversy involving the positions of realism and antirealism. And it is necessary to bring these into sharper relief (French, Vehling, and Wellstein 1988) and to be as clear about what they are *not* as about what they are if we are to understand the implications of these arguments for social science. Both are distinctly post-LP/E in that they reject the major tenets of that school; yet both are troubled, and catalyzed, by the dilemma of how to vindicate science (and themselves), which, they believe, has been precipitated by arguments such as that of Kuhn. Despite the merits that might be attributed to each as philosophical accounts of science and despite the fact that they both place emphasis on the actual practice of science, they reflect more attempts to cope with problems generated and defined by LP/E and its aftermath than something that is, in some obvious way, essentially mysterious about science. Realism in the philosophy of science today is not, or not merely, theoretical realism in the sense, for example, that Sellars propagated it or Kuhn implied it (e.g., Aronson 1984). While I have called Kuhn a theoretical realist, his claims are starkly at odds with what is usually classified as scientific realism (Hoyningen-Huene 1993). In its principal forms, it actually involves claims that are closer in content and spirit to prerevolutionary philosophy of science. And although certain aspects of contemporary antirealism have something of a traditional empiricist flavor, it would be a mistake to assume that it involves a return to the older form of instrumentalism.

IV

Empiricism with all its talk about facts and observation is sometimes construed as a kind of realism, but as hard core philosophical realists from

V. I. Lenin (1950) onward have pointed out, it is grounded in regressive idealist premises that make reality or the "given" elusive by reducing it to some form of sensory experience (Hindess 1971; Putnam 1987). Its claim about grounding knowledge in experience was actually an antirealist position that opened it to constant skeptical doubts and to a kind of solipsism insulated from both the world and other minds. There is an important sense in which contemporary realism is as much a reaction to traditional empiricism as it is to what it perceives as the dangers inherent in philosophies that seem to endorse the "fragmentation of reason" (Stitch 1990) or what, more neutrally, might be called cognitive pluralism, or the view that truth and reality are functions of the theories available. Such pluralism, however, seems difficult to deny that even it is viewed as in some way reflecting deeper universal human needs and general epistemic values (Ellis 1990).

It is possible to distinguish, at least analytically, one family of "realisms" that in various ways attempts to give ontological preference to common sense. Within this genre one could include certain Aristotelian positions, phenomenology, Strawson's descriptive metaphysics, and certain arguments in the philosophy of science (Strawson 1963; Koerner 1966; Cornman 1975). Although this kind of claim could be construed as supported by reference to certain theories in science such as quantum mechanics (Heisenberg 1958), it tends, conceptually and historically, to slip over into attempts to posit an incorrigible experientially grounded language. It is one thing to suggest that, historically, science arose from common sense, but it is quite another thing to claim that the latter is ontologically privileged. The everyday account of the world, or what Sellars calls the "manifest image," is not the foundation of the "scientific image" but rather an incommensurable and competing first-order scheme. Sellars embraces not only theoretical realism but a kind of scientific realism that, for him, means privileging the scientific image of the world. Sellars, as well as Kuhn, might be interpreted as embracing what might be characterized as a philosophical version of the kind of functional realism that is often associated with scientific practice, that is, the idea that the language of science reflects the world it encounters. It was, however, precisely the failure of functional realism as a theory *of* science, the belief that Newtonian mechanics was a true picture of the world, that in part precipitated the late-nineteenth-century crisis in the philosophy of science and the worry that theories might not correspond with the facts. Although most scientists might be understood as functional realists, radical changes in scientific theory do not seem to shake their faith in the business of science and its ability to give an account of the world. Where theoretical change creates uneasiness is less in the interpretation of nature than in the interpretation of science.

Contemporary realism and antirealism each wishes to square its vision with the practice of science, but much of the contemporary conversation takes place within a context that would strain the attention span and competence of many natural scientists as well as that of the most intrepid social scientific pilgrims in search of the grail of scientific authority. One of the continuities between the old and new philosophy of science is the concern with the logical formalization of theories in the natural sciences. The principal differences are that the old did not focus on actual theories, and it squeezed its analysis into the Procrustean framework of classical logic. The new, following Tarski and others, concentrates on the development of a "semantic conception" of the structure of theories in the natural sciences (Stegmuller 1976; Suppe 1989). Although lurking within such technical and mathematical projects is the residue of many of the formative issues involving the relationship between philosophy and science, such issues have been attenuated and submerged. The attitude is often largely that actual scientific theories are the subject matter of philosophy but that the philosophy of science has its own agenda and should not be confused with science.

There are, as the philosopher Hilary Putnam has suggested, "many faces of realism" (1987), and over a period of years, he himself has represented several of these visages. Among the "varieties" (Harré 1986), which all make some kind of claim about the difference between the world and how it is conceived or represented, metaphysical, or ontological, realism offers the strongest profile. Sometimes its proponents are also materialists or physicalists (Devitt 1984), but their key point is that objects referred to in science have an existence independent of mental constructions. Realism views its task as saving reality, and scientific truth, from dangerous philosophical trends. Latent in such a position, however, are still the assumptions that philosophy has a decisive role in constituting reality and truth and that reality is itself some kind of philosophical object. For some realists, such as Michael Devitt, who recognize that criteria of truth change, there is a need to separate realism from truth. Roger Trigg, for example, claims that truth and what we believe or "what reality is and how we conceive it are always separate questions" (1989:xi). This kind of argument gains its force by moving back and forth between a context in which the point makes sense and one in which it does not. The claim that concepts and reality are fundamentally different is cogent within a particular theoretical discourse and community of scientific practice, but as a general epistemological proposition, this attempt to dispel unnatural doubts is empty. This brand of realism is motivated by the idea of philosophy as a kind of superscience that guarantees a timeless transcontextual world and that both validates science and empowers philosophy by accessing a world that is constant and not hostage to changing ideas in either science or common sense. Few philosophical positions can live up to this standard. It is not only Kuhn, Feyerabend, Rorty, and Goodman who are deemed too weak to hold on to truth and reality but a variety of others such as Nicholas Rescher (1987) who, while maintaining an idea of reality as a regulative ideal object, would admit to an ultimate inability to peer through the screen of our concepts. There is also an uneasiness about the holistic account of theory and fact in the work of Quine (1969) as well as about the claims of philosophers such as Davidson who would collapse reality and concepts, or the world and our beliefs about it, in a nonidealist manner (e.g., Siegel 1987). Without a strong distinction between language and reality, there cannot be an enterprise devoted to establishing how they fit together.

While once embracing philosophical materialism, Putnam subsequently moved to, and then from, metaphysical realism to "internal" or "pragmatic" realism (1978, 1981, 1983, 1988, 1990). And these shifts were often characterized by changes in political and social commitment ranging from Maoism to Judaism. The first time that I encountered Putnam, he was the model of a straightlaced Quinean analytical philosopher. The next time I heard him speak he was dressed in denims, urging his audience to buy copies, which he was carrying with him, of the Progressive Labor Party's newspaper and supporting Lenin's realist critique of positivism. His realism, in its later incarnations, attempted to reconcile American pragmatism and pluralism with a commitment to an attenuated vision of correspondence. This internal realism, however, is an inherently ambivalent position that often seems to be little more than a modulated epistemological faith in the face of the fact of conceptual relativism. His argument is that while our concepts are relative to theoretical and cultural contexts and while the "world" does not determine what we can say about what exists, we must assume, on pragmatic grounds, that truth and falsity are not just a matter of decision and that there is an external reality that constrains our conceptual choices. This would seem to be a very historicized form of realism, what one more hard-core advocate (Lewis 1986) calls "feigned realism," but Putnam still attempts to separate his internal realism from a position such as that of Rorty, which he believes surrenders the idea of representation altogether (1994). He is still caught up in attempting to give a metatheoretical answer to the question of reality and cannot seem to exorcise the fear that various forms of contemporary philosophy might endanger the claim of scientific reason. In his most recent work, he has returned to a kind of modulated external realism that he views as consistent with classical pragmatism but as a rejection of "epistemological skepticism" (1992, 1995). Once, however, we give up the traditional correspondence theory of truth, it is impossible to separate ontology and epistemology, and thus *"there remains no possibility of precluding a robust relativism at the center of the philosophy of science"* (Margolis 1986:133).

There are many subtle variations among arguments that are usually understood as belonging to the narrower class usually designated as *scientific* realism (which should not be confused with a position such as that of Sellars), but those arguments have a common core of concern and commitment, as well as argumentative strategy (Glymour 1980; Newton-Smith 1981; Miller 1987). The principal concern is still to justify, as scientific realism's proponents believe postpositivists have failed to do, the belief that science is progressive. Since progress seems to be inherent in science's ability to predict and control, or its experimental "realization" of theoretical entities (unless, as the slogan goes, science is a "miracle"), it is necessary, scientific realists claim, to embrace the assumption that theories are at least approximately true and in some important sense referential. The truth of realism, then, is supposedly secured by the efficacy of science. Many such accounts thus employ some form of retroductive or abductive argument with respect to both the truth of theories and the progress of science, that is, they claim that epistemological realism is a kind of empirical hypothesis that is confirmed by the practice and history of science (Leplin 1984; Mackinnon 1974, 1978; Hacking 1983; Harré 1986). Despite the emphasis on a world beyond theory, scientific realism is very much rooted in an antipositivist (antiinstrumentalist) position, and most of its adherents believe that antirealism implies a swing back toward positivism. Antirealists, however, also abjure the legacy of positivism and maintain that it is realism that is still tainted with such premises. The exact dividing line between these positions is often difficult to specify (Wright 1987)—even for the parties to the debate.

Most "antirealists," such as Michael Dummett (1978), who largely introduced the term into the contemporary conversation, will allow that theories have truth-values in that they are effectively decidable within the practices in which they appear. Thus antirealism in this sense is much like internal realism. Truth, in this view, is what can be justifiably asserted, and reality is a function of accepted evidence. "Global antirealism," such as that advanced by Dummett (1991), is skeptical about starting from metaphysical positions regarding such philosophical entities as the world, minds, moral principles, and the past. Antirealists stress starting from logic and meaning in reaching a notion of truth and argue that the idea that realism, as an epistemological claim, can be tested by the history and practice of science, an idea that Laudan (1981) has dubbed "convergent epistemological realism," is in fact and in principle incorrect and futile. Furthermore, much of actual scientific practice, they suggest, is based on antirealist premises, that is, it does not assume that good explanations and theories are necessarily and/or literally true. That a theory is true, they argue, is not why it is successful, and there is no way that success can be parsed as explanation. Probably the leading antirealist account of science, and certainly at the center of much of recent discussion and controversy, is that of Bas van Fraassen (1980; Churchland and Hooker 1985). He holds that theoretical claims, by which he largely means claims about unobservables, are meaningful, have truth-value, are to be literally construed, and cannot be reduced to observables. Thus it could be suggested that if viewed in terms of the older debate about the interpretation of theory, he is a theoretical realist as opposed to an instrumentalist. But he also argues that a theory need not be true to be good, that is, to solve problems and save the phenomena. This makes him, like Laudan, an epistemological or methodological antirealist or, in his words, a "constructive empiricist." Quasirealists such as Frederick Suppe, who emerge from the same philosophical tradition as van Fraasen, maintain that accepted scientific theories should be viewed as true but should not be literally construed.

So, how do we assess all this, and what, if anything, does it have to do with social science? There is at least one important lesson to be learned from this latest phase in the literature of the philosophy of science. Among the rival positions such as realism and pragmatism, instrumentalism, and the kind of empiricism in which it was rooted, is dead as an account of scientific theory (Boyd, Gasper, and Trout 1991). It was a mistake to believe that any philosophical account of theory could provide a guide to substantive theorizing, but instrumentalism, by its very nature, forestalled realizing theory in social science. Today's realists and antirealists are, in an important sense, both theoretical realists, and if social scientists wish to take lessons from philosophy, theoretical realism is more conducive to taking theory seriously and to thinking about what it is and what it means to engage in it. We should be practical realists in that we should recognize that scientific theories are real claims about the world and constitutive of "the world." Theoretical realism as a philosophical position means that the "world" is rendered in terms of our theories and entails the assumption that truth is not an object or datum but a concept applied to what in any practice is taken as justified belief. As Wittgenstein noted, "The harmony between thought and reality is to be found in the grammar of the language" (1967:sec. 55). And as Goodman argues, "The uniformity of nature which we marvel at or the unreliability we protest belongs to a world of our own making" (1978:10).

> While we may speak of determining what versions are right as learning about the "world," the world supposedly being that which all right versions

describe, all we learn about the world is contained in these right versions of it; and while the underlying world, bereft of these, need not be denied to those who love it, it is perhaps on the whole a world well lost. (1978:4; see also Goodman 1972 and Rorty 1972)

"Truth cannot be defined or tested by agreement with the 'world,'" since "the actual world is the worlds that we create in our theories, and our passion for *one* world is satisfied, at different times and for different purposes, in *many* different ways" (Goodman 1978:17, 20). Goodman suggests that this does not mean that "everything goes" but only that "truth must be otherwise conceived than as correspondence with a ready-made world" (1978:94).

We must, however, recognize the continuing inhibitions to such a notion of theory in social science, both to examining the theories that lie dormant in its "facts" and to articulating challenges to them. There is, first, the burden of the instrumentalist cognitive perspective, which in a variety of forms and in various fields still rests heavily on the practice of social science (Gunnell 1986a). Second, much of academic social and political theory inhabits a world of abstract discourse where there is no longer much attachment to the vocation of social research. The activities of theory and empirical inquiry have tended to move apart. Third, epistemology is, after all, more romantic than most science. Why be a scientist when one can be a superscientist? Fourth, and maybe most cruel to mention, is the fact that metatheory is simply easier than theory—particularly when it comes prepackaged in the literature of philosophy. But in the end, there is yet another problem.

It is difficult, in the insecure and nonhegemonic world of the social sciences, to engage in theory without apology. This difficulty tends to perpetuate, as in the early days of natural science, a rhetoric of inquiry devoted to justifying both particular claims and the enterprise in which they are produced. This draws social science to epistemology and exposes it to the danger of displacing theory. While some form of realism might be a more defensible philosophical account of scientific theory than alternatives, there is a risk of forsaking practical theoretical realism for epistemology and of committing the same *kind* of mistake that was inherent in adopting instrumentalism. If theorizing is to be bolstered by epistemology, the theories must come first. What we tend to have today in the social sciences, however, and particularly political theory, is epistemologies in search of theories. And they are often not really even epistemologies of our own making.

V

Since many of the issues in the philosophy of science today revolve around matters specific to natural science and are generated by internal controversies in philosophy, social scientists must be very careful in borrowing arguments. While the philosophy of science is now trying harder to make sense of existing scientific theory, the propensity of social science is still to put epistemology first and see it either as a path toward theory or as leverage for particular images of the practical role of social science. It is important not to perpetuate these mistakes of the past and assume that one can extract from philosophy a scientific identity, take it as a descriptive account of science, or apply it as a methodological guide to scientific practice. While philosophy might, in various ways, have much to offer to social scientific self-reflection, we have for too long accepted the authority of philosophy without much attention either to its inherent limitations or to exactly how it might be brought to bear on issues in social science. These assumptions, however, persist and are manifest in the recent turn to realism in political theory, just as they are in work that seeks sustenance from arguments such as those of Davidson.

The philosophy of science today is to some extent an academized and institutionalized form of the rhetoric of inquiry. Its seemingly endless absorption with the abstract issues of how science is possible and how it progresses makes it in some respects a dubious enterprise in its own right. It is less than clear about its own identity and exact purpose as well as its relationship to its subject matter. While the philosophy of science originally offered a distorted image of science in order to save it, and then to save itself, it now often distorts science for various intrinsic philosophical purposes. If social science needs a rhetoric of inquiry, it might do well not to be confined by the horizon of this discipline and its agenda. If social science abandons substantive theory for metatheory, it will continue to find itself bound to the fate of arguments created by others. The propensity to repair to this material is, however, difficult to jettison. The insecurity of social science leads it to seek authority about the meaning of science, and the philosophy of science is the only systematic source. But as stressed earlier, there is a deeper dimension to the issue. Social science seeks answers from philosophy in part because it shares with philosophy the problem of the relationship between second-order discourses and their subject matter. Social science, and the discourses on society and politics that were the functional and historical precursors of these disciplines, were themselves at one time tied to the first-order universe of politics. Now, at least in the United States, as highly differentiated and institutionalized forms of second-order discourse, they must sort out their relationship to their objects of inquiry. This is why the issue of relativism looms so large in social science—as it does in the philosophy of science—and why the problem of theory and practice is constantly at the heart of metatheoretical reflection.

Metatheory in political theory does not so much justify particular views of political reality as it does images of itself possessing the ability to say something authoritative about politics. Like the philosophy of science, it has tended to be an inherently foundational enterprise. And foundations are what political theory now seeks in philosophies such as scientific realism. The difficulty, however, is that in this case, as in previous instances of attachment to philosophy, political theory is in danger of devolving into an alienated rhetoric of inquiry dispossessed of substantive theories or devoted to underwriting debilitated ones. The search for foundational authority has transformed many dimensions of political theory into a kind of metatheoretical transcendentalism.

As I have already noted, one impetus behind the latest involvement with the philosophy of science is to provide some sort of coherence within the highly pluralistic world of social scientific research as well as to reconcile humanistic and scientific modes of analysis or empirical and interpretive methods. Is there not a real world to which all these approaches refer and in terms of which the results and progress of inquiry as a whole can be judged? And given the current skepticism about the foundations of knowledge engendered by postmodernism and other dimensions of contemporary philosophy, how is it possible to justify the cognitive claims that support practical aspirations of second-order disciplines? There have, at this point, been few systematic excursions by political theorists into the realm of realism (e.g., Keat and Urry 1975; Outhwaite 1975), and my concern is not to survey and analyze these somewhat tentative explorations (Layder 1990) but rather to focus on one salient example and to bring the underlying issue into focus before this route becomes a popular itinerary.

Realism in the philosophy of science, as well as philosophical realism in a number of fields such as ethics, literature, and legal theory (Gillespie 1986; Sayre-McCord 1988; Fuller 1988; Brink 1989; Tannsjo 1990; Levine 1993), are appealing to social science because they offer the hope of critical purchase and access to the foundations of judgment in, and with respect to, its subject matter. Although contemporary moral realism is not simply a return to natural law, it maintains, as opposed to what some philosophers insist (Harman 1977), that the world does, at least in some very limited way (Williams 1985), regulate our normative beliefs. Realists worry about making the notion of the world so thin that it is absorbed into changing discursive formations. While the problem of relativism continues to structure the discourse of a field such as the philosophy of science, this field tends to view itself as simply a very specialized academic activity. Although political theory may in some respects be construed as proceeding in the same direction, its memory of its practical roots and concerns is, in general, sharper, and it remains more sensitive to the manner in which the problem of relativism reflects issues in the relationship between first- and second-order discourses. But the problem of theory and practice continues to be played out in surrogate form on the artificial turf of metatheory. Realism in social and political theory has largely taken the form of what has been called "critical realism" (Isaac 1990). This is a somewhat loosely defined class of arguments that can be identified by certain family resemblances and mutual influences, but they are essentially metatheoretical or epistemological. Although in various ways critical realism incorporates and refers, or alludes, to theoretical claims, it is primarily a theory of social science and not a theory of social phenomena.

It should not be surprising that realism and Marxism have been closely linked ever since Lenin attacked the instrumentalist premises of logical positivism and its claim that theory was "only a systematization of experience, a system of empirio-symbols" rather than an account of " 'ultimate' . . . reality." He was concerned about scientists being "led astray by professional philosophy" and the *"partisan* science" of epistemology (1950:44, 287, 356). Lenin grasped well the rhetorical character of the epistemological enterprise. Marxism very distinctly qualifies as a theory in the sense that I have attempted to explicate that concept. As a theoretical endeavor, and especially one that frontally challenges other accounts of the world, it is naturally sensitive to philosophical construals of theory that reduce it to conceptual instruments or embrace the idea that scientific theories are mental constructs and ideal types and assume that reality is somehow given in immediate experience and common sense. Since Marxism also exists in a world in which it is cognitively insecure vis-à-vis other theories, it quite naturally resorts to epistemological defenses. In addition, like nearly all social theories, it involves praxis or a demand for theoretical intervention. This requires establishing cognitive authority as a basis of practical authority. For all these reasons, there should be little mystery about why Marxism has evolved a rhetoric of inquiry that has involved both a critique of empiricism and a defense of realism. And it should not be surprising that the main tributary of realism in social science and the philosophy of social science has had a strong Marxist current despite various eddies (Althusser 1969; Hindess 1971). Yet while all this is quite reasonable, the project became derailed when the epistemological defense of Marxism was cut loose from its theoretical and practical roots and became largely an alienated metatheoretical academic exercise. I will focus on the work of Roy Bhaskar, which is both influential and typical.

Bhaskar's work contains a cogent critique of empiricism and a defense of realism, but as a project, it, like the work of Habermas and others, inhabits a discursive demimonde somewhere between ideological rhetoric and academic analysis where the audience, both in terms of type and persuasion, is difficult to specify (1973, 1979, 1986). What emerges is a kind of metatheoretical collage in which diverse ideas, extracted from everyone from Plato to Marx to contemporary philosophers and social theorists, are formed into an epistemological mosaic. Arguments are more summarized and characterized than analyzed and explored, and issues and claims belonging to various levels of discourse are persistently conflated. In this intellectual tour de force, all things are possible. Hermeneutics and structuralism, theory and practice, natural science and social science, rationalism and relativism, and theory and epistemology are reconciled and compounded into a formula that promises nothing less than "human emancipation." What stands out in the end is the fact that there is really neither a coherent theory here nor an actual consideration of what, in practice, would constitute a critical social science. Bhaskar calls for a philosophy that is both an ontology and an epistemology, the latter reflecting the former. Like traditional realism, it posits the existence of objects independent of the framework of inquiry; yet it recognizes, taking account of Kuhn and Gaston Bachelard, the inseparability of inquiry and the world. The formulation of the problem is, however, skewed from the beginning by perpetuating the worry that arguments such as that of Kuhn cannot explain how there can be a clash between paradigms and a resolution. This is to thrust onto Kuhn the very problem that he denied as a valid philosophical issue without confronting his actual argument.

As much as Bhaskar agrees with the "anti-monistic" revolution in the philosophy of science, he claims that it cannot deal with change and amounts in the end to "subjective super-idealism" (1986:2). The point of the revolution to which he refers, however, was that there was no general philosophical answer to change. But we cannot, Bhaskar stresses, leave the issue of reality to science and scientific theory. What is required is a "metaphysical realism" quite apart from the content of any particular scientific theory. Philosophy, he argues, treats the very same world as the sciences but only "transcendentally" (12). Although it is constrained by the parameters and content of science, it must go beyond scientific practice and demonstrate how science is possible. It is a Kantian project that, in order to avoid circularity and self-validation, proceeds by an "immanent critique" of other philosophical positions (14). This line of argument holds that "a realist philosophy of science and a qualified or critical naturalism provides the best metatheoretical framework" for social science (Outhwaite 1987), but the questions that must be posed with respect to this project are who, in principle, needs this scientific theology and why and to whom is this plea for philosophy as a kind of superscience addressed. The epistemological claims are both weakly reconciled and theoretically underdetermined, and there is little in the way of an argument that can be distinctly joined at any point.

Ian Shapiro has also attempted to draw upon realism as the basis of a critical theory. His *Political Criticism* (1990) is primarily an attempt to reconcile foundationalism and contextualism and to ameliorate the perceived dangers of relativism with respect to developing a critical social theory. His version of "critical naturalism" or "pragmatic realism," even as a metatheoretical intervention, does not emerge very clearly, but there is no elaboration of a theory that would support the epistemological commitments. Critical realism is, in general, a rather amorphous metatheoretical family (Isaac 1987). In orientation, it is committed to a historical and hermeneutic view of social reality, yet one that is consistent with a notion of scientific causal analysis; it tends to accept epistemological relativism but insists on an objective ontological realm as a basis of claims to truth; it emphasizes human agency but also the manner in which social structures determine action; it is a synthetic position emerging from an immanent critique of other philosophical positions; it often has roots in Marxism and allied ideas of critical social analysis but seeks to overcome certain elements of Marxist essentialism; it is postmodernist in its rejection of a theory of the subject but wishes to constrain the relativism that it detects in this line of thinking. It is the height of epistemological pluralism, but it is also a very porous position.

Critical realism does not carry us very far in realizing theory, and it does not face up to the practical problem inherent in the relationship between public and academic discourse. Yet its emphasis on realism and its focus on criticism does point positively in the direction of confronting the two most fundamental problems in social science: the need to join in creating and arguing about a coherent account of social reality that would engender and support cognitive claims about its subject matter and the need to come to grips with the historically situated practical relationship between social science and its object of inquiry (e.g., Ball 1987; Manicas 1989). But we can also gain a less positive lesson from the manner in which it continues to exemplify the dangers of metatheoretical seduction. The critical function of a social science is not a matter that can be solved metatheoretically. It is a matter of the commitments and attitudes of its practitioners and of the relationship between academic and political practice in a particular social and historical context. Epistemologies do not logically entail a certain form of social scientific practice. We can, for example, fantasize at length about the connection between Rorty's antifoundationalism and his liberalism and which informs which, but the real fantasy is to believe that a wimpy philosophy entails a wimpy politics. It is a fundamental mistake to assume that we can make judgments about which metatheoretical account (Winchian, Habermasian, etc.) of social science is more critical. These are, first, not social scientific practices but spiritual images of such practices. The critical function of a social science is also not basically a theoretical matter even though certain theories might be construed as having greater critical implications. But theory is a necessary and sufficient condition of social science whatever the latter's practical uses.

All theories and entailed singular claims are inherently critical in that they challenge other accounts of the way things are. Whether social science as such can be a critical practice in more than an academic sense, institutionalized as it is in the United States within the highly professionalized and insulated scholarly world where such visions are generated, is a complex matter that requires historical and sociological sensitivity to its evolution and current context. What we must face up to is the fact that the critical import of political theory is not a function of metatheoretical attitude and epistemological enthusiasm. Any social scientific claim (explanatory, descriptive, critical, etc.) is ultimately grounded in theoretical propositions about social reality. If contested, such claims are ultimately pushed back to those propositions. There is no social science without, so to speak, foundations, but the foundations are theories and not metatheories. Antifoundationalism is, properly understood, an argument about the limits of philosophy (epistemology)—not about the practices of life and knowledge. Without foundations, there would be no practices. Foundation, however, is a poor metaphor to the extent that it implies that conceptions of reality and knowledge are erected upon a priori and temporally prior bases. It is primarily an empiricist epistemological metaphor and not one that is particularly helpful in understanding theories and how they function in the practices of knowledge.

Realizing theory requires that we embrace theoretical realism as both a practical and metatheoretical attitude. Theory, as I have argued in chapter 2, must, in a systematic and detailed way, make sense of the concepts in terms of which we speak about human action and its artifacts. We might, then, either in principle or as a reflection of social scientific practice, develop a metatheoretical explication and defense of this mode of theoretically informed explanation. Chapter 5 confronts what many would consider to be the most basic epistemological issue in the social sciences and humanities, that is, the nature of interpretation, but I approach this issue in light of my analysis of the orders of discourse and the theory of conventional objects.

CHAPTER

Interpretation

It is the primary task of interpretation . . . to rediscover the original relationship between the writer and his audience.

—Friedrich Schleiermacher

The real meaning of a text, as it speaks to an interpreter, does not depend on the contingency of the author and whom he originally wrote for.

—Hans-Georg Gadamer

For the day that there will be a reading of the Oxford card, the one and true reading, will be the end of history.

—Jacques Derrida

If interpretation can never be achieved, it is simply because there is nothing to interpret, because at bottom everything is already interpretation.

—Michel Foucault

I will begin by describing an instance of intellectual intersection and coincidence that points up some of the difficulties inherent in contemporary debates about textual interpretation as well as in accounts of the broader universe of metapractices. In 1977, a colleague of mine visiting at Oxford University sent me a postcard derived from a drawing in a manuscript at the Bodelian library. I subsequently commissioned an enlarged photograph of the drawing as the basis of a cover for a book that I published in 1979. The picture was of Plato standing behind, and apparently dictating to, Socrates, who was seated and writing. This image had a double significance for me. First, my book was largely devoted to a critique of the widely held assumption that the classic texts of political theory, from Plato to Marx, represented an actual tradition of discourse that constituted a genetic explanation of contemporary political thought and action and to which synoptic philosophical and historical meaning could be attributed. My purpose was to signify the manner in which the so-called tradition was an image conjured up in academic discourse and projected backward to create a virtual history. But there was another, less obvious, point represented in my use of this picture. A decade earlier, I had written a book on Plato (1968a, rev. 1986a) and his confrontation with Athenian politics. I argued that despite his overt deprecation of writing, inscription was, in fact, Plato's vehicle for an incursion into the oral tradition that governed the traditional culture as well as the sophistic enterprise and that writing was central to his conception of philosophical knowledge. I also questioned common assumptions about Socrates as a historical figure and as the teacher of Plato. I suggested that in Plato's dialogues, Socrates was a symbolic surrogate for Plato even in the case of the story of Socrates's trial and death. I represented this picture as "saying" both that Plato had employed the image of Socrates to express himself and that writing was the critical form of expression. In Jacques Derrida's *The Postcard* (1987; originally published in 1980) the same picture was utilized to support some very different arguments. There was, first, the substantive historical claim that Plato was the instigator of a phonocentric tradition that has governed subsequent Western philosophy and, second, a number of assertions and intimations to the effect that interpretation is always a claim about an object that is constituted in the interpretive process. Given the diverse meanings attributed to the postcard, it might seem that Derrida's position is confirmed, but I will argue that neither Derrida nor I were involved in what could reasonably be construed as an interpretation. Not all understandings and attributions of meaning and significance are interpretations even though a wide range of philosophical positions, including those of Davidson and Derrida, tend to construe the concept of interpretation in such a broad manner.

I

Interpretation, I will argue, is the negotiation of meaning. The Latin root *interpres* suggests a concept implying some sort of mediation or exchange between two parties that pivots on explaining or rendering the meaning of a conventional object. On its face, this might not seem to be a contentious point, and it is one that, abstractly stated, is compatible with a number of hermeneutical positions. What I am assuming, however, is the discursive autonomy of both the interpreted object and the interpretation, and this is why speaking about the interpretation of nature can be only metaphorical. Although this duality is generically present in all circumstances and instances of interpretation, both internal to a practice and among practices within the same order of discourse, my particular concern is with second-order metapractices such as history, literary analysis, and social science. My contention is that the concept of interpretation, despite common extensions of its meaning, applies particularly and paradigmatically to the activity of metapractices. As I have already stressed, abstract epistemological talk, and debate, about interpretation is fruitless without theoretical grounding and attention to the orders of discourse. The critical issue is the theoretical constitution of the object of inquiry and the implications of this theory for accounts of, and practices of, interpretation. My concern is to say something about interpreting conventional objects, and thus the argument is essentially an epistemological and methodological one, but the discussion, in both its critical and positive dimensions, is theoretically informed. Since my focus, for exemplary reasons, is on texts, I am also taking account of the pragmatic criteria peculiar to texts as a particular class of conventional objects. All texts are conventional objects, but despite the theoretical homology, not all conventional objects are texts. One difficulty with many contemporary arguments that attempt to extend the image of textuality to all social phenomena is that they extrapolate the generic from the specific.

Despite all the literature that has emerged in recent years dealing with the issue of interpretation, most of it, in the end, still revolves around the axis of the question of whether interpretation is a search for objective meaning or whether it is the creation of meaning. As E. D. Hirsch notes, "There is not much that is new, or can be new, under the hermeneutical sun" (1976:3). And as usual in such cases of abstract epistemological confrontation, there are a number of attempts to find a middle ground. J. L. Austin's advice applies here: when confronted with such a dichotomous problem, it is best to dissolve it rather than resolve it. The theory of conventional objects does not automatically settle the question of what constitutes interpretation, but it does offer a basis for a distinct argument about the matter and one that steps away from a confrontation between theoretically unanchored epistemologies. The futility of the metatheoretical search for some general transtheoretical and transcontextual criteria of objective meaning as well as the emptiness of the conclusion that the concept of objective meanings makes no sense are illustrated in versions of the, probably apocryphal, story (e.g., Cushman 1995) of the council of rabbis seeking to determine how much of the Torah really represented the word of God and how much could be ascribed to interpretive commentary. After much debate, a tentative consensus was reached suggesting that at least the Ten Commandments could be construed as unmediated. But there still seemed to be no demonstrative proof, and after considerable further discussion, agreement seemed possible only with respect to the First Commandment. Some, however, questioned even this conclusion and forced the group to accept tentatively the position that only the first word, *anochi,* of the First Commandment was indubitably the word of God. One skeptic, however, still persisted, and finally unanimity could be achieved only with respect to the first letter of the first word—"A" or *aleph.* This primal sound, they agreed, must have represented God's voice, yet ironically, this letter in Hebrew is silent.

Although this parable might conceivably be used to defend a variety of hermeneutical positions, I will take it as indicating, first, that interpretation is a metapractical activity and often implies a community of interpreters but, second, that at the same time, without some notion of the autonomy of conventional objects, there is a tendency to slip into an epistemological abyss where the difference between text and interpretation recedes. If we think carefully about the situation of these rabbis, we will see that they were operating within a third-order discourse and were attempting to sort out strands of first- and second-order discourses, that is, texts and interpretations. Their failure suggests only that such sorting is sometimes difficult. It does not signify either that a text cannot be distinguished from interpretations or that there is some philosophically distinct realm of objective meaning. Both of these polar positions are examples of what Umberto Eco has called "epistemological fanaticism" (1990:24), an extremism that only tends to accelerate as it loses touch with both a theoretical ground and the particularities of concrete interpretative problems.

There are few areas in which the battle among alienated epistemologies has been so prominent, and perennial, as in discussions about the nature of historical and textual interpretation. I take hermeneutics, for the most part, to be basically the same order of discourse as epistemology and methodology, that is, claims about a form of knowledge and how it is acquired. Despite some quite dramatic changes in philosophical warrants, the positions represented in the quotations at the head of this chapter have persisted as paradigms for thinking about the nature and method of interpretation. It may not be possible to settle, or even fully clarify, the differences between these positions, but there cannot be any rational exchange unless the theoretical underpinnings and practical motifs, or lack thereof, are exposed. It is often noted that the hermeneutical tradition originated in pragmatic concerns about how to interpret the word of God or the Bible (Palmer 1969; Ormisten and Scrift 1990a), that is, that hermeneutical arguments were adjuncts to forms of interpretive practice. This corresponds to the arguments that I have advanced earlier about the historical origins of fields such as social science and the philosophy of natural science, that is, how they evolved from legitimating and critical discourses entwined with substantive first-order claims to practices bearing an inherently problematical cognitive and practical relationship to their object.

In the case of Schleiermacher, the problem was largely one of supplying a justification for the practice of literal rather than allegorical interpretation of the Scriptures and classical texts, but he also shifted the concern from practical methods of exegesis to the general issue of textual understanding. Similarly, Wilhelm Dilthey attempted to provide a rationale for the practice of the human sciences, such as history, both by distinguishing them from the natural sciences and by defending the superior intelligibility of the artifacts of human consciousness. With Schleiermacher, Dilthey, and others, hermeneutics had already begun, much like the early philosophy of science, to detach from the contexts of practical inquiry in which it originated and to embrace the general question of how it is possible to reach understanding. This was, almost necessarily, countered by an equally abstract skeptical tradition that questioned the very possibility of reaching understanding (Ormisten and Schrift 1990b) or separating texts from their interpretation in a manner that would prevent interpretation from becoming, as Montaigne feared, an endless process. As some substantive practices, such as academic historical inquiry, became more disciplinary and routinized, epistemological issues and the rhetoric of inquiry receded *and* became largely the property of philosophy as a scholarly field. When, however, disputes have arisen in interpretive practice, practitioners have, ironically, tended to turn to philosophy for justification. Even though the concept of "real" meaning has often been more the concern of those who focus on "original" meaning or on what authors intended to say by saying what they said, those such as Gadamer who stress the autonomy of the text also assume something that can be called the "real" meaning and that emerges in the process of interpretation. And even those who seem to deny the existence of any "real" meaning are actually often mortgaged to the concept in that they find themselves forced to articulate what they claim does not exist. My basic answer to the question of the *real* meaning of a text (or any other conventional object) will be that it does make sense to speak about such a meaning but not in a way that reflects any of the classic positions. All of these claims about the existence and nonexistence of real meaning are presented in an order of discourse in which there are no adequate criteria for applying the concept. Such claims are like arguments in the philosophy of science about the real world. There is a real meaning of a text just as there is a real explanation of a physical phenomenon—one that is real in light of criteria operative in an interpretive context informed by a theory and further specified by the pragmatics of that context. Real is not a property of something but a concept referring to statements positing the existence of something. Metatheoretical claims about "real" meaning, or its lack, that is, those divorced from such a context, are just so much generic talk. Specific interpretive claims are constitutive of real meanings just as specific claims in natural science constitute the real world. The difference among these spheres is that of the difference between claims in first- and second-order discourses. While interpretation produces (external) claims about real meaning, it is in competition with preconstituted (internal) meanings as well as with other second-order renderings. A text, of course, cannot itself contradict an interpretation—this requires another interpreter or a member of a community who has appropriated the text and acquired an understanding of it.

When someone argues that real meaning is to be found by inducing, from speech or a text, the initiating mental states, or when it is claimed that meaning is a function of the perspective of a reader, a contestable theoretical position may be implied, but it is often thinly articulated. Arguments at this level, however, do not tell us very much about either how to produce an interpretation or how to judge one, and they reveal only in a tangential manner how the object of interpretation is theoretically constituted. Theory is a matter of the nature of what is interpreted, and only theory can support an epistemology of interpretation or a hermeneutic. There cannot, strictly speaking, be a theory of interpretation, in the sense that I use the concept, any more, or less, than there can be a theory of explanation. My purpose, however, is not so much to legislate severely the meaning of *theory* in this instance or quarrel with looser uses of the concept as simply, once again, to distinguish what I am calling theory from epistemology and methodology and to make some analytical distinctions among the levels or orders of discourse in which questions are posed and claims are made as well as among the practices in which they occur. The basic distinctions that guide the following discussion are among matters of *theory, epistemology,* and *methodology,* which compose what I will refer to as the realm of *general* hermeneutics, or problems revolving around the issue of the nature of interpretation as such, and matters of *method* and *technique* that are particular to specific research areas and that involve what I will call *regional* hermeneutics.

II

There are, as I noted in the introduction, several reasons I have chosen to discuss, at some length, the arguments of Quentin Skinner. In a positive sense, his work has, over the past three decades, contributed significantly to inspiring a new wave of substantive research in intellectual history, and it has played a major role in generating reflection about the nature of historical and textual interpretation. At the same time, however, it has manifested, and perpetuated, a number of problems relating to the relationship between the philosophy and practice of inquiry (Tully 1988). There is, however, one distinct difference between Skinner and many epistemologists of social science and history. He is a practicing historian involved in the activity of intellectual history and textual interpretation. What brought him to issues of meaning and understanding in the history of ideas (1969) was both a dissatisfaction with current modes of practice, particularly in the history of political theory, and a concern with justifying the norms and methods of a certain approach to historical inquiry. What evolved was largely an epistemological rhetoric of inquiry or metatheory of interpretation. In the process, he articulated and expanded more fully some of the theoretical propositions to which he subscribed and which were already embedded in the kind of historical enterprise that he wished to defend, but he also presented his metatheory as a method, even as *the* method, of intellectual history.

My differences with Skinner involve several specific dimensions. The first is a disagreement with certain aspects of his theoretical claims, particularly his view of intentionality. The second involves what, I argue, is his ultimate inversion of theory and epistemology, or at least a failure to distinguish between the two. My argument, quite simply, is that his epistemological, disciplinary, and, maybe, ideological commitments have, as in the case of Habermas and so many others, led his theory. Third, he tends to equate epistemology with method. Finally, despite the emphasis on textual interpretation in Skinner's work, his treatment of texts often tends, in practice, to be secondary to a focus on contexts. His epistemological and methodological commitments draw attention away both from a close internal analysis of the structure and from the thematic content of texts. These problems are manifest not only in Skinner's own work but in the genre of intellectual history or the history of ideas that he has influenced. There is, so to speak, a considerable conceptual and practical gap between hermeneutical windup and interpretive delivery with respect to the treatment of texts.

We can understand something about the path of Skinner's arguments by noting his attachment to a certain kind of intellectual history. When J. G. A. Pocock claimed that past scholarship in the "history" of political theory had been unhistorical and that it was now necessary to employ the rigorous "methods of the historian," he was attempting to privilege a certain kind of scholarship. It would be difficult to specify anything that resembled what Pocock referred to as the "emergence of a truly autonomous method" of the historian (1971:9, 11). Even though it would be quite fair to make a general distinction between earlier work in the history of political theory and the concerns and approach of those who by the late 1970s were identified as revisionists and proponents of a "new history" (Gunnell 1979a), it would be considerably more difficult to make the case that the difference turned on a matter of method. Skinner still claims, however, that he has "exclusively been concerned with how we should proceed" to understand texts (1988:232), and the answer remains, basically, to put them in their proper context and to focus on isolating intentional meaning. Skinner claimed that his historical scholarship exemplified his methodological "precepts" and represented "a particular way of approaching the study and interpretation of historical texts" (1978a:x). It is far from clear that there has, in fact, been such an exemplification, but I am less concerned with settling this issue than with examining the nature of the precepts and their connection to the activity of interpretation. In the most general terms, Skinner's position, as he acknowledges, is closely allied to that of R. G. Collingwood's vision of history as the recovery of lived meaning. He finds support in Max Weber's claims about the explanation of action as well as in contemporary postempiricist accounts of interpretive social science. W. H. Greenleaf described this general position as one committed to the view that the first task of interpretation is to "perceive and describe the original meaning" and "re-create or re-experience" the thought of the past. This was to be accomplished by the "historical" task of understanding authors and texts "in their own terms," which in turn involved illuminating their "intellectual background" (1964:2).

What, exactly, is the nature of such a claim? In what order of discourse do we locate it? It is certainly not a theory. Neither can it be construed as a method or technique, since it is too abstractly stated to determine what would be involved in such a performance. It belongs to the realm of epistemology and methodology. It is a methodological norm regarding the acquisition of knowledge, which is, in turn, the entailment of an epistemological position. Although it may both serve a rhetorical function and reflect some features of a certain form of historical practice, it is a theoretically underdetermined claim. The idealist tradition of historical inquiry, with which Skinner tends to associate himself, as well as early Continental accounts of social scientific and historical inquiry that stressed the function of *Verstehen,* were revitalized in postempiricist philosophy of social science by the adoption of Wittgensteinian and Austinian analyses of language. Since language was viewed as having a public character and as an instrument or expression of thought, ideas could be construed as having an objective and recoverable status and as the basis of explaining overt action and texts. Skinner, much more than most associated with this line of argument in the philosophy of social science, set out to give theoretical depth to this epistemology. Yet his theoretical claims have in large measure been shaped by his prior epistemological and historiographical commitments.

Skinner characteristically speaks of his discussion of conventions and speech acts (1969, 1970, 1971, 1972a, 1972b, 1978b), what I would refer to as his theoretical claims, as if it logically yielded a method. He explicitly claims not only that his model of speech acts is of "theoretical" interest but that it offers an *"appropriate methodology for the history of ideas,"* by which he means a "method" for "investigating the motives of political theorists" and for the "interpretation of historical texts" (1978a:10). The theory might arguably be construed as supporting a methodological argument such as Skinner's about the need to situate texts in their context, but it is not a method. And there is no necessary connection between the theoretical claims and the norm of approaching interpretation by reconstructing contexts. Theories are less like instruction books on how to find one's way around in a certain landscape than an account of the features of that landscape. Method and methodology are also easily confused, since they are both couched in prescriptive terms, but to state that understanding a text requires closing the context, to say that this is how the meaning of a text is determined, does not entail any distinct method, and certainly not a specific technique, for doing so. In the matrix of a practice of inquiry, particularly in the social sciences, theory, epistemology, methodology, method, and technique are likely to be only analytically distinguishable, but it is possible to consider which claims belong to what sphere and how they do, and should, relate to one another.

Skinner's theoretical claims were developed in defense of a prior epistemological position holding that understanding social action, and texts, is a matter of recovering ideas, beliefs, or other prior mental states. Skinner notes that "with the ebbing of confidence in empiricist epistemologies and their accompanying claims to provide us with a methodology for the human sciences, *those of us who practice these disciplines . . . come to feel an increasing need to look for renewed philosophical help*" (1978b:69). "Philosophical" in this instance encompasses both theory and epistemology, but what is being pursued is principally an apology for a certain form of historical practice. Skinner has a great deal to say about intentions and intentionality, and mental predicates such as motives, but it nearly all revolves around demonstrating that these mental phenomena are represented in language and can, in principle, be recovered by locating a text in its appropriate linguistic context and within a wider set of social conventions that would aid in determining what an author was doing, and seeking to accomplish, by saying what was said. Skinner never really confronts many of the theoretical issues involved in such a theory of intentionality, since his principal concern is to detail a method for the recovery of the mental, for determining what an author "intended to mean, and how this meaning was intended to be taken." This is to be accomplished, he argues, by reconstructing "the whole range of communication which could have been conventionally performed on the given occasion of the utterance of the given utterance, next, to trace the relation between the given utterance and this wider linguistic context as a means of decoding the actual intention of the given writer" (1969:28–49).

This injunction is a methodological norm that conforms to his hermeneutical claim that the meaning of a text is "actually *equivalent*" to the intention of the author (Skinner 1972b:404–6; 1974:285; 1975–1976:214, 219). But there can be little doubt about the theoretical presupposition. Intentionality is presented, linking H. P. Grice and Austin, as a mental state expressed in illocutionary conventions that are manifest in speech-acts. Although, following Austin, Skinner acknowledges that there is more than one dimension of meaning, the essential meaning is the intention. He recognizes that there is a difference between lexical and intentional meaning and that both are relevant (1988:269), but illocutionary intention, and what he believes to be the mental state it expresses, are the focus of his concern. The interpreter, he argues, analyzes language as a way of "decoding" the "nonnatural meaning," that is, the "motives" that "prompted those particular speech acts" (1975–1976:214; 1972b:400). This decoding is explained as a matter of situating speech, and belief, in a wider conventional context and determining whether what was said "would be appropriate" for a rational actor in that situation. Much like Lakatos and Hollis, Skinner assumes that rational action is largely its own explanation and that "to exhibit a social action as rational *is* to explain it," since otherwise it is necessary to explain why the actor in that context "*believed* it was rational" to act in that manner (1978b:60; 1974:295). Skinner is not entirely clear about how this notion of rationality squares theoretically with his other claims, since he also specifically distances himself from those who argue that it is "fatal to introduce the question of truth into social explanation" (1988:239). But even though he is relatively explicit about the identity of his core theoretical position, it is still the issue of method that is his focus.

Although Skinner suggests that most practicing historians "assume that the explanation of action is a matter of recovering meanings and motives," most historians are, in fact, notoriously vague about what such recovery theoretically entails. What Skinner wants to determine is whether the historian's method can be formalized, "whether it is possible to lay down any general rules about how to interpret a literary text" in such a manner that, given the fact that it is never possible to achieve complete closure or "arrive at '*the* correct reading,' " an interpreter can recover the "message" of the text and offer the "best reading" of it (1978b:64; 1972b:393). In response to skeptics who claim that "it is actually impossible to recover a writer's motives and intentions," Skinner argues that such a position "seems straight-forwardly false" and states, "I assert this as obvious, and shall not attempt to prove it" (1972b:400). Skinner's "rules" turn out to amount to the same general methodological precept, that is, to look not only at the text but at the wider context of issues and conventions in which it is situated in order to grasp the "writer's mental world" and "beliefs" (1972b:400, 406–7). Exactly what intentions, beliefs, motives, attitudes, opinions, and so on are, however, remains theoretically nebulous.

Although Skinner certainly does not claim that the meaning of a text can be determined simply by placing it in context, his account of interpretation consistently slides in the direction of equating exegesis with contextual reconstruction. He states that a text is "a meaningful item within a wider context of conventions and assumptions," that understanding authors is a matter of determining the "general social and intellectual matrix out of which their works arose," and that "to surround a given text with an appropriate context of conventions is an indispensable key to decoding the meaning of the text itself." In doing all this, "we are not merely providing historical 'background' for our interpretation; we are already engaged in the act of interpretation itself" (1978a:x, xiv; 1975–1976:221, 224). Some texts may be more "autonomous" than others, but even the least "heteronomous" require that we assume that textual interpretation and historical contextual reconstruction are inseparable (1975–1976:217). This is considerably more than a claim about the need for contextual or historical sensitivity. For Skinner, the classic texts of political theory, for example, are a "record" of the "history of ideologies," of "how political thinking in all its various forms was carried on in the past," and one purpose for studying this material is "to establish the connections between the world of ideology and the world of political action" (1974:279–80). What is evident in this formulation is the theoretical assumption that there is an ontological distinction between the realms of thought and action and that the former generates and explains the latter. The point, he states, is to put the classic texts in "their appropriate ideological context" in order "to recover their different mentalities" (1978a:xi). This account raises a number of obvious difficulties that Skinner tends to deal with in a somewhat ad hoc manner. One example is his treatment of rationalization. Skinner's whole account of political thought is predicated on demonstrating that ideas are not epiphenomenal and that, opposed, for example, to Marxist accounts, they are ultimate explanatory factors. Although he does not accept the view that an actor's reference to principle can be simply taken as an adequate account of motives or as a sufficient cause of action, he does want to preserve the preeminence of ideas. Even when principles are used to legitimate behavior, there is still "a causal connection between the principles" and "actual social and political actions," since an actor "will be obliged to behave in such a way that his actions remain compatible with the claim that these principles actually motivated them" and to act within the scope of available principles that are the "key determinants" (1974:292, 299–300).

Skinner responds to those who find it difficult to see a direct connection between his hermeneutics and his substantive historical claims by suggesting that such skepticism amounts to denying that historiographical considerations and "philosophical reflection about the concepts of meaning and explanation have any bearing upon the intellectual historian's task" (1988:232). The problem, however, is that of differentiating between theory and epistemology within "philosophy" and of examining the relationship between them as well as the bearing of each on historical practice and matters of method and technique. It is important here to distinguish also between the general and regional aspects of hermeneutics—a distinction that seems to blur in Skinner's work. Method and technique are elements of the latter and largely reflect particular research concerns and problems. Theory, epistemology, and methodology belong to the former. There is a relationship between these realms, but method, for example, cannot be logically extrapolated from theory. Skinner, however, seeks to present contextualist analysis as a method demanded by his theory.

There is surely something to be said, both theoretically and epistemologically, about the concept of context in the case of phenomena such as speech-acts, that is, about how such objects are holistically situated and what this implies in terms of acquiring knowledge about them. But too often, as in the case of Skinner, this is translated into research imperatives; at the same time, pragmatic attention to contexts is universalized into a general methodological injunction. Sometimes an interpretive problem may not require elaborating a context, and sometimes it may, and what is the "appropriate context" and how to construct it are matters that are very difficult to generalize about in a manner that exceeds the level of shibboleth. A generation ago, E. P. Thompson claimed that, like anthropology, "the discipline of history is, above all, the discipline of context; each fact can be given meaning only within an ensemble of other meanings" (1971:43). A decade later, it was said that "contextualization is the strongest feature in the area of the history of ideas that has made the strongest progress in the last decade: the history of political thought" (Darnton 1980:339). Today there appears to be no reason to amend this judgment. Whether it is the emphasis of Skinner on situating texts and concepts in their appropriate linguistic context; J. G. A. Pocock's insistence on identifying texts as participating in the vocabulary of a particular political language; the emphasis on social history and political contexts in the *Begriffsgeschichte* (Koselleck 1988; Richter 1995) various forms of the sociology knowledge; or the holism of the "new historicism" and cultural studies, contexts are, in some manner, presented as the basis of historical understanding. James Farr notes that most conceptual history "inclines

toward a fairly strong contextualism" and that the kind of approach represented in Skinner's work constitutes something like a "United Front" (Farr
1989:41). There has, however, been little careful analytical consideration
of the concept of context.

While few would deny that interpreting past works must in some respect involve resurrecting an image of the circumstances in which they
were written, what, exactly, is entailed is far less clear. Skinner, and others,
repeatedly offer statements to the effect that we must "be able to fit the
major texts into their appropriate intellectual context, pointing to the fields
of meaning in which they arose, and to which they contributed" (1985:51),
but what this would require in a particular case is far from evident. Even
some of those who generally embrace a contextualist approach admit that
despite the logic suggesting that language must be understood contextually, "in general, the 'social context' of intellectual activity turns out to
have a limited explanatory role in practice" (Collini 1985:47). And constructing broad contexts too often becomes a surrogate for a careful internal interpretation of a text. If we begin with a dictionary entry for the
term *context,* we find that it is defined as a written or spoken verbal configuration in which a particular word or passage that we may be concerned
with occurs and that often serves as a basis for apprehending and specifying the meaning of a particular expression. In the case of events, a context
is the situation or circumstances, implying dimensions of both time and
space, in which a particular event occurs. The concept of context suggests
both sequence and coherence *(contextus)* and a weaving or joining *(contextere)*
together. We need not necessarily refer to the dictionary or etymologies
for authority, but while this narrow explication of the concept is widely
accepted, it is also frequently transgressed and unreflectively expanded.

This kind of context is what I will call *natural,* in the same sense that I
have spoken of conventions as natural, that is, that it is preconstituted and
has an integral relationship to the contextualized words, expressions, or
events. The context and the contextualized object are organically related
as whole and part. They are, however, different things. Wittgenstein often
spoke of the "atmosphere" that surrounds words and things, and this is
largely what I mean by a natural context. But he also stressed that "the
atmosphere that is inseparable from its object—is not an atmosphere"
(1953:183), that is to say that the atmosphere must be itself identifiable
and not merely an aura or flavor that one might attribute to an object. We
are, in effect, talking about the familiar notion of the hermeneutic circle.
While what is designated as an object and a context is a matter of second-
order selection, both the object and the context must be assumed to be
given, even though the identity of each, as well as the character of their
relationship, may be contested. A text, for example, becomes a context

only in relation to a claim about an object, such as a sentence, which in turn is factored out of the text, but neither the text nor the object gain their primary identity in terms of this second-order designation. We are talking about such objects and contexts as a move within a game, a chapter within a book, an argument in a conversation, and a measure within a musical score. The logical force of the concept of context that I have described is frequently employed and implied in various claims, but it is also often used inappropriately. There is often a tendency to begin with something such as a passage in a book, locate the book in a genre, relate the genre to a certain kind of activity, and situate the activity in a particular historical setting—all the while assuming that we are moving through a logical progression of connections between objects and contexts or tracing relationships that appear as expanding concentric circles like the ripples produced by dropping a pebble in a pond. Along the way, however, there is a category mistake. In the case of a text that is "re-presented" as the context of a statement or passage in that text, we are dealing with what I have called natural, albeit conventional, entities. But the word *context* also carries the connotation of fabrication and artifice. What are often, maybe even most often, referred to as contexts are configurations that are *analytical* and *constructed* rather than *natural* and *reconstructed*.

In the case of projecting a set of historical circumstances and offering it as the context of the text, we are often dealing with a constructed rather than reconstructed context, that is, one that is analytically constituted. This is something quite different from the more narrow construal of the concept of a context, yet this is closer to what historical inquiry employing the idea of contextual understanding usually embraces. Often historians are dealing with *both* objects and contexts that are constructed, and although this may be perfectly legitimate, it is crucial to distinguish such analytical and constructed objects and contexts from those that are natural and reconstructed. The concept of context refers not to specific things but to a class of things, and there is a profound difference between specifying and circumscribing an instance of the subclass of natural or prefigured context and positing an analytical one, that is, between reconstructing and constructing, just as there is a crucial difference between a first-order historical tradition and one that is retrospectively and analytically constituted from the perspective of a second-order discourse.

When we are talking about contexts in the natural sense, we are usually talking about things that are logically comparable to the object that is contextualized. When we are talking about contexts in the analytical sense, we are talking about something that is not comparable to the specified entity and, therefore, not something that can be spoken of as causing, influencing, determining, related to, or interacting with it in the same manner that we might speak of such connections between an object and its natural context. In the case of a text such as Adam Smith's *Wealth of Nations* and a context in which one might choose to locate it, such as the Augustan Age in England, we are dealing with a natural object and an analytical context. An analytical context is a *rhetorical* construction designed to support an argument about the identity and character of certain conventional objects. By speaking of them as rhetorical, I am not suggesting that they are merely devices of persuasion but that they are formed in the course of making an argument about the identity, meaning, and significance of conventional objects. Interpretation, like scientific explanation, is always an argument and therefore, in principle, defeasible or corrigible. The relationship between such contexts and the object that is interpreted is contingent and can be viewed much in the same way as the relationship between a speech-act and the situation in which it was prompted and uttered, understood, and had results, effects, and consequences. While the conventions that constitute a speech-act can be analytically distinguished, they are elements of one complex. The conventional configuration that one might posit as the context of such an act is, however, even if construed as natural, such as a conversation, not a component of that act. And in the case of constructed contexts, there is a lack of logical comparability. What is crucial in the case of analytical or rhetorical contexts is to draw actual empirical connections between the object and context rather than merely juxtaposing them and implying that the latter thereby explains the former. There are, however, other difficulties with the use, and abuse, of the concept of context.

The contexts that are often advanced by historians and other second-order practitioners are not the product of primary research but rather summary constructions drawn from diverse, and sometimes not necessarily compatible and comparable, secondary sources that themselves are the subject, and often in need, of interpretation. Only in a derivative manner are these even constructed contexts. These, usually rather large, historical configurations are then often labeled by sociological abstractions such as crisis, revolution, modernity, and the like that in the course of their use begin to lose their categorical ideal-typical status and become reified and imaged as a natural, preconstituted, historically identifiable context comparable to the object of investigation and posited as something that can make the object intelligible by its participation in it. In Skinner's work, the overriding theoretical presupposition is that meaning is a linguistically expressed mental intention, and the emphasis on context is a function of the assumption that closing the context must be the basic path to isolating that unseen mental entity. This approach, however, is largely a consequence of issues that arise from the concerns of the guild historian. There are more pointed defenses of the equation of meaning and intention and of the interpretive or methodological norm of seeking it. The work of E. D. Hirsch is one such case, and it is worth examining his claim and how it relates to an argument such as that of Skinner.

III

While Skinner and Pocock are really less concerned with an internal analysis of texts than with situating them within and understanding them in terms of historical contexts and traditions, Hirsch is primarily concerned with texts and with the issue of what constitutes textual meaning. He does not offer any particular method for arriving at meaning, but he does defend the possibility of such an arrival and the norm of traveling that route. Although he ventures into philosophy and touches upon such issues as Husserl's account of intentionality, his work, unlike that of Skinner, has little explicit theoretical content, even though numerous theoretical issues are implied and broached. He speaks, for example, of such things as the "will" and "mind" of an author, but these concepts seem to have little more theoretical depth than terms in folk psychology. What Hirsch explicitly defends is the interpretive norm of seeking an author's meaning, which he understands as the "contents of mind" objectified in "intentional acts" (1976:79–80). Although Hirsch once equated meaning strictly with "original meaning" or authorial intention and insisted that the author is "the determiner of his text's meaning," he later conceded that this is too narrow a construal. Seeking the author's intention "is not the only possible norm for interpretation" and not necessarily required by the " 'nature of the text,' " but it is nevertheless the norm that Hirsch wishes to defend (1967:3, 24–25; 1976:7, 79). He does not discuss what he calls the "ontology of the text" (or what I would refer to as theory) in detail. What he designates as theory, as in the case of most literary critics, is hermeneutics that is best understood as a framework or approach that, in Hirsch's words, "codifies *ex post facto* the interpretative norms we already prefer" (1976:76), that is, what I would refer to as epistemology. This is the basic locus of Hirsch's argument.

Hirsch argues that in principle, original meaning can be recovered, but even if, in some circumstance, it cannot, the idea of original or "best meaning" *should* define the project of interpretation. This position can be distinguished from an argument such as that of Skinner or, more pointedly, P. D. Juhl (1980). Juhl defends seeking an author's intention on the basis that this is both "what our common concept of the meaning of a literary work is" (3) and what one is necessarily in effect involved in when engaged in interpretation. Hirsch takes on Gadamer as his nemesis, and while this might seem reasonable at a certain level of abstraction, since Gadamer challenges the norm and possibility of pursuing original meaning, it is difficult to find distinct points of contact, even at the level of epistemology. Hirsch bases much of his argument on a distinction between "meaning" and "significance," and he argues for the value of seeking the author's meaning as opposed to the growing popularity of the idea of "semantic autonomy" and the "banishment of the author," which valorize significance as defined from the perspective of an interpreter (1967:3, 8, 10). He maintains that the author's meaning is "changeless" and, in principle, "both determinate and reproducible," since the genres, norms, and conventions expressed are sharable even across barriers of time and historical circumstances (1976:27, 45–46, 75–76). Like Skinner, he claims that it is the public conventions of language that allow meaning to be recovered and, also like Skinner, claims that meaning is not reducible to conventions. Despite changes in the audience, and even in the position of an author, meaning, he argues, must be viewed as "stable," since anything qualifying as "knowledge" requires an object independent of a knowing subject. Hirsch does not claim that these meanings are automatically discoverable but only that seeking them should be the basic goal of interpretation, since "all valid interpretation of every sort is founded on the re-cognition of what an author meant" (1976:126, 136). Such claims, he maintains, are not indefeasible, and, he argues, following Popper's account of the methodology of science, that they should be conceived as hypotheses that are more or less probable depending on the degree to which they can stand up to criticism.

Although Hirsch notes that there may be ways in which it is possible to suggest that an interpreter understands authors better than they understood themselves, this, he claims, is true only in the sense that the latter might not always be conscious of certain dimensions of their meaning. Although he insists that his preference for "original meaning" over "anachronistic meaning" is ultimately a matter of commitment and decision, he sees this as an ethical or moral choice. The search for original meaning represents, he believes, a recognition of "cultural pluralism," a definite goal for interpretive practice, "a sense of community in the discipline," and a common criterion of "objectivity" (1976:77–79). But in a more cosmic sense, he believes that searching for original meaning is simply the right thing to do, since

> when we simply use an author's words for our own purposes without respecting his intentions, we transgress . . . "the ethics of language," just as we transgress ethical norms when we use another person merely for our own ends. . . . To treat an author's words merely as grist for one's own mill

is ethically analogous to using another man merely for one's own purposes. (90–91)

The meaning "anarchy" that results from imposing alien meanings on a text "is the direct consequence of transgressing the fundamental ethical norms of speech and its interpretation" (1976:90–91). The connection between epistemology and ideology is apparent here but not quite as stark as in the case of another Hirsch who argues that rejecting this norm springs from tainted philosophies associated with Nazism and Marxism—such as those of a "discredited French wife-killer" and "an American post-modern Marxist academic who proves his own beliefs in the evils of wealth, unequal distribution, and commodification by living on a handsome salary provided by the generous overflow of a tobacco fortune" (Hirsch 1991:171).

In any event, E. D. Hirsch claims that the author's meaning is something that persists despite changes in significance or in "textual meaning in relation to a larger context" (1976:50, 1–2). He argues that without a distinction between meaning and significance, there could be no such thing as knowledge in the humanities—"Meaning is the stable object of knowledge in interpretation," while significance belongs to "the unstable realm of value" (1976:146). It is this fundamental distinction that, he believes, has been challenged by the "dogmatic skepticism" of philosophers such as Heidegger and Gadamer who not only reject the norm of seeking original meaning but really reject, because of their claim about our inability to surpass our historical horizon, the goal of recovering textual meaning altogether. These philosophers, he claims, are the consorts of "relativists," "perspectivists," "subjectivists," historicists," "skeptics," "cognitive atheists," and all others who "deny the possibility of a distinction between meaning and significance" and who join in recommending "that we vitalize the inscrutable texts of the past by distorting them to our own perspective" (1976:3, 39). In his polemical enthusiasm, Hirsch sometimes forgets that he has liberalized his notion of meaning, and he often reverts back to the claims that "a text cannot be interpreted from a perspective different from the original author's" and that "any other procedure is authorship" and a relegation of interpretation to "fiction and poetry" (1976:49, 147). For Hirsch, the answer to this kind of "dogmatic relativism" in interpretation is to provide a defense of knowledge based on what he believes is Popper's demolition of Kuhn's theory of science. For someone so intent on recovering original meaning, however, Hirsch plays rather fast and loose with the work of individuals such as Gadamer, Kuhn, and Popper. But once we separate his rhetoric from the core of his argument and set aside some of his dubious attributions to other authors, it is possible to characterize his position.

The same epistemological commitments and interpretive norm embraced by Skinner are being defended, but there is little in the way of claims about either methodology or method. And there is no explicit theoretical argument. Rather than an inversion of theory and epistemology, Hirsch's argument comes close to detaching epistemology from any coherent theoretical ground. But, as in the case of Skinner, the position is largely articulated in defense of a certain kind of interpretive practice and, at least in Hirsch's case, ideological concern. Since both Skinner and Hirsch, in varying degrees, attempt to identify their position by distinguishing it from that of Gadamer, who becomes the symbol of epistemological anarchy in interpretation, it is worthwhile examining Gadamer's work in more detail and situating it within the orders of discourse. One of the most egregious, but still common, mistakes in describing Gadamer's work is to assume either that he is defending and recommending a method for social scientific inquiry and textual interpretation or that he is defending a particular interpretive norm. But I also want to suggest that Gadamer's work is not easily classified as a theory of the text or of conventional objects in general.

IV

When Hirsch, for example, approaches Gadamer as his opposite number, he really does not designate the proper enemy and formulate the appropriate rules of engagement. Gadamer is quite explicit that his purpose is neither to propose "a methodology of the human sciences" nor to specify "how they must change in order to become philosophically legitimate" (1975:xiii–xvii). His goal is in part, however, to break the dominance of the positivist reconstruction of knowledge that, he believes, has prevented the social sciences from giving an adequate "account of themselves" (1975:90). Neither is he sympathetic to attempts to purge methodologically the subjectivity of an interpreter in order objectively to recover the subjectivity of an author. Gadamer's project might best be specified as an attempt to provide a general account of human understanding, that is, what is "common to all modes of understanding" (1975:xxxi). What appears to bring Gadamer into confrontation with arguments such as those of Hirsch or Skinner is his claim that in reading a text, "the mens auctoris is not admissable as a yardstick of meaning" (1975:xix), but Gadamer is not primarily defending a particular interpretive norm. And although he has a great deal to say about the nature of texts and about such things as the fundamental "metaphoricity of language" (1975:431), his argument is difficult to construe as a theory of such phenomena. For the most part, his focus is on understanding, and this produces essentially an epistemology or hermeneutic, albeit one with some distinct theoretical intimations. One of those intimations, which would suggest a fundamental difference between Gadamer on the one hand and Skinner and Hirsch on the other, is Gadamer's suggestion that there is no ontological distinction between thought and language.

Gadamer argues that the claim that understanding requires a nullification of the perspective of the interpreter obscures the fact that understanding always takes place within a language and tradition of discourse that not only cannot be eliminated but is productive of understanding and actually makes it possible, much like participating in a game. He argues that one can step neither outside language nor the "horizon" of the present, since "the experience of the world in language is 'absolute' " and language is virtually constitutive of the world (1975:44, 364–65, 401, 408). Since there is a fundamental unity of thought, language, and the world, it makes little sense to speak of being imprisoned within language or a historical context. According to Gadamer, the fact that "understanding is language bound" should not be construed as "leading us into any kind of linguistic relativism" but rather as indicating the universality of language and the possibility of communication (1976:15–16). Gadamer maintains that it is our "preconceptions" and "prejudices" that provide the "initial directiveness" in an interpretive encounter. Although we should ideally be reflective about such predispositions and take account of them, they allow a text to first "speak" (1975:263, 267; 1976:9, 16). Our particular horizon is only a manifestation of the historicity of human being, and the problem of understanding the past or interpreting a text is only a particular aspect of the human condition in general. This standing in a tradition provides what Gadamer calls an "effective history" or the basis of understanding, since it mediates between, and allows a "fusion" of, the horizon of the interpreter and the horizon disclosed by the text. Thus temporal distance is not "primarily a gulf to be bridged" but the medium of tradition that holds promise for communication between horizons.

Gadamer maintains that "in view of the finite nature of our historical existence there is . . . something absurd about the whole idea of a uniquely correct interpretation" (1975:289). It is, however, important to be clear about what he is actually saying. He is not suggesting that in practice it is meaningless or useless to speak about the meaning of a text or even about what an author means, or even that we should not attempt to revise or clear away our preconceptions, but rather that there is no philosophical vantage point from which to make the concept of a "correct interpretation" intelligible. If we try to find some basis for comparison between Gadamer and someone such as Hirsch, it would be reasonable to suggest that they both see interpretation as a process of formulating corrigible hypotheses about meaning and that significance changes in different contexts. Yet for Gadamer any distinction between meaning and significance is pragmatic. His consistent rejection of the notion of canonical interpretation is closely tied to his thesis that understanding the meaning or message of a text is not equivalent to recovering the author's intention and its context and that a "hermeneutics that regarded understanding as the reconstruction of the original would be no more than the recovery of dead meaning." Interpretation is, he suggests, always in some sense a replication but, like playing a musical score, one where "every repetition is equally an original of the work" or, in a more passive sense, like the aesthetic experience of being "grasped" by a work of art (1975:149, 110). Here, however, Gadamer's analysis begins to slip over into something that sounds like the defense of an interpretive norm. He argues that "understanding means, primarily, to understand the content of what is said and only secondarily to isolate and understand another's meaning as such," but this claim follows from his more fundamental premise that "always, the meaning of a text goes beyond its author," since the interpreter confronts it from within effective history (1975:262–64).

Gadamer maintains that "what is fixed in writing has detached itself from the contingency of its origin and its author and made itself free for new relationships," but, he argues, like the indissoluble link between a whole text and its parts, this dimension of the hermeneutic circle, the fact that no reading is, so to speak "authorized," should not be construed as a "methodological dilemma" but as a fundamental "structural element in understanding." The meaning of a text arises in the dialogue between text and interpreter, and understanding and interpretation, the passive and active dimensions in this relationship, merge (1975:357, 261). Understanding is not simply a matter of method and "technical virtuosity" in reading but "a genuine experience, i.e., an encounter with something that asserts itself as truth." The truth of texts "lies in what is said in them; and not in a meaning locked in the impotence of subjective particularity"—"not something that pertains to the speaker, but to what is spoken" (445). Thus "it is senseless to speak of a perfect knowledge of history," and it is not possible to speak of a truth that can be recovered by "scientific methods" (252, 446).

One of the difficulties in dealing with Gadamer's arguments is that, unlike some of his predecessors in the tradition of hermeneutics, his account, despite the fears of individuals such as Skinner and Hirsch, is difficult to tie to any specific interpretive practice. His work belongs to the same order of discourse as that of Hirsch and Skinner, but although it could be construed as a rhetoric of inquiry, it is less than clear what it is defending even though it is directed, in a negative sense, against positivist theories of meaning. Thus it frees itself for rather abstract confrontations such as that represented in Hirsch's critique or in the debates with Habermas, who views Gadamer, as he does Winch, as undercutting the ground of transcendental reason. Gadamer's account of interpretation is also compatible with a number of theoretical positions (e.g., Farrell 1994), even though his work can reasonably be understood as reinforcing what the literature in literary criticism refers to as a position that is "against theory" (Knapp and Michaels 1982; Mitchell 1983). For those who defend what individuals such as Jonathan Culler (1982) call theory, the emphasis is on standing outside a text and approaching it as an object that is subject to a systematic semiotic analysis. Gadamer's purpose, however, is "not to offer a general theory of interpretation" (1975:xxxi) and particularly not to lay down regulative principles or provide a critical hermeneutics (Bleicher 1980). His concern is not with what we ought to do in the process of interpretation but with what happens when we actually do it.

One of the problems with Gadamer's work is that he is still fighting a Quixotic battle with natural science and scientific method, which he construes in positivist imagery. The most significant problem, however, with respect to illuminating or informing the situation of the social sciences and second-order practices in general is that he fails to confront, in any very pointed manner, their status as second-order discourses and metapractices. At the level of the universality of human understanding, the human sciences would of course be implicated, but his analysis pivots on the experience or condition of standing *in* a tradition or activity rather than on that of understanding another tradition or activity. Such analogies as that between textual understanding and aesthetic experience, for example, or the idea of tradition bridging temporal distance, might work well in illuminating intradiscursive forms of life, but they are more problematical as explications of relations between different orders of discourse. At a certain level of abstraction, the image of interpretation as dialogue is compelling. It encompasses dimensions of the public or communal aspect of understanding as well as the practical relationship between social science and its object. But in many instances, there may be little more than language as a generic medium connecting interpreters with what is interpreted, unless, like Davidson, for example, we assume comparable truth-conditions. In the case of social science, the truth of the "text" may not be the overriding consideration, and the idea of the unity of understanding, interpretation, and application, which Gadamer stresses, may not obtain. If there are difficulties in isolating Gadamer's proper audience and the realm of discourse to which his claims belong, it is even more difficult in the case of Paul Ricoeur.

V

Ricoeur's multidimensional eclectic synthesis, or maybe fusion, of meta-physics, epistemology, theory, and method is similar in kind to projects such as those of Habermas and Bhaskar, but exactly what the ultimate purpose may be in his case is more opaque. Borrowing from Ferdinand de Saussure, Austin, Frege, Husserl, Hirsch, Habermas, Claude Lévi-Strauss, and a variety of others, Ricoeur weaves a hermeneutical tapestry that is abstractly symmetrical and lucid but structurally tense if not theoretically contradictory. He may not so much exemplify epistemological fanaticism as hermeneutical schizophrenia. Although he claims to be concerned with bringing philosophical reflection to bear on interpretative practice and wishes "to initiate a truly reciprocal discussion between philosophical hermeneutics and the methodology of historical inquiry" (Ricoeur 1976b:683), the point of intersection is even less specified than in the cases of Skinner, Hirsch, and Gadamer.

Drawing upon Saussure's distinction between *langue* and *parole,* Ricoeur argues that a science of interpretation requires a two-dimensional ap-proach—semiotics and semantics. This, he claims, would take account of discourse as both "event and meaning" and recognize the dialectical rela-tionship in which they stand to one another (1976a:8). In speech, a system of language is actualized and given propositional content or meaning that reflects "the intentionality of language" and makes understanding pos-sible (1976a:5). Although meaning, in general, includes the utterer's mean-ing, the meaning of the utterance, that is, its propositional content, must be given its due if meaning is not to be "a mere psychological intention." Ricoeur, however, suggests that this psychological dimension has a se-mantic basis in various grammatical structures and linguistic conventions, and thus no "mental entity need be hypothesized or hypostazised" (1976a:13). Ricoeur, like Skinner, adopts Austin's analysis of speech acts in distinguishing between locution (sense and reference) and illocution (performative force) as well as stressing what he terms the "inter-locutionary" dimension of meaning or the fact that discourse is addressed to someone and communicated. Propositional content, he suggests, is most easily understood. Even though misunderstanding may arise because of the "polysemic" character of words and the ambiguities that attend sense and reference, the context usually limits the plurality of possible interpre-tations. While the illocutionary act is more difficult to convey and appre-hend, it is also signaled by a variety of linguistic conventions. The perlocutionary dimension of meaning, the purpose of the speech-act, is the least communicable but belongs to the world of convention. Finally, there is what Ricoeur terms the "intention" that is experienced by the speaker, but again, even these "mental acts" are expressed in language "which is the process by which private experience is made public" and the "psychic" is exteriorized (1976a:19).

Meaning, then, for Ricoeur, has a subjective side in its self-reference, illocutionary force, and intention, but it also has an objective side represented in what Frege called sense and reference, that is, the "what" and "about what" of discourse. Sense is a function of the system of language, but in reference, language "transcends itself" and touches the world in that we both "bring to language" experience of the world and make claims about the world in language (1976a:21). Ricoeur argues that this objective aspect of discourse releases hermeneutics from the psychological prejudices that were introduced by Schleiermacher and Dilthey. He does not want to substitute a structural approach that would obscure the dialogic character of discourse, but he claims that if discourse theory is to also be a theory of the text, it is necessary to understand how discourse is transformed into writing where meaning is transformed through transcription and detached from the event of speech.

Ricoeur claims that inscription "fixes" what is said in discourse, but "the author's intention and the meaning of the text cease to coincide." What Ricoeur terms the "semantic autonomy of the text" emerges, and what the author meant and what the text means diverge in such a way that the "text's career escapes the finite horizon lived by its author" (1976a:29–30). Here, he suggests, the problem of exegesis begins. Ricoeur does not want to let go of the idea of authorial meaning and commit the "fallacy of the absolute text" in the course of avoiding the "intentional fallacy," so he moves, in effect, to the position that authorial meaning is a dimension of the text. A text, however, he argues, is freed from its original audience, and the audience is universalized. Significance is now in part a function of the response of the reader, and the horizons of the reader and text converge in the process of interpretation. In written discourse, the sentence also gives way to, or is surpassed by, the larger structural units of literary genres created and employed by an author. Finally, in written discourse the situational reference is broken, and reference becomes the world projected by the text. Ricoeur argues that writing must not be viewed (as he claims it was by Plato, Rousseau, and others) as a form of temporal and spiritual alienation but as productive *"distanciation"* that, rather than weakly representing reality, creates "a real more real than ordinary reality" (1976a:42–43).

Ricoeur insists that in answering the question of what constitutes an understanding of a text and how it is achieved, it is necessary to transcend the emphasis on subjectivity characteristic of "romanticist hermeneutics" and grasp the dialectic of understanding and explanation, *Verstehen* and

Erlaren inherent in discourse and rooted in the fundamental duality of event and meaning. Traditional dichotomies must be jettisoned, since both explanation and understanding, the methods of the natural sciences as well as those peculiar to the human sciences, are involved. He argues that "in explanation we ex-plicate or unfold the range of propositions and meanings, whereas in understanding we comprehend or grasp as a whole the chain of partial meanings in one act of synthesis" (1976a:72). Explanation focuses on the analytic structure of a text, while understanding emphasizes the intention. Together they represent the dialectic of interpretation. This dialectic begins, he suggests, with understanding or a primitive grasp of the meaning of a text, moves to the complementary and mediating process of explaining, and ends in "comprehension." The initial interrogation of a text involves a "guess" about its meaning, since the author cannot be queried and intention must be hypothesized "in light of the text itself" and the objective semantic evidence. There is no "simple return to the alleged situation of the author" (1976a:76). There are, he maintains, no rules to be followed in discovering meaning, but like Hirsch, he turns to Popper for a method of validating our guesses. Once a guess about understanding is offered, we can explain or empirically support our hypothesis by examining the structure of the text, locating it in a genre, and other procedures. These moves can be based on the logic of probability and make possible "a scientific knowledge of the text" that can be subjected to tests of falsification. Ricoeur maintains that "it is not true that all interpretations are equal," since "there are criteria of relative superiority . . . which can easily be derived from the logic of subjective probability" (1976a:79).

The dialectical culmination in what Ricoeur refers to as "comprehension," however, involves reconciling the polarities of sense and reference. This requires a type of analysis such as structuralism or semiotics whereby a text is explained as a closed system of signs, but this analysis must be complemented by understanding the nonostensive reference of the text or "the world opened up by the depth semantics of the text." Here "understanding has less than ever to do with the author and his situation" as it "points toward a possible world" (1976a:87). While historicism seeks the intelligibility of a text by locating it in a social context, Ricoeur defends the "anti-historicist trend" toward seeking an objective noncontextual meaning. The text, "objectified and dehistoricized . . . becomes the necessary mediation between writer and reader" as existential distanciation becomes methodologically productive. What is "appropriated is the meaning of the text itself, conceived in a dynamic way as the direction of thought opened up by the text." In this sense, it becomes possible to understand an author better than he understood himself" (1976a:91–93).

The most obvious way to identify Ricoeur's argument is as a hermeneutical variation of the genre that sought in the early postpositivist period to find a reconciliation between naturalism and humanism or explanation and understanding (e.g., von Wright 1971). Ricoeur's analysis is the furthest removed from any distinct practice or purpose. Certainly no one can accuse him of failing to appear at all the checkpoints in this rally through the literature of hermeneutics. His work is a tour de force that attempts to amalgamate and reconcile all the salient norms, methods, theories, and epistemologies that have surfaced. One of the difficulties with an account such as that of Ricoeur is that it is almost impossible to find a point at which to engage it. One would have to strain to disagree with many claims, given the level of generality in which they are couched. No theoretical issue, such as the relationship between thought and language, is held in view long enough to allow an examination, and many of the epistemological and methodological claims cohere only through juxtaposition. The image of dialectic is not sufficient to provide a reconciliation and a hermeneutical whole that has any distinct relevance for either method or methodology. The question is what purpose is served by this kind of exercise and how it would yield a science of interpretation—if such a science were, even in principle, conceivable.

VI

In recent years, certainly the most dominant voice in discussions of interpretation has been that of Derrida. His work has become a prominent authority for those who wish to address the general issue of the nature of interpretation as well as for those who wish to pursue the idea of social science as an interpretive, and even critical, activity. Derrida's claims about interpretation and language are, however, theoretically porous, and they inadequately confront the complexities involved in the relationship between the orders of discourse. Much of what is interesting in his work, as in the case of Foucault, is less the general claims about language than his interpretations of particular texts; yet these deconstructive readings are often, at once, so oracular, detailed, esoteric, and unsystematic that they nearly defy engagement in terms of either substance or approach. In reading a work such as *The Postcard* one cannot but be struck by the fact that there is not only a "gag in this picture" (1987:13) but a "gag" in the act of interpreting it. And given his comments on Austin, Searle, and others who might be associated with an emphasis on "ordinary language," part of the gag is the fact that the postcard was sent from Oxford. The suggestions of meaning and significance that are rapidly proffered are provocative but also lacking argument and evidence. Similarly, while a work such as "Plato's Pharmacy" is, almost perversely, loaded with the accoutrements of erudition, it cries out at every juncture for alternate readings, a closer look at the movement of the texts in question, a more linear argument, and some extended discussion of such matters as the extent to which one can assume an identity between Plato and Socrates and the place of writing in Athenian society. It also seems to violate, by glibly attributing intentions to Plato, some of Derrida's own claims about textuality and reading. While Derrida seems to be suggesting how texts escape the control of an author, he seldom confronts the possibility that what may from one perspective appear as unconscious may have been quite conscious.

Although it may be possible in some sense to describe Derrida's position and approach, or even schematically to lay out the "tenets" of deconstructionism (Lehman 1991), we probably miss the point of much of his work if we approach it as a theory of language or as a statement of a method of analysis that can be replicated and deployed. The uses of Derrida's work reflect less his urging than the epistemological hunger of much of his audience. Certainly some of the most disappointing literature in recent years has been so-called Foucauldian and Derridean analyses of various issues and texts as well as attempts to suggest that they provide the basis for the development of social theory (e.g., Martin 1992). While there would seem to be some basic theoretical assumptions in Derrida's work, it is difficult to extract a coherent set of claims about such matters. Inserting Derrida into this discussion of meaning, along with individuals such as Skinner, may, then, seem anomalous, but it also points up just how disparate the projects are that are often treated somewhat homogeneously and one-dimensionally when confronting the issue of meaning and interpretation in the human sciences. Although there may be a great deal of contention with respect to issues such as whether Derrida is a philosopher or a literary ironist and the intellectual implications of deconstructionism, there is surprising unanimity among commentators regarding the major elements of his account of language and meaning. Summarizing Derrida is often approached, however, with nearly religious deference, trepidation, and apology, as if it can be achieved only through personal discipleship and iconography (Harvey 1986; Bennington and Derrida 1993). There seems to be a quite general belief that one cannot say what Derrida says without contradicting what he says—and does—or without somehow transgressing the ineffable, but if that should be the case, it may be best to follow Wittgenstein's advice regarding the occasions of silence.

What is appealing in Derrida's work, for those who hold anti-foundationalist sympathies, such as Rorty, is the extent to which he has added to the mounting critique of the epistemological quest. Much of what Derrida has to say moves in the direction of confirming the view that philosophy cannot transcend language, or even metaphor, and reach a world beyond language. This has not, however, prevented some from seeking foundationalist support in his work and from viewing it as an antidote to postmodernist relativism; a "convergence" with Habermas (Norris 1987:169; 1990); and an example of transcendental philosophy (Culler 1982; Gasché 1986; Wood 1992). All of this indicates that one can find largely what one wishes in Derrida's work and that it does not carry us very far in the search for a theory of the text. What we find are a number of concepts or ideas that seem to indicate attributes of language and textuality, but they lack a distinct theoretical context. One might, as I would, agree with Derrida's attribution of idealism to Searle's image of intention (Searle 1977; Derrida 1977), but its glib extension, as well as other claims, to Austin is quite another matter (Cavell 1995). But exactly what Derrida's position is on such matters would be difficult to specify in any manner that allows a clearly joined argument.

It is interesting to note, as Derrida does, that many, or even all, texts may have, at least at their margins, implicit and unconscious and often unrecognized conceptual tensions, structural oppositions, hierarchies, contradictions, and aporias. These attributes, which are presented as something on the order of revelations and paradoxes, may seem to add up to the notion that meaning is, by its very nature, always elusive and transient. But this image depends in a peculiar manner on its reified opposite. Only against the background of an abstract image of meaning as reference, or some other kind of meaning determinacy, do these claims about such matters as the inherent slippage between sign and signified gain coherency. As a philosophical proposition, the claim that meaning is always fluid carries force only in terms of the ghost of its binary counterpart. To suggest, for example, that something always "escapes" in the reading of a text does not say very much if we cannot articulate what it is that escapes. *Différance,* dissemination, intertextuality, iterability, trace, drift, grafting, undecidability, and the other concepts that to a large extent circumscribe and define the core of Derrida's work are predicated on a nebulous theoretical ground and often seem to add up to little more than the idea that meaning as such is a reification and that meanings must be viewed holistically. What is disturbing, but maybe less explicit in Derrida's own work than in derivative voices, is the idea that since there is no way philosophically to delimit meaning, in terms of either what is signified or illocutionary intent, interpretive claims are performances to be judged by their virtuosity. For Derrida, there are really neither determinate texts nor contexts but only signs detached from authors and audiences and open to endless attributions. Although he posits a kind of "archewriting," which generates speech and writing, this is deemed to be beyond cognitive reach. The problem is that when undecidability or any of these other concepts connoting the fluidity of meaning are pitched at this contextless level, they only speak against their transcontextual opposite. They have little to say to, and about, practices in which there are criteria of meaning, even though both deconstructionists and their critics sometimes view Derrida's work as subverting substantive communities of truth and meaning.

Derrida's attempt to rehabilitate writing, and to demonstrate that what is at the heart of language must be grasped in terms of the model of writing rather than that of speech, is part of his confrontation with what he argues has been the logocentric and phonocentric tradition in Western philosophy. Although viewing language in this way may arguably present a challenge to some traditional philosophical positions and the attempt to keep philosophy pure, it is not without significance that writing is quintessentially the vehicle of philosophy and the intellectual elite, for whom interpretation is a form of authority. Derrida's work represents, in the end, yet another defense of philosophy and an attempt to maintain its preeminence vis-à-vis the specialized social and human sciences. Derrida may in some respects present a challenge to Kantian foundationalism, but he has his own version of the special status of philosophy. Metaphysics may be a "white mythology" (1982:213), but so is the very idea of the authority of philosophy. In the end, Derrida, like Nietzsche and Heidegger, cannot cut himself loose from the hold of the metaphysical tradition—or the belief in its existence.

VII

The principal problem in dealing with arguments such as those of Skinner, Hirsch, Gadamer, Ricoeur, and Derrida is to sort out the levels of discourse. At the risk of doing some summary injustice to the claims, I would characterize them as follows. In the case of Skinner, we find an epistemological argument, albeit theoretically supported, employed to defend an interpretive norm, presented as a method, associated with a particular kind of historical practice. Hirsch provides, from the standpoint of literary criticism, an extended epistemological argument in favor of the norm of seeking an author's intention. Although theoretical assumptions are involved and although he sometimes suggests that this is an approach or method of interpretation, there is little explicit discussion of either theory or method. Gadamer's work, notwithstanding his concern with what might be construed as the ontological conditions of understanding, does not really provide a theory of the text. His argument, his hermeneutical "theory," is basically an epistemological account. Ricoeur's synthesis of all things great and small creates a very heterogenous composite that, despite his announced concern, has little bearing on any concrete practice of interpretation and that leaves numerous theoretical issues hanging. Derrida is the most anomalous case, but it is that very characteristic that suggests the need for caution in thinking of his work as either a theory of the text or a method of interpretation. How difficult it is to join some of these claims is evident in something such as the exchange between Searle and Derrida regarding Austin or in the "encounter" between Gadamer and Derrida (Michelfelder and Palmer 1989).

In addition to differences in style and the tensions among the projects that are pursued, there is not a sufficiently articulated theoretical core in this literature to make the various positions comparable. It is not that it is, in many instances, wrong so much as that its claims are suspended in rarified epistemic air and that they are tied, and molded to conform, to a variety of particular concerns and purposes. The theory of conventional objects elaborated in chapter 2 represents, among other things, a theory of the text, and the task is to extrapolate from this theory a theoretically grounded hermeneutic and to explore some of its implications with respect to issues of interpretive practice. And just as the theory of conventional objects encompasses both texts and social phenomena, I am assuming a certain degree of symmetry between textual interpretation and social scientific inquiry.

Unlike general claims about the epistemology of social science, however, the theory of conventional objects is a theory about a class of phenomena and not a claim about the scope and purpose of disciplines. As I have stressed previously, a theory, by providing criteria of judgment, does shape interpretive practice, but a theory is not a method or procedure, and it cannot provide discrete answers to pragmatic aspects of interpretation. It is, therefore, important, once again, to distinguish between general and regional hermeneutics. Primarily what I wish to demonstrate is the manner in which epistemological issues have theoretical solutions or in which epistemological differences are really, in the end, theoretical differences.

The first issue that I wish to confront is that of the autonomy of the text. One kind of claim about the autonomy of the text is that advanced by someone such as Gadamer. It is a claim about the independence of the text from its original author and about the manner in which the text participates in a dialogue with the reader. Another kind of autonomy is that advocated by Hirsch. It posits the text as possessing a meaning that is a product of the author's intention and that is in principle distinct and recoverable and not reducible to its significance for an interpreter. While these two views of autonomy can be construed as in conflict, someone such as Stanley Fish might appear to oppose both by arguing that "there is no such thing as literal meaning" and that there is no text against which to check our interpretive accounts. Meaning, he claims, is a function of interpretive communities (1980:4, 144). Meaning is, of course, a function of readers and interpretive communities if we are speaking about how the meaning of a conventional object is rendered in second-order practices of knowledge. And meaning is even more a matter of communities if we are talking about the meaning of first-order concepts. What Fish is saying, however, is that the meaning of a text has little status other than that accorded by a community of interpretation, and he is addressing claims such as that of Hirsch. But although one might suggest, for example, that the meaning of Hobbes's *Leviathan* is the history of its interpretation or even that for classic texts such as this the meaning has increasingly become something generated less by concrete textual puzzles than by conflicts between interpretive perspectives and traditions of interpretation, this does not entail the generalization that texts are creations of interpretation. Although in this respect meaning is a product of interpretation, a text is not an indeterminate entity like the "world" that is endowed with meaning only as it is given substance in scientific theories. My attribution of the quality of autonomy to a text is not a claim that textual meaning is evident or uncontested but rather a recognition that, from a third-order perspective, we can peek around second-order interpretations and see a text that is not merely a discursive product of such interpretations. A text is itself a discursive artifact, and its autonomy is a matter of neither its material substance nor the immaterial intention of an author. Even though a text cannot be queried about its self-understanding, this pragmatic limitation does not alter its conventional autonomy.

In terms of the theory of conventional objects, there is no reason to think of meaning as inherently "unauthorized," but it is redundant to speak of intention, and meaning, as something distinguishable from what is manifest in the text. The autonomy of the text is not based on something outside it—either an author's mental intention or the imposition of significance by a reader. It is rather a matter of its internal constitution, of both structure and content. There are some definite pragmatic differences between texts and, for example, instances of social action that turn on the former's diminished practical relationship to an interpreter. The relationship between readers and texts is largely cognitive. Texts cannot, literally, or maybe we should say except literally, fight back or contradict their interpretation. The image of dialogue between text and reader and the notion of a horizon created by a text are not without import, but they must be construed somewhat metaphorically. Texts are relatively defenseless against hermeneutic violence, but as a minimum, chapter 1 of some work cannot easily be read as chapter 2, and grammar, syntax, and lexical meaning are relatively given. No one seems to dispute, for example, the claim that the postcard represents Plato and Socrates.

The differences between texts and other conventional objects is, then, entirely pragmatic. There is no theoretical ground on which action or speech can be privileged over writing as more accessible, immediate, or genuine. Certain kinds of problems such as the inability to query an author may be so characteristic of a particular sphere of interpretive practice, such as history, that they may almost appear to be inherent in the nature of the phenomena, but to assume that historical objects are unique would be very much like construing dinosaurs as other than biological because we never find them alive. To say that texts have meaning that is not dependent on interpretation is not to say, any more than in case of forms of social action, that these are neutrally accessible in terms of some ideal metapractical vantage. This is not so much an epistemic point as a theoretical one, not a claim about how meaning is derived but about the nature of the object. While the theory of conventional objects does not inherently distinguish between understanding *in* and understanding *of* conventional configurations, this is a significant pragmatic difference suggesting that interpretation is something closer to the idea of radical translation. We know that radical translation is possible, as in the case of ancient languages, but it is incorrect to assume that this either requires sharing truth-conditions in Davidson's sense or raises the issue of Quinean indeterminacy. Learning or understanding a language presupposes already possessing a language, as any number of arguments, including those of Chomsky, Gadamer, and Davidson, assume. Skinner, however, reacts sharply to this idea and poses the problem of how we could have learned our first language (1988:251), but his concern emerges as a response to the Gadamerian claim that interpretation involves a fusion of horizons that, for Skinner, suggests difficulties in separating subject and object. Although problems of understanding are more pronounced in the case of interpretation, that is, understanding between orders of discourse as opposed to intradiscursive communication, understanding is always an intertextual affair.

When we ask how understanding is possible, it is necessary to be clear about the level at which the question is posed. How it is phylogenetically possible is one issue, and an interesting one (e.g., Pinker 1994). Whatever the answer, whether genetic programming, as claimed by Chomsky, or initial operative conditioning, à la B. F. Skinner, radical translation is possible. To suggest that translation is, philosophically speaking, indeterminate implies a retention of the questionable scheme/content image and means very little as far as interpretive practice. How it is possible in specific instances can be addressed in terms of those contexts. The open question of how we can ever really know something is pointless unless we can articulate the criteria of *really* knowing as opposed to knowing as the category of propositions in which we have what we take to be justified belief. Interpretation is a matter of giving an account that is in principle corrigible, and there is no need to subscribe to Popper's notions of probability and falsification to indicate the hypothetical and conjectural character of second-order interpretive claims. Social science not only involves a general linguistic and cultural horizon, which its object may or may not share in some degree, but a disciplinary and theoretical horizon. This brings us back to the tensions characteristic of interdiscursive relations for which there is no theoretical and epistemological relief.

One issue that has been part of the epistemological repertoire, particularly in the case of textual interpretation, is that of the significance of temporal distance. For many, temporal distance signifies an attenuated grasp of the object of inquiry; for others such as Gadamer, it is the medium of productive understanding. This issue is basically parallel to that of cultural or spatial distance—for example, how to understand an alien society. Temporal and spatial distance do not constitute any intrinsic attenuation of meaning. These issues are fundamentally pragmatic rather than theoretical. We might, for example, in some instance have a much better evidential and perspectival basis for understanding something in the past than something more temporally proximate. It is necessary to associate agency with all conventional objects, since manifestations of these objects involve temporally and spatially bounded instantiations by someone or something. But it is not agents that are understood or interpreted except in a trivial sense. It is rather what they do, say, write, or think. In that sense, it is the text that is interpreted and not the author, but interpreting the text might very well involve returning to the circumstances of its instantiation.

It is the structure of conventional objects that both opens up and delimits possibilities of meaning. Almost all attempts to define meaning, and thereby interpretation, involve valorizing and universalizing some dimension of the structure of the object and consequently reifying the concepts of meaning and interpretation. Conventional objects are instantiated by the actions and speech of persons but also, for example, in texts and institutions. It is necessary to jettison the idea that, for example, in understanding speech, texts, and actions we are attempting to understand an agent or author, or mental state, that lies behind them. This claim is not a version of eliminative materialism. It is eliminative conventionalism or conventional realism. And it is not the same as the variety of arguments in hermeneutics and postmodernism about the autonomy of language and the banishment of the author and subject. We might still accept Lionel Trilling's precept that we must always begin with "the animus of the author" (1965:15) without carrying along all the epistemological baggage that often accompanies such a claim. Texts have authors, embodied and historically situated ones, and if we know who they are, it is relevant. Where there is knowledge of an author, for example, interpreting the text *is* interpreting the author. What are we interpreting when we decipher ancient script if not an unknown author? But what is it to interpret an author if we are not talking about what the author has written, and what other criteria are there for deciding what an author or agent intends than what they do or say?

Although it is quite reasonable, in some instances, to use the concepts of understanding and interpretation interchangeably, it is also important to distinguish between them. Wittgenstein, for example, noted "that there is a way of grasping a rule which is *not an interpretation,* but which is exhibited in what we call 'obeying the rule' and 'going against it' in actual cases." He suggested, and I agree, that it would be best to restrict the concept of interpretation to an account of a rule (1953:201). One might tend to say that individuals in the course of a conversation interpret one another, but it seems more accurate to say that they understand or do not understand and communicate with one another and to reserve the concept of interpretation, like that of translation, for referring to a rendering, either verbal or written, of understanding. An understanding is not a thing but rather a property that we attribute, often on the basis of verbal or physical behavior. An interpretation of a text, however, is, always "another text" (Garcia 1995). We can say that an interpretation reflects an understanding, but this does not mean that we can separate the understanding from the interpretation. Every interpretation is an account of a text, that is, a reconstruction *of* an "other" and a representation to "an-other." Unless the object of interpretation is presupposed, the concept of interpretation loses its primary force.

Interpretation is a rendering and conveyance. Interpretations may or may not belong to an order of discourse different from their object, but they are logically distinct from such an object. Thus it is not possible to suggest literally that texts gain their identity in terms of their interpretation. It might be more cogent to suggest that texts gain their meaning through interpretation, but there are also problems with this claim. Meaning is a property of a text about which an interpretation makes a claim, and although texts are artifacts with the special characteristics that attend that class of conventional objects, that is, for example, they cannot reply or defend themselves, they are not hermeneutically inert. The very concept of interpretation implies the identity and autonomy of meaning. This is why, for example, to speak of natural science as interpreting the world is to speak metaphorically. Those who argue that everything is interpretation fail to see that it is not that we are confronted by innumerable free-floating interpretations but rather that we encounter numerous texts and numerous interpretations. To put this point in Wittgensteinian terms, we might say that a rule is open to infinite interpretations, but this does not create identity between the rule and its interpretation. There is a relationship between a text and an interpretation of it, but there is no third realm against which to compare them. As Wittgenstein puts it, "Any interpretation still hangs in the air along with what it interprets, and cannot give it support. Interpretations by themselves do not determine meaning" (1953:198).

Texts are neither identical with their meaning nor independent of their meaning. It is possible, although not probable, for example, for numerically different texts, as in the case of lexically different speech-acts, to have the same meaning. Texts are constructed to embody and convey meaning, and they are constructed of conventional signs, in either natural or artificial languages, represented by marks, which are arranged in a particular manner and constitute a *textus,* or structure. Texts, then, are made out of language and have authors and embody intentionality even though interpreting texts is not a matter of understanding some prior intended text in the mind of an author. Thus although the meaning of texts may appear very fluid in cases where there are contentious and diverse claims about their meaning, texts have certain dimensions of inherent resistance and determination and are less flexible than the languages from which they are constructed. There are, then, always limits on textual interpretation and the rendering of meaning even though it would be a mistake to suggest that there is some a priori criterion for isolating and discerning a core of meaning. These limits involve numerous factors such as the author, audience, contexts, language, structure, and propositional content. A dialogue about the existence of a determinate meaning, when carried on at the level represented by many of the individuals discussed earlier in this chapter, is something like a battle between rock-and-roll bands. To interpret a text is neither to reproduce it nor to add to it, but it is to create an account of it.

There has traditionally seemed to be a series of paradoxes that, together, we might speak of as the interpreter's dilemma. If a text is understood, why must it be interpreted? Or once it is interpreted and understanding is achieved, can we not do away with the interpretation? Is there not an infinite regress whereby one interpretation is piled upon another and we see texts increasingly through a glass darkly? These problems arise in part from their formulation at a high level of epistemological abstraction. Interpretation is a particular kind of activity involving re-creation, evocation, and mediation through the construction of a supervenient text. But in the end, like the putative theoretician's dilemma in the philosophy

of science, the interpreter's dilemma reflects a distinction between interpretation and what is interpreted. While the dissolution of this dilemma in
the philosophy of science rests on demonstrating the lack of an ontological distinction between "theory" and "fact," the interpreter's dilemma is
not based on the myth of the given. Conventional facts are given. This
proposition requires focusing yet more closely on the issue of textual autonomy.

The recent history of literary criticism has become an increasingly familiar story that I will not rehearse in full here. Much has pivoted on the
"new criticism," or the approach represented by I. A. Richards, T. S. Eliot,
William Empson, W. K. Wimsatt, and others, which stressed avoiding what
was designated as the intentionalist fallacy and, instead, emphasized viewing canonical texts as aesthetic objects with self-sufficient meanings. Although this position was countered to some degree by the new contextualism and other renewed concerns about recovering the intentions of
authors, it could be argued that poststructuralism and postmodern-ism
further pursued emptying texts of anything that could be isolated as *the*
meaning and distinguished from the genealogy of their interpretation. It
is not unusual, however, to notice that those who pursue the idea of the
radical fluidity of textual meaning seem to assume that *their* claims have a
certain root lexicality and that the claims of others that they either endorse or criticize also have an identifiable character. Attributing such recursive guilt does not solve the problem posited, but it may point toward
some of the difficulties in the formulation of this kind of claim.

Probably Rorty, as literally as anyone, has attacked attempts to make a
distinction between texts and their interpretation. Throwing his lot in with
what he takes to be Derrida's position, he argues that such a distinction is
just one more dualism of Western metaphysics that should be eliminated.
Rorty argues that "there is no point at which we can draw a line between
what we are talking about and what we are saying about it" and that there
is no fundamental difference between interpreting a text and "using" it
(Rorty 1992:98). Rorty claims that a reader simply "beats the text into a
shape which will serve for his purpose" (1982:151). There are, however,
several closely related difficulties with Rorty's account. First, his arguments
are directed against some rather easy targets such as Hirsch's extreme view
of authorial privilege. Second, he moves from a rejection of foundationalism as a philosophical argument to the rejection of internal or theoretical foundationalism or, in this case, the criteria operative within an interpretive practice. The vulnerability of metatheoretical claims about the
autonomy of texts does not entail the defeasibility of theoretical arguments and particular substantive interpretive claims. Third, Rorty seems
to extrapolate from a rejection of the "myth of the given," with respect to

an account of facts in natural science, to an account of conventional facts, but this extrapolation fails to confront the discursive independence of such phenomena. What, exactly, this independence involves, however, is both a theoretical matter and a matter peculiar to texts as a species of conventional objects.

The tendency toward overstatement in some recent claims about the position of the reader, or communities of readers, with respect to determining the identity and meaning of texts has led to a reaction even among those who have emphasized the role of the reader in producing meaning. One example is that of Umberto Eco, who while strongly advancing the idea of the active role of the interpreter (1976, 1979, 1984), believes that the claims of literary critics such as Hillis Miller and Paul de Man have gone too far—from interpretation to "overinterpretation"—and failed to recognize the "limits of interpretation." They represent, he suggests, the resurrection of ancient Hermetic and Gnostic antirationalist traditions and the idea of interpretive *Übermenschen* (1990, 1992).

Eco claims that his Peircean idea of "unlimited semiosis," while rejecting the interpretive norm of recovering an original intention, never assumed, unlike some contemporary versions of this concept, that there were "no criteria" of interpretation grounded in the nature of the object and in the pragmatics of interpretive circumstances. He argues that there is something that can reasonably be called the "intention of the text," or *intentio operis,* in addition to the *intentio autoris* and *intentio lectoris,* which is a function of "internal textual coherence." While Eco still holds the idea of an "empirical author's intention radically useless," he maintains that it is nevertheless often important to know the identity of authors and the circumstances in which they wrote if one is to make a "conjecture" about the meaning of a text. Such a conjecture implies forming a conception of a model author just as a writer must have formed an image of a model reader (1992:65–66). The central point of Eco's argument, and mine as well, is that the very idea of semiosis implies the nonidentity of text and interpretation. It might be too strong to suggest, as Eco does, that "texts have rights," which sounds something like Hirsch's notion of the moral parameters of interpretation, but "if there is something to be interpreted, the interpretation must speak of something which must be found somewhere, and in some way respected" (1990:7). What, however, exactly is it that must be respected?

First, just as in the case of the object of any metapractical discourse, there is what I would call the discursive and theoretical integrity of a text, which involves the dual recognition that the object is not epistemologically a function of claims about it, any more than a society studied by the social scientist is constituted by the claims of a social scientist, and that it reflects an internally constituted theoretical/factual domain. But then the issue might seem to be whether the interpretive object is actually accessible, and this can be addressed on three levels, the first of which I would deem illegitimate or at least illogical. This level involves the open question, such as that posed by Derrida, of whether we can ever *really* or *truly* or *finally* understand a text. The reply to this challenge must, again, be to ask for the transcendental criteria imputed to such modal concepts. What the open question is suggesting is that there are no such criteria, but that is hardly a basis for suggesting that there are no criteria at all. What it should indicate is that we must retreat from the abstractions of epistemological fanaticism—the polemics and compromises between the claim that texts have some objective essence and the assumption that they are open to infinite and unconstrained interpretation. Where we retreat to is interpretive practices and the issues confronted in such practices. Embedded in practices are, in principle, criteria at the levels of theory, epistemology, method, and technique as well as more pragmatic criteria based on the particular text in question and on the circumstances surrounding it.

Eco relates the story, taken from a mid-seventeenth-century journal, of a plantation owner who instructs his illiterate Indian slave to deliver a basket of figs. The basket also contained a letter explaining the gift and mentioning the quantity of figs. During his journey, the slave consumed a number of the figs, which prompted the recipient, after reading the letter, to reprimand him for stealing. The slave, amazed at the letter's ability to inform on him, accused it of bearing false witness. Although cautioned by his master when sent on a second mission of this kind, the slave once again consumed some figs but hid the letter under a rock so that it might not observe his transgression, but then, on his arrival, found to his consternation that the letter once again revealed the truth of what he had done. This story might, conceivably, be used to illustrate a number of things, but it indicates both the practical power of language and the fact that "within the boundaries of a given language, there is a literal meaning of lexical items," in terms of which interpretation always proceeds despite where it may end up. And there are pragmatic bases, both within and around texts, that point toward a "contextual disambiguation of the exaggerated fecundity of symbols" (1990:5, 21). Eco argues that there is reason to distinguish between what he refers to as "semantic" or "semiotic" interpretation, which I would refer to as understanding, albeit from a metapractical perspective, and "critical" or "semiotic" interpretation, which is a supervenient metalinguistic description and explanation. There is surely some abstract sense in which all interpretations are equal, but this is hardly the case in particular instances. And this equality does not logically entail, even at the most abstract level, that there is no distinction between *interpretans* and *interpretandum*.

Behind all the contemporary emphasis on the slippage between signified and signifier, there is actually an implicit depreciation of the power of
convention. What is lurking in some of the arguments associated with
individuals such as Derrida is really the idolatry of the nonconventional—
of the God that is dead—and a sense that nothing can really replace it.
There is also a depreciation of the practices of life in which conventions
feature; to the epistemologist and antiepistemologist, these practices appear, respectively, hopelessly or hopefully lacking in solidity despite their
solidity. But this is only one indication of the cognitive and practical
distance between the academic voice and the practices of life about which
it professes to speak.

CHAPTER
6

Speaking Politically

At no time since their youth have philosophers known their way
to the agora, nor do they know where the courthouse is, or the council chamber,
or where the popular assembly is held. Neither do they hear or read the laws or
care for the results of popular voting.

—Plato

How, in the end, can a mere writer affect political life?

—T. S. Eliot

If political philosophy is to survive as the perpetual quest for
the betterment of a common interest then I believe we must look to those
old despised pack-horses, the Universities. . . .

—Rt. Hon. Jo Grimond, M.P.

Once we cut through all the abstract discussion of the relationship between theory and practice, the intellectual agony surrounding the problem
of relativism, and the displays of epistemological *machismo,* we encounter
a real dilemma and one that has attended the historical career of social
science and other academic metapractices. Most university humanists, social theorists, and political theorists, at least in their professional capacity,
have little direct cognitive and practical contact with the particularities of
politics; yet while engaged in the performances associated with their normal academic pursuits, many wish to affect politics, or even be understood as participating in it. This dilemma springs in part from the very
nature of metapractices and the basic character of their relationship to
their subject matter, but what is most crucial is the historical and existential context. Although the dilemma can be construed as a generic aspect
of the relationship of intellectuals to politics, from Plato to the present, it
has been specific to the social sciences since their institutionalization in
the nineteenth century. The issue is largely one rooted in and defined by
the genealogy of these disciplines (Gunnell 1993) and in the contemporary relationship between the university and public life (Freeland 1992;
Geiger 1993). The paradox of the social sciences has been that they arose
from reform movements and moral philosophy, and while social scientists
believed that the university offered scientific legitimation for claims
that would have practical purchase, it largely, in the end, insulated these

disciplines from public life and partisan politics (Gunnell in press). The residual image of "social science as public philosophy" is still very much alive, as indicated in work such as that by Robert Bellah and the other authors of *Habits of the Heart* (1996), but it is an image that must be historically and analytically scrutinized.

I

Maybe the most striking differences between the philosophers to whom Socrates referred and those in our own time are that, for the most part, the latter, even in their youth, were not involved with politics and that, in ancient Greece, philosophy was not an institutionalized professional activity. At least in the United States, not only are the bourdaries between academic and public discourse quite distinct but the career paths that bring individuals to these respective spheres are largely separate. And increasingly, in a world marked by professionalization and specialization as well as by the demise of such diversions as general military service, scholars often have not significantly experienced any way of life other than that of the academy. They are not, and seldom resemble, Gramscian organic intellectuals, and neither can they be cast in the image of the amateur public figure that Ralph Waldo Emerson referred to as the American scholar. Despite a great deal of discussion about the relationship between intellectuals and politics or public life (e.g., Fink, Leonard, and Reed 1996; Eyerman 1994; Boggs 1993; Lemert 1991; Robbins 1990; Johnson 1988; Bauman 1987), specific consideration of the academic intellectual has been minimal. The academic intellectual, then, is not a "mere" writer but rather a writer of a particular kind in particular circumstances. There are many American scholars but few American public intellectuals, even though scholars often mimic the voice of such intellectuals.

There is, as I have stressed, an important sense in which it is in the very nature of metapractices to seek authority and to seek it in epistemic terms. This is evident, for example, in all the classic texts of political theory, but there are some distinct differences between the spirit of many of these works and the modern academic theorist. While it is tempting, and common, to characterize the classic literature as foundationalist, the claim of reason that it advanced was usually consciously rhetorical and often ironic. What these texts reveal is an awareness that the issue of theory and practice is indeed a practical issue and that the claim to epistemic privilege is not only tenuous but without demonstrable grounds. What emerges most clearly, from Plato to Marx, is the realization that what characterizes human beings is that they are naturally unnatural and that their world is ultimately held together by convention and agreement—however obtained

(Gunnell 1979a). Contemporary academic foundationalism is of a different order. It has not only taken seriously the rhetoric of epistemic privilege but often pursued it exclusive of the circumstances in which it has been asserted. Despite the inherent pull toward foundationalist formulations, however, it is neither natural, in the sense of necessary, nor, in any obvious way, prudent for metapractices to follow this path. In the contemporary world, the rhetoric of foundationalism is no longer very convincing, and taking foundationalism seriously only inhibits thinking contextually.

Although Max Weber's essays on the vocations of science and politics have usually been construed as, for better or worse, encouraging a separation between social science and politics, the actual motive, as for others such as Mannheim, was to find a way to connect them (Gunnell 1993). The paradox was that given the character of the twentieth-century university and in a pluralistic society, the only authority that social science could claim was the authority of science, which was gained through a claim to objectivity and to knowledge that stood outside the realm of politics. The Weberian paradox has been at the very core of the history of the social sciences, and although Weber never offered any very clear answer to the problem of exactly how social science was to advance its claims in the world of politics, the general answer, that is, to achieve proximity through distance, has been consistent. Even positivism, which has been understood as eschewing value judgments, was rooted, in both philosophy and social science, in a search for the social uses of knowledge.

It might be argued that there is a way in which positivism was correct about the fact/value dichotomy. It was correct in recognizing and stressing the logical distinction between two kinds of statements. Where it went wrong was, first, in assuming that one kind of statement was inherently cognitively privileged, and, second, in assuming that the basic distinction was categorically exhaustive with respect to what can be done with words. Those who attacked the positivist distinction on the basis that there inevitably were value words that crept into ostensibly empirical claims and that there was always a normative slant inherent in any such claim bought into both the positivist assumption that particular atomistic words were the fundamental carriers of meaning and the assumption that the dichotomy was the fundamental issue for joining the conversation. But there was also another insight that was implicit in the positivist agenda—even if incorrectly pursued. Positivists claimed, for example, that in the case of social science there could be credible descriptive and explanatory statements but that value claims were not really capable of adjudication.

If we think about social science in terms of its place in the realm of second-order discourse, there is something to be said for this position.

The descriptive and explanatory claims of a second-order discourse about a first-order activity are probably more supportable than normative injunctions. We might be able to make a better case for a description of American politics that goes beyond what political actors may perceive than a case for the ability of social science to devise values and performances to which such actors should subscribe. This is true in much the same sense that second-order analysts might be better able to describe and explain what is going on in the game of baseball than to prescribe strategies and plays or even make a case for why one should play that game as opposed to another. That social scientists should have something of normative significance to say about politics is no more a given than that sportscasters should be heeded by baseball players or actors by theater critics. The essential import of this chapter is not that the academic intellectual does not, cannot, or should not affect politics, but I challenge some prevailing and persistent assumptions about each of these matters and urge a more realistic assessment.

Many political theorists and philosophers propagate an image of themselves as public moralists, and while I do not wish to suggest that academics retreat from normative claims, I question the belief that metapractical adherents to a number of persuasions, ranging from natural law to neo-Marxist critical theory, possess, or should possess, any inherent ethical authority and even the assumption that their influence in public life would necessarily be salutary. While there is, as I have already stressed, at least a latent claim to first-order authority on the part of most metapractices, there are, for example, few, either in philosophy or science, who would overtly argue that philosophical discourse actually does, or should, play a significant role in scientific practice. It would be unlikely that anyone would suggest that philosophers of science are, in any significant manner, participants in science or could be construed, in the course of their normal activity, as "speaking scientifically." As with so many metapractices, whatever practical connection to their subject matter may have once existed has long since become attenuated, and what remains is largely discursive traces. What is it, then, about politics that engenders the assumption that a variety of metapractices, which present themselves as in some way attending to this sphere, have something to say to it or actually perform in it? What is the basis of the claim that such metapractitioners as social scientists, historians, philosophers, political theorists, and even literary critics are, in some general manner, acting in or on politics or should do so?

These metapractitioners have tended to adopt a dualistic, and sometimes contradictory, strategy: on the one hand, claiming that the vocations of political theory and politics can be assimilated and, on the other, asserting that the former is both distinct and epistemically privileged. As I stressed in chapter 1, this simultaneous search for identity and difference is an endemic feature of those practices of knowledge that study other forms of human activity, and it is rooted in both cognitive and practical motives. Immanuel Kant's defense of the preeminence of theory, and philosophy, more than two hundred years ago may be the paradigm case. There can be little doubt about the immediate impetus. He was apprehensive both about the status and role of philosophy vis-à-vis other fields and about its relationship to political authority or what he designated, respectively, and prejudicially, as the realm of truth and theory vis-à-vis power and practice. Statesmen, and other practitioners, he claimed, were "of one mind in going after the *academician,* who concerns himself with theory on their behalf and for their good; but since they imagine themselves to understand this better than he, they desire to banish him to his academy . . . as a pedant, who, unfit for practice, only stands in the way of experienced wisdom" (1983:62–63). Like many after him, Kant set out to demonstrate that although theory and practice represent different activities, there is a kind of functional unity as well as an intrinsic basis for the priority of the former and its relevance to the latter. Kant's assumption was that theories, or rules and principles, were indigenous to practice, and thus theory and practice were, in effect, one; at the same time, theory, as an activity, merited a privileged position.

Metapractitioners today still employ such idioms as "speaking truth to power" and "theory and practice" that rhetorically obscure some of the most fundamental questions about the relationship between metapractices and their object. There is, first, a propensity to blur the line between academic and public discourse. The boundary separating these realms may not always be clear, rigid, or impermeable, but neither is it merely analytical. Derrida, for example, claims that "every philosophical colloquium necessarily has a political significance" and that the "essence of the philosophical" and the "essence of the political" are "always entwined" and joined by an "a priori link" (1982:13). It is precisely such unsupported assertions and semantic erasures that spawn an obfuscating rhetoric that perpetuates the failure to come to grips with the actual relationship between academic and public discourse. As Rorty has noted, the impact of Derrida on the American left has, despite all the intimations about a critical philosophy, been in the direction of disengagement. Despite all the talk about deconstructive reading, there simply is no *political* notion of how to resist (1994:117). Although claims about political theory as a form of political discourse or phrases such as the "politics of interpretation" (Mitchell 1983) may, in some instances, be illuminating, they often reflect conceptual strategies for displacing or repressing the issue of the actual relationship of metapractices to their object of inquiry.

It is sometimes suggested that political theory is simply an abstract and reflective form of political discourse; that politics is ultimately a linguistic practice and therefore not really unlike academic metapolitics and its confrontation with texts; that in a world of ultimate textuality, the master of texts is the consummate political actor; that human affairs are, at least in the modern world, a holistic entity and that, as George Orwell noted, "in our age there is no such thing as 'keeping out of politics.' All issues are political issue ... " (Orwell 1968:137); that since there is no clear boundary between the academy and politics, academic practice, through cultural dispersion, educational osmosis, and various other avenues, inevitably has political consequences; that a cultural object like politics gains identity only in relation to other cultural objects, and thus neither disciplines nor their subject matters can be viewed in isolation; and that academic analysis and prescription with respect to public issues such as feminism, abortion, and gay rights are themselves a kind, or dimension, of political practice. While all of these propositions may have some general merit and while each may be true in some set of historical circumstances, they often are advanced less as arguments than as pleas for an excuse not to confront the real issue of the relationship between the academy and politics. The assumption seems to be that to admit difference is to deny contact, but as I argued earlier, it is impossible to speak cogently of relationships without assigning criteria of difference to the things in question.

There might seem to be some intuitive basis for suggesting that a field such as political theory or political science, which is specifically concerned with political phenomena, can be construed as a means or form of political action. Furthermore, politics is, after all, a relatively familiar activity and one that is often encompassed by the same culture to which the metapractitioner belongs. Under these circumstances, problems of practical and cognitive distance seem mitigated. We might, however, be less inclined to think, for example, of the anthropologist studying cannibals as participating in cannibalism (Gunnell in press), and we would also probably not be likely to say that a sociologist studying the family is engaging in family life. Suggestions of an identity between politics and political theory often seem, in the end, to have little more than a lexical basis. One common conception of theory and practice is to conceive of both as contained within, as elements of, a particular field or activity. Literary critics, for example, speak about the theory and practice of literary interpretation. Here theory is understood as a set of principles of inquiry, or an epistemology, and as something that can both guide the practice of interpretation and serve as a basis for judging it. This notion of theory and practice is often extended, sometimes consciously and sometimes unreflectively, to the relationship between metapractices and their object.

Even the concept of theory as an internal guide to practice is dubious, but the extension of this concept to the relationship between second- and first-order practices, and the claim of epistemic and, consequently, practical authority on the part of the former, are misleading.

The assumption that a field such as academic political theory is in some way relevant to, or may have an effect on, politics is often based less on evidence than aspiration. When the same claims are made for literary criticism, and this enterprise is advanced as a critical social practice, credulity seems even more strained. But as university practices, one activity has probably as great, or small, a claim as the other. Asking whether political theory has a closer tie to politics than literary criticism is something like asking which liberal arts major is the best preparation for law school. They are both academic enterprises that are subject to the contextual and internal restraints and possibilities of such pursuits. But since claims about political theory as a means to or form of political action are so familiar, it is interesting to look at an extended argument for literary interpretation as "politics by other means" and "itself a way of changing the world" (Mitchell 1983:1, 5).

Frank Lentricchia, like Norris, Terry Eagleton (1976, 1983), and others, has argued strongly for the idea of literary criticism, and university education, as not only *means* of social change but *modes* of social action. He asks if it is possible to "do radical work *as* a literary intellectual," that is, a person "who works mainly on texts and produces texts." He concludes that scholars, "in their work in and on culture, involve themselves inescapably in the political work of social change and social conservation." Lentricchia claims that the role of the "university humanist . . . as a social and political actor has been cynically underrated and ignored." He refers not to an academician who engages in supplementary extrinsic political activity but rather the person whose work "is carried on at the specific institutional site where he finds himself and on the terms of his own expertise, on the terms inherent to his own functioning as an intellectual." Lentricchia argues that "our potentially most powerful political work as university humanists must be carried out in what we do, what we are trained for."

> I would go so far as to say that those of us in the university who conceive of our political work . . . not as activity intrinsic, specific to our intellectuality (our work as medieval historians, for example) are being crushed by feelings of guilt and occupational alienation. We have let our beliefs and our discourse be invaded by the eviscerating notion that politics is something that somehow goes on somewhere else, in the "outside" world, as the saying goes, and that the work of culture that goes on "inside" the university is somehow apolitical—and that this is a good thing. (1983:1–7)

Appropriating, but reversing the meaning of, Marx's aphorism, Lentricchia claims that "the point is not only to interpret texts, but in so interpreting them, change society" and the structure of power through the transformation of culture. By doing what they quintessentially do, academicians, he argues, can play, or play upon, politics. Theory in literary criticism is advanced as a form of rhetoric and persuasion and a vehicle for a radical and "oppositional critic, seeking to amplify and strategically position the marginalized voices of the ruled, exploited, oppressed, and excluded" and to create a new "community." In the end, "all literary power is social power" (1983:10–12, 15, 19).

This vision is often less audaciously articulated, but it is widespread even if pointedly rejected by others. Harold Bloom, for example, maintains that "criticism is not a program for social betterment, not an engine for social change" (1993:205), and Fish has offered an extended response to arguments such as those of Lentricchia. He argues that while some wish to "blur the boundaries between academic subjects or between the academy and the world," interdisciplinarity does not produce a more total vision of society, and, at least in the United States, the very condition of being an academician is to "remain distanced from any effort to work changes in society" (Fish 1995:viii, 1). His assessment is that the rewards and demands that govern the life of the contemporary academic professional are such that "the relationship between art and the production of civic virtue is thin to the point of vanishing," that "artistic freedom has been purchased at the expense of artistic efficacy," and that "if you want to send a message that will be heard outside the academy, get out of it" (2, 32, 36). It is necessary, he claims, to distinguish between actual politics and the "general (and trivial) sense in which everything is political" and to realize that changes in the language and issues defined by academic practice do not "make it into an instrument of political action" (45, 97).

Fish's scenario may, typically, be rhetorically overdrawn, but it is less extravagant than many of the claims presented by those he criticizes. My claim, again, is not that, in either principle or practice, metapractices have no first-order consequences, but rather that one cannot assume that they do or should have such consequences. There may be, or have been, instances in which something approaching Lentricchia's image may come close to corresponding with the historical situation, but most of those who embrace generically the notion that there is an identity between textual analysis and politics offer little in the way of evidence. They rarely fully explore the analytical dimensions of the relationship, let alone examine the actual institutional and historical setting and the operative connections among the orders of discourse. Arguments for both identity and privilege have begun to surface in a number of areas such as cultural studies and the new historicism. Oppositional literary theories are presented as forms of social criticism and "cultural politics" (Brantlinger 1990; Agger 1992; Grossberg, Nelson, and Treichler 1992). This kind of imagery encourages a neglect of the actual configuration of discursive practices and of the relationships among them, but often the assumption is that the recognition of boundaries is implicitly to defend the insulation of "theory" from "practice." "Practice," however, tends, in these discussions, to lose any substantive reference.

Neither I, nor, I think, Fish would claim that an activity and body of academic literature such as feminist theory is not relevant to politics and has not had a political impact. The issue is exactly what impact it has had and whether one can extrapolate from such a case to generalizations about the academy and politics. Patrice McDermott, for example, argues that "feminist academic journals have played a central role in breaking the boundaries between politics and scholarship" (1994:12), but her study of such journals does not explore and assess their impact on feminist politics. Feminist theory is somewhat unique in that it *represents* what might be construed as a political constituency, but there is a question of what is meant by representation. It is reasonable to say that feminist theory refers to and sometimes addresses an identifiable political or social movement. It has, for the most part, however, not been chosen as a representative any more than Marxist critical theory has been chosen by the unemancipated writ large. The idea of representation is unilateral. In the case of feminist theory, there may be a certain form of identity between the theorist and her subject matter, but this case also presents a salient example of the paradox of the academic intellectual. As McDermott puts it, feminist theory exemplifies the problem of "ironic reflexivity," that is, the attempt to meet the demands of academic "detachment" while being "passionately engaged," but the tension is yet deeper. It is not only a matter of attempting to meet such general formal academic standards as objectivity, which are actually often not pressed very strictly, but the more subtle demands of speaking in the idiom of various philosophical authorities who informally govern academic discourse but who often both render it inaccessible to the very constituency that one hopes to address and persistently draw discussion away from the particularities that initiated concern.

I have, to this point, been focusing primarily on the situation and internal characteristics of metapractices, but an important part of what is at issue is the character of their subject matter—or at least their perception of it. One reason that politics has so often been abstracted and romanticized by metapractices such as political theory is that its actual manifestations have been perceived and encountered, in a variety of ways, as pathological, banal, dangerous, and mundane. Politics, it seems, has required discursive purification and sublimation before it could be approached. As in the case of the philosophy of science's reconstruction of science, politics, in the literature of metapractices, often emerges as a philosophical object that is only vaguely, if at all, related to the various actual conventional phenomena manifest in campaigns, city councils, school boards, town meetings, legislatures, and numerous other venues. The "practice" to and about which "theory" speaks is largely a metapractical caricature or an abstraction.

It is symptomatic that a volume devoted to a consideration of "social science as moral inquiry" (Haan et al. 1983) essentially ignores the concrete practical dimensions of the relationship between the academy and public life. More recently, in a series of essays in a *Nomos* volume on "theory and practice" (Shapiro and DeCew 1995), philosophers and political theorists embrace positions such as "critical race theory," argue that Rawls's conception of justice as fairness demands the use of solar technology, assess the quality of life in developing countries, and make a variety of other claims about practical matters, but there is no discussion of exactly how such philosophical analysis bears on the practices and issues toward which it is supposedly directed. "Theory" is used generically to encompass everyone from Aristotle to Rawls, and "practice" appears as an abstract and equally undifferentiated datum. There is scant attention either to the situation of the academician, who for the most part, either explicitly or implicitly, is the principal reference for "theory," or to the historical and concrete manifestations and permutations of politics. As the literary critic Edward Said has suggested, there tends to be "a complete divorce between the academy and the world. The American academic in particular has a unique kind of arrogance, a presumption that he or she can talk about these general issues without any form of commitment to any social or political institution except the academy and the furthering of a certain career" (1993:119).

Metapractical talk *about* politics is quite different from talking *to* and *in* politics, yet the assumption persists that, as one contributor to the *Nomos* volume put it, "political theory is simply conscientious civic conversation without a deadline" (Shapiro and DeCew 1995:148). There is characteristically a failure to recognize that the "theory/practice problem" is less a universal with various manifestations than a category for subsuming historically situated issues that have a certain family resemblance. Political and social theorists may conjure up all sorts of philosophical grounds for the claim that metapractices should be heard and heeded in the world of first-order activities such as politics, but there is wide resistance to a concrete, historical, and contextualized examination of the moral relevance of social science and its practical relationship to its object of analysis. One reason the social sciences, as a whole, have not adequately confronted this issue is, as I have stressed throughout this volume, their peculiar and perennial involvement with philosophy. The social sciences have become too philosophically encumbered.

It is perhaps understandable that a professional philosopher might claim, for example, that "the philosophy of the social sciences . . . is the indispensable starting-point for all social science" (Trigg 1985:205), but why this should be the tacit or explicit premise of so many social scientists requires some explanation, particularly since few philosophers find much virtue in social science (see, however, Bunge 1996). During the past century, the philosophical validation of science has really amounted to a validation of philosophy, and we might assume that philosophy will continue to valorize whatever first-order enterprises it takes to be authoritative. Social science, however, has seldom been the subject of such validation. Part of the explanation is historical. From the beginning, philosophy, particularly in Germany and England, struggled to defend itself against what it perceived as incursions from the specialized empirical human sciences, and the residue of this concern is still evident in many dimensions of contemporary philosophy. But social science, as is so evident in a work such as that of Winch as well as various humanistic critiques of the enterprise, is a competing metapractice. The social sciences have, strangely, seldom recognized their historical, if not natural, enemy. It is something of a paradox that their endemic condition of cognitive insecurity and practical guilt has led them to seek identity and authority in philosophy. The search for philosophical justification has, however, produced both theoretical atrophication and a failure to come to grips with the practical issue of the relationship between academic and public discourse.

Throughout this volume I have pointed to the persistent inversion of theory and epistemology, the manner in which self-reflection in social science has taken place through the medium of an alien discursive screen, how philosophical doctrines have often become the premises of the practice of social scientific inquiry, and the extent to which social science finds itself attached to the destiny of ideas that may be intrinsically problematical. Am I saying, then, that social science does not need philosophy or that it should practice philosophical abstinence? This is too large and complex a question for any general response. My concern has been less to offer blanket judgments and prescriptions than to detail past problems and to signal persistent and characteristic concrete dangers. I would caution, yet once more, against construing my strictures regarding philosophy as tantamount to a call for reflective abnegation. My references to philosophy are specific and not a wholesale assault on this universe of discourse, but the problem is less with philosophy per se than with its use and abuse by social science. With respect to the relationship between natural science and the philosophy of science, my assumption and claim is that it has been an attenuated one. Often what philosophers meant by science was a logical construct that had little to do with actual scientific practice, and natural scientists, for the most part, have had little knowledge of, and have seldom been touched by, philosophy. Despite the pretensions of a philosopher such as Popper to have been a participant at crucial junctures in the development of modern science and to have grasped the essential contours of scientific rationality, the history of contemporary natural science has been little affected by the philosophy of science. There may have been some instances, such as in the cases of Heisenberg and Einstein, where the interaction of philosophy and science has been both significant and felicitous, and even though my hypothesis regarding this matter is largely a null one, the issue deserves careful exploration. The traditionally closer relationship between social science and philosophy might lead one to suspect that there have been instances in which contact with philosophy has propelled the social sciences in fruitful directions, and this, too, is a matter open to argument and investigation.

Nothing I have said about the dangers of intercourse with philosophy should be construed as an attempt to deny social science a rhetoric of inquiry and an epistemological vindication of its theories and methods. It is unlikely, for a number of closely related reasons, that the pluralistic universe of social science, as well as specialized subfields such as political theory, will become more intellectually homogeneous or paradigmatic. First, the conventional and historical character of the subject matter is characterized by diversity, change, and ideology that are reflected in the world of inquiry. Second, there are internal rivalries among the social sciences for cognitive and practical authority as well as external challenges to their status that limit their capacity to become theoretically hegemonic. Third, such internal factors as the historical peculiarities of professional structure inhibit consolidation. Fourth, the endemic practical concerns of social science engender differences based on the purposes of inquiry and the normative concerns often attached to these purposes; fifth, justifying their cognitive authority—both to their subject matter and to other metapractices—is a persistent problem. Finally, these fields cannot, by their very nature as metapractices, detach themselves from the general problem of their relationship to their subject matter. For all of these reasons, social science will, unlike the natural sciences, continue to be involved with a rhetoric of inquiry that will inevitably find inspiration and sustenance in external authorities such as philosophy.

There is, however, always a danger of becoming a prisoner of one's own rhetoric and allowing that rhetoric to govern or even displace what it justifies, and much of the criticism that I have advanced revolves around this problem. While the purpose of a rhetoric of inquiry has often been to secure the cognitive autonomy and identity of social science and to advance its practical aspirations, it has, paradoxically, tended to divert attention away from such matters and function more to advance the fortune of professional enclaves and reinforce existing persuasions. There have been few instances when someone has been converted from one social scientific paradigm to another through the force of argument rather than professional pragmatics, and the rhetoric of inquiry has had little external impact on first-order discourses and the practical relationship of social science to its object of inquiry. Rhetorics of inquiry, however, and the philosophies that inform them, are matters of fundamental choice that have implications for the conduct of metapractices.

While most images of critical theory have been predicated on some version of rationalism or foundationalism, it is now common to find a basis for critical metapractice in deconstructionism and the work of individuals such as Derrida. Such a move indicates, in part, that the issue is less foundationalism per se than a philosophical justification of the cognitive authority of metapractices. While Habermas and others maintain that postmodernism is an instance of a wider crisis of reason, precipitated by Gadamer, Rorty, Lyotard, and others (e.g., Habermas 1987), that denies the possibility of philosophical privilege and undermines the idea of critical theory, postmodernism is sometimes invoked as a kind of reverse transcendentalism. Rather than empowering, for example, political theory with privileged access to knowledge, the claims to truth in the practices it studies are devalued so that both seem to occupy the same playing field. Theory seems to retain an attenuated but still superior reflective position even in Rorty's image of an "edifying" philosophy that would join in the "conversation of mankind."

Antifoundationalist tendencies in contemporary philosophy, such as the work of Rorty, have caused strong reactions simply, in part, because of their challenge to traditional philosophical practice. But this alone is not sufficient to explain the controversy that has arisen and its impact on other second-order fields such as social science. Although social scientific disciplines have suffered an identity crisis in the wake of the critique of specific philosophical doctrines to which they had subscribed, such as positivism and other forms of foundationalism, the deeper issue raised by postpositivism and antifoundationalism involves the nature of the relationship between second- and first-order discourses. It has precipitated a crisis in the general claim to authority on the part of all metapractical discourses. But while one strategy has been to shore up rationalism and attack "relativism," another has been to find ways within newer philosophical persuasions to assert philosophical privilege and to seek assimilation to their object of inquiry. While the traditional claim to authority of social science was based on postulating knowledge above power, much of poststructuralism and postmodernism seeks to demonstrate both that knowledge is power and that language and discourse, the province of philosophy, are at the core of power relationships. While the attack on traditional epistemology has challenged the authority of philosophy, political theory has turned to seeking grounds of normativity within the heart of the contemporary antifoundationalist challenge.

Although I have identified strongly with antifoundationalist arguments in philosophy, it is not because I wish to join many of the controversies in which these claims are usually featured—such as whether foundationalism or antifoundationalism offers the better basis for a critical social science or whether there are connections between such philosophical positions and certain ideological dispositions. I have argued that much of antifoundationalism, and what is often called relativism, is not just another philosophical stance but an argument against a whole conception of philosophy and an argument that forces a reevaluation of basic assumptions about the orders of discourse. I take the core of antifoundationalism not only as raising serious questions about much of the enterprise of modern philosophy and the "epistemological quest" but, more important, as indicating that metapractices have no inherent cognitive authority over their subject matter, that epistemology is not a substitute for theory, and that the practical role of social science is not a function of metatheoretical potency.

The fundamental claim of antifoundationalism, as implied by Winch and Kuhn and forcefully advanced by individuals such as Rorty and Cavell, is that traditional epistemology has been a misguided attempt to speak generically about the criteria of knowledge. These arguments, however, must be recognized as largely a gloss on Wittgenstein. What has defined the epistemological quest, and continues to shape much of philosophical discourse, is a classic case of alienation, that is, the abstraction and projection of natural or ordinary certainty beyond a theoretical and practical context and then its reification as a realm of transcendental knowledge that is advanced against an equally alienated skepticism. This philosophical theology, as we experience it today, began with Kant and was perpetuated by individuals such as Frege and Husserl, and it set the tone of modern philosophy. What the epistemologist has sought is a transcontextual supradiscursive basis for underwriting or undermining substantive first-order claims to knowledge, but what has been achieved is only a fetish incapable, in the end, of creating or dissolving doubt. But it is a fetish to which social scientists and social theorists have been attracted long after much of philosophy has forgotten what it originally represented. If the transcendental illusion were merely an aberration of professional philosophy, it would be simply an intradisciplinary curiosity. This is sometimes the manner in which it appears in the work of Cavell and Rorty, who often seem to have little sense of the effect of the siren call of epistemology in the odyssey of fields such as social science.

Rorty originally suggested that the epistemologist's overtures have been "shrugged off by those who wanted an ideology or self-image" (1979:5), but the response to his work by social theorists, on both the left and right, should by now have disabused him of this idea. His claim that "there is no wholesale, epistemological way to direct, or criticize, or underwrite, the course of inquiry" (1982:162) has, along with similar claims associated with postmodernism, traumatized social theorists of various persuasions. While the intense reaction to Rorty's pragmatic liberalism is in part a consequence of the discursive heritage of this concept in the history of social science, it is more generally a manifestation of the degree to which the identity and claim to authority of social science has been predicated on various forms of philosophical foundationalism. The concern of some with what is taken to be Rorty's conservatism, or the conservative implications of his work, as well as the worry about the socially destructive impact of his relativism, derives from the assumption that a different attitude toward epistemology would have different practical import with respect to both ideology and the authority of metapractices. Although questions of epistemology, narrowly conceived, revolve around the status of knowledge, what propels the obsession with epistemology in second-order practices is often less a cognitive than a practical concern. From Aristotle's idea of political science to Marx's notion of praxis, there has been a recognition of the peculiar character of second-order claims, and this is still reflected in contemporary social science.

When Aristotle spoke of political science as a practical, rather than a theoretical, science, he meant, first, that it was *about* a conventional or practical world. Even more explicit was his claim that it was a practical science in that it had an end in action and was directed toward a world created and changed through human agency. It was practical in intention and purpose, and its object was the subject of, and subject to, human artifice. His point was not that political science was lacking theoretical grounds, that it did not possess a theoretical understanding or a detached perspective and language, or that it was merely instrumental. It was rather that there was something about the character of its claims that rendered them less than meaningful if detached from a practical context of human action. When designating political science as practical, Aristotle did not mean that, like the knowledge and art of the statesman, it was embedded in practice but quite the opposite. Although in some sense it might be based on, or a distillation of, the practitioner's moral and factual knowledge as well as knowledge of *how* to do certain things and although it might have utility for practice and be directed toward practice, it was distinctly still knowledge *about* politics. Yet it professed to say something authoritative—descriptive, explanatory, evaluative, prescriptive—with respect to politics. This entailed potentially, and maybe necessarily, a clash of authorities—the authority of knowledge about politics versus the authority of politics. It also involved the question of how these universes of discourse were and could be related—both in principle and with respect to the limitations and possibilities of specific historical instances.

What Aristotle meant when calling political science practical was not only that it had an end in action and a practical purpose but that unless it in some way became part of practice, it had a diminished status as knowledge. Part of the sense of urgency that we might discern in many of the texts that have come to compose the classic canon of political theory derives from the assumption that what is advanced as knowledge is lacking full significance if not instituted or in some way made practically effective. Consequently, the focus was often on the vehicle of theoretical intervention. The very idea of pure practical knowledge has an oxymoronic aura, while the notion of practical pure knowledge does not seem as strange even if it implies the problem of how to translate from one sphere to another. While knowledge of natural things is ultimately validated by the conventional acceptance of claims about the existence, and manner of existence, of the objects in question, there is an important sense in which knowledge about politics, which is itself a conventional object, is validated only through institution. There is a way in which it is not knowledge of anything unless put into practice or unless practice descriptively and prescriptively conforms to it. All this is true of practical knowledge that is most essentially practical in that it is exemplified in practice, but there is a special poignancy and sense of paradox attached to those claims that are "practical" in the Aristotelian sense, that are advanced by an external activity. They are claims to practical authority on the basis of something outside of practice. The question is what kind of authority outside a practice can command the attention of practice?

It is this conflict between knowledge "about" and knowledge "in" that has given unity and continuity to the venerable discussions of "theory and practice." The second-order/first-order discourse relationship is the "truth" of the "theory/practice" problem. Second-order discourses are, by their nature, derivative, with respect to both their origins and current practice, and although various species of second-order activities, and different manifestations of each, have their own particular history of their relationship to their subject matter, the fundamental problematic has been generic and constant. Part of that problematic has been to justify their existence and their authority to speak to and about their subject matter— in both principle and practice. Most second-order discourses such as the philosophy of science, ethics, and social science continue to reflect their genesis. Even though they are institutionally and discursively distanced from the practices from which they sprung, they conduct themselves, in many respects, as if they were still involved in, or significantly interacting with, those practices, but when the problem of the practical relationship between metapractical discourses and their object is approached as an epistemological issue, what continues to be missing is any direct confrontation with the practical issue of the relationship between social science and politics. Even when it is confronted, however, the discussion has, in a peculiar way, become decentered.

II

In the mid-1990s, a political theorist challenged his colleagues by asking why, as obsessed as many were with issues surrounding liberalism and democracy, they had failed to address events and ideas associated with the 1989 revolution in Eastern Europe when the "walls of communism came tumbling down." Jeffrey Isaac argued that "American political theory responded to this situation with a deafening silence" that amounted to a "shocking indictment" of the field (1995). While political theory, he noted, is quick to embrace every new intellectual or philosophical fad, the "reticence" to comment on, or even "interpret," such "current events" seemed odd in the case of a profession that claims to be the "heir" of Plato, Machiavelli, Locke, Kant, Tocqueville, Paine, Hegel, and Marx. Were these events, he asked, too recent, too foreign, too lacking in theoretical and historical significance? Isaac concluded that such explanations were not sufficient and that the most fundamental sources of political theory's alienation from politics were its professionalization, its focus on the classic canon, an absorption with "metatheoretical" issues and an "aversion" to "first-order" inquiry, and the peculiarly American character and setting of the enterprise. While this general diagnosis, which closely mirrored arguments that I had earlier presented at some length (1979a, 1986a, 1993), pointed to continuing problems with the enterprise of political theory, it did not confront certain underlying issues that were also elided by most of the symposiasts and others who responded to Isaac's critique. Some begrudgingly admitted that political theory must do better, but much of the commentary defended the current practice of political theory and suggested that by being "untimely" it was more relevant than many realize

(Connolly 1995) and that there were dangers involved in premature ejaculation (Gillespie 1995). One later response claimed that the integrity of political theory is compromised "if it becomes trapped by responding to events" (Brown 1997:2), and another suggested that the real problem is less with political theory than with the conditions of the modern world in which "political theory is so difficult" (Wolin 1997:1).

What Isaac's criticism indirectly points to is the disjunction between what political theorists do and what they claim to do. There is certainly no lack of pretension to public relevance. The fundamental issue, however, is not how political theorists responded to the events in Eastern Europe. Isaac's complaint could as easily have been directed toward political theory's estrangement from the particularities of politics in the United States, and the problem has hardly been limited to the last quarter of the twentieth century. The basic problem is what political theory and other academic metapractices *could* and *should* be doing, and have done, with respect to engaging politics. Isaac's claim that the failure of political theorists to "address" and make "intelligible" the events of 1989 amounted to a "serious ethical abdication" is premised on the assumption that political theory has some particular ability, obligation, and authority to perform in this manner. Isaac pointedly criticized what I have called the "myth of the tradition," that is, the assumption that contemporary academic political theory belongs to a lineage that includes the classic canon (Gunnell 1979a, 1986a). And he also noted, as I have stressed, that the image of political theory as a "vocation" separate from political science, evoked by Sheldon Wolin and others, signified more the emergence of a professional academic identity than the recovery of an epic past (Gunnell 1993). Yet heroic images of academic political theory as the descendant of the "great tradition" still resonant in Isaac's critique and distract attention from what kind of an enterprise is represented in the contemporary discipline and the context in which it actually exists.

Why, one might ask, should political theory, or a variety of other forms of university scholarship, have something empirically and normatively significant to say about current events and on what basis can philosophers and political theorists make authoritative judgments about such matters? These activities certainly have no priestly or other form of institutional relationship to their subject matter. While we might reasonably expect relevant commentary from, for example, journalists or even mainstream political scientists who study particular areas such as Eastern Europe, it is less clear why we should attribute this role, in any general manner, to academic political theorists and political philosophers. In most instances, neither graduate training nor the typical modes of professional research prepare them for such a task. Isaac seemed to assume that political theorists should and can play a role as public ethicists, and what his challenge to the field prompts is a consideration of this assumption, which both he and many of those he criticizes hold in common.

One of the difficulties in confronting the issue of the relationship between the academy and politics derives from the prismatic ambiguity attaching to the term *politics* and its cognates. The facets of meaning that give shape to the concept of politics often support rhetorical and distorting refractions, since the concept refers not only to a historically and culturally circumscribed activity but often to the study of that activity as well. Many academic university programs in political science officially call themselves departments of government or politics, and there are historical reasons for this that involved establishing a sense of identity with their subject matter. Because we have become familiar with such designations, we forget that this practice is logically equivalent, for example, to philosophers of science constituting themselves as a department of science. This abstruseness attaching to the term *politics* allows, either purposively or unselfconsciously, the propagation of a sense of both assimilation and authority. It is easy to be seduced into believing that by talking *about* politics, one is in some manner engaged *in* politics, that such commentary is at least a virtual politics if not a more reflective dimension, or even microcosm, of political life. And it is common to assume that arrogating politics as an object of inquiry carries with it some natural authority to evaluate and prescribe with respect to it.

While there may be, for example, despite the alliterative and semantic resemblance, little likelihood of confusing anthropology with anthropophagy, or even sociology with society, political theory has often been understood, popularly as well as professionally, as something in politics as well as commentary about politics and thus as in some way bridging the orders of discourse. This has been the case in the history of academic political theory, and the general assumption is still evident. For example, in a recent article in the *New Yorker* magazine comparing the actions of President Clinton with the ideas of Oakeshott, the author suggested that "these days, political philosophy exists in two varieties—as a specialized subject taught in universities and as a thing that every politician just has." He noted that "sometimes the academic and the popular senses of the term meet up, so that what the professors teach and what the politicians talk about resemble each other, and sometimes they don't" (Gopnik 1996:194). There may well be reasons both politicians and academicians might wish to play on either the differences or similarities between these spheres, but the real issue is exactly how and if they in fact "meet up."

Often lurking behind, or coupled with, notions about an underlying affinity between politics and political theory is the image of culture and society as a seamless web in which every strand ultimately resonates when another is tweaked. This image is now bolstered by references to "intertextuality" and the assumption that a "mere writer" must necessarily have an impact on, or in effect participate in, the social practices addressed. Richard Harvey Brown, for example, argues that social science is necessarily a mode of "civic discourse" that, in its positivistic form, has, albeit often inadvertently, abetted repressive social forces characteristic of the bureaucracy and market. He urges a change in ideology and methodology that would provide a more rhetorical focus and "transform the human sciences into a fully democratic civic discourse" and provide an "agency for the empowerment of citizens" (1989:ix; 1987). Probably many would agree with the sentiment expressed in such a position. There can be little doubt that in various ways the practices of social science have an impact on other dimensions of society, and few would quarrel with the notion that it would be salutary to enhance the democratic character of any social practice. The difficulty with arguments such as that of Brown is that they do not directly address such crucial issues as exactly how this internal transformation is to be effected, how social science actually intersects with politics and various social structures, and why professed practitioners of a democratic social science should be invested with the influence and authority that is presumed. Skepticism about such images need not imply that there cannot be situations in which they are relevant but only that they have limits as general accounts of the relationship between particular forms of human conduct and the metapractices that study them.

Another crucial ambiguity attaching to "politics" and "political," however, as already noted in chapters 1 and 2, involves the difference between the functional, generic, and stipulative uses of these words, on the one hand, and their particularistic or historical referential role, on the other hand. Although there is nothing invidious in this distinction, a problem arises when it is not recognized or when it is strategically obscured. It is neither incorrect nor surprising that activities manifesting certain functional characteristics such as power or struggle are referred to as politics. There are, however, many well-known examples of conflating the particular and generic uses of "politics"—such as when images abstracted from the structure and processes of political practice in the United States were employed by political scientists as a basis for analyzing and describing the "politics" of third-world countries. There are the problems both of reifying an abstract or analytical definition of politics, albeit maybe one originally derived from observing particular cases, and of extrapolating from the particular to the generic. Similar conceptual problems emerge in discussions about political theorists and historians as political actors, the politics of interpretation, political theory as a form of political practice, and the like. These are, if taken literally, category mistakes, and it is necessary to heed the subtle dangers of conceptual slippage.

III

The relationship between politics and disciplined, or disciplinized, political science and political theory, from the last quarter of the nineteenth century to the present, is a matter that does not lend itself easily to analysis in terms of abstract philosophical pronouncements about theory and practice. What is, in the end, most fundamentally at issue, as I suggested earlier, is the relationship between the university and politics. What can be said, in general, may amount to little more than noting that quite a bit of politics seeps into the university but very little of the university leaks out into politics. Much of what we may see in the academy as representing social and political forces in society is less the catalyst of such forces than a reaction to them. How, exactly, the relationship between the academy and politics plays out, however, has much to do with the situation of the modern university in particular societies. We often fail to recognize how much contemporary political theory bears the genetic imprint of its nineteenth-century origins and subsequent evolution. Social science originated as a surrogate for religion and moral philosophy, and the implantation of German philosophy complemented and accentuated this perspective. No matter how much the demography of the field has changed, it still reflects the Protestant evangelical spirit from which much of it originally sprung as well as several complementary infusions from German philosophy. What political theorists have failed to figure out, however, is exactly how this academic community with its vast production of claims about public morality has, could have, and deserves practical significance.

The political theorist Michael Walzer, for example, has advanced the idea of the theorist as a "connected critic" who, while seeking necessary "critical distance," enters the "mainstream" and pursues criticism as "interpretation" and "opposition" and seeks to mediate between "specialists and commoners" or "elite and mass" (1987, 1988). Yet none of Walzer's many historical examples, from the Hebrew prophets to Michel Foucault, touch directly upon the circumstances of contemporary institutionalized academic metapractices. Charles Lindblom, the dean of American policy analysts, has grappled intensively with the problems of whether social science can provide "usable knowledge" (Cohen and Lindblom 1979) and of how social scientific inquiry can contribute to social change (Lindblom 1990), that is, with the issue of relating knowing about to knowing how, but in the end, the matter seems to come down to the place of the university in contemporary society.

Russell Jacoby has advanced the thesis that the American university has come to function as a sort of "brain drain" that has attracted but also absorbed and neutralized the potential public intellectual, particularly on the left (1988). This is a provocative claim, but it is based on a romanticized image of the past existence and impact of public intellectuals in American political life. Thomas Bender, for example, has more carefully explored the impact of the modern university on certain dimensions of the participation of academics in public life (1993). While there may be something to the notion that academic discourse is a kind of surrogate politics, those attracted to the university were seldom those who really had a stomach for political life and dirty hands. Jacoby's more recent analysis, in the *Chronicle of Higher Education,* probably hits closer to the mark. He suggests that the university is at once politicized and apolitical (1996). Academicians take positions on a variety of political and moral issues but in a universe, and language, that are quite disconnected from practical politics; instead a kind of virtual politics is represented in academic discussions of public issues. Just as scientific issues resonate in the philosophy of science, political issues are reflected in the discourse of social science, but neither the philosophy of science nor social science has much impact on its subject matter.

There are spheres of academic discourse that would seem to have distinct external constituencies, and some may believe that this is evidence of a connection between virtual and real politics. I would suggest that it is evidence of a connection but not the kind that many would suggest. It is evidence that the academy tends to reflect what is already happening in society, that it is reactive, not that its intellectual concerns lead political life. We might very well ask what political movement ever originated within the American university, and at the same time, we might speculate about how much the university is responsible for the lack of both conservatism and socialism in the United States. The question then becomes one of whether the virtual politics of the academy reverberates back on what initially inspired it. One can reasonably assume that there are many ways in which it does, but the empirical questions of how and how much and the normative question of the extent to which this is good for either politics or the academy are not easy to answer. The dream that scholarly activity is a form of, or a route to, speaking politically in America is deeply rooted in the history of the academy, but it is largely an academic fantasy.

We may learn something from the example of someone such as Said, who is, by anyone's standards, both a scholarly virtuoso and a public intellectual—if not a political actor. He notes that even though he is professionally "certified" only to teach literature, he is moved by political "causes and ideas" that relate to the "values and principles" in which he personally believes. But with respect to the latter, he considers himself "a rank ama- teur," and as much as he makes "a conscious effort to acquire a new and wider audience for these views," they represent arguments that he would "never present inside a classroom" (1994). The academy, he claims, "is *not* a place to resolve sociopolitical tensions" but to "understand them" (1993:122). We may feel no need to subscribe to such neo-Weberian as- ceticism, but we should be able to sense the resonance of the deeply em- bedded belief that only by holding our academic and political commit- ments apart can we be efficacious in either domain. Said, much like Noam Chomsky, seeks neither political credit for his academic status nor aca- demic recognition for his political views. Many would see these individu- als as exemplars because they are in some measure politically effective academicians, but whatever symbiosis we may believe that we discern be- tween their vocation and avocation, their political work is carried on quite separate from their academic work and they possess skills that are hardly the product of their academic training. To the typical academic, Fish of- fers the challenge, "Were you to wake up one morning and say to yourself, 'I think I'll become a public intellectual,' there would be no roadway or sequence of steps whose negotiation would lead to the implementation of your new resolve" (1995:117). Since to be a public intellectual requires at least a hope for public attention, "academics, by definition, are not can- didates for the role of public intellectual" (117–18).

Allan Bloom's claim, and lament, that leftist ideology has taken over the university is strangely complementary to Jacoby's position. Bloom assumed that the university was less the prison of ideas than a staging zone for political education (1988). Probably either position would be difficult to sustain empirically, but Jacoby probably has a better grasp of the place of the university in contemporary American society. Despite abstractly voiced concerns about, and attestations to, relevance, most scholarly activity is generated and propelled by academic concerns and professionalism. Much of political theory, characterized by a self-image that seems quite unre- lated to its actual practice and condition, bespeaks, however, of a wider syndrome.

A dominant theme in many humanistic social scientific fields is that they are, in one way or another, a form of political action or that they can exercise significant influence on public life. While most of these claims are advanced by individuals who fancy themselves radical and oppositional thinkers, conservatives such as Bloom, Roger Kimball (1990), Dinesh D'Sousa (1991), Martin Anderson (1992), and Lynne Cheney (1995) pro- test the influence of these individuals in the American academy and warn of their corrosive impact on public life and morals. The question is whether they do have any such influence. "Have hordes of tenured radicals, the flotsam and jetsam of the countercultural 1960s, who failed to take over the government, reappeared two decades later to take over the English departments and to threaten Western culture from inside its former citadels of defense?" (Edmundsen 1993:3). The truth of the matter is that many of such an ideological bent have so reappeared, but they are not even a threat to the academy, let alone civilization. Despite radical rhetoric, they rarely do anything to change or democratize the very habitat in which they reside. What the commentators on both the left and right, those who see academic pronouncements as a form of political action and those who fear those pronouncements, have in common, however, is the belief that what takes place in the university really has consequences. Specifying, or determining, the exact nature of these consequences is another matter.

Claims about the alienation of the academy from politics are answered in a number of ways, as in the case of the responses to Jacoby in the wake of his comments in the *Chronicle,* but they often do not squarely confront the issue. One response is to point to what is sometimes called the "crossover" phenomenon, that is, instances of academics entering political life or politicians moving to the academy, but this response fails to take account of what the metapractical dream has been all about, that is, to have authority over practice without joining it. And "crossover" has other difficulties attached to it. While examples may seem intuitively significant— Woodrow Wilson, Henry Kissinger, and Hubert Humphrey moving in one direction and Jimmy Carter and others in the other direction—these are exceptions that do not prove the rule. What these classic cases, as well as instances of Straussians joining the Reagan and Bush team or the influence of communitarian liberals and academic advocates of strong democracy in the Clinton White House, tell us about the general relationship between political theory and politics is difficult to say. To some extent they indicate that these realms are actually quite disparate and that what is involved is more a choice between vocations than articulation. But what Shadia Drury's study of Leo Strauss's influence on the American right suggests is that it is a unique case (1997). It is fascinating in part because it is so unusual, not because it represents the manner in which the ideas and students of political theorists are characteristically involved in politics. And even though we might wish to think that this is an example of theory leading practice, it may represent more an instance of practice using theory, even though it is often difficult to disentangle reasons and rationalizations.

Another line of argument is based on the "trickle-down" hypothesis that the university can, and does, play, through education and other processes of cultural diffusion, a major role in shaping the public consciousness. Some also subscribe to the view that there are many individual theorists who are actually talking about politics and confronting pressing political problems, both by dealing with the philosophical dimension of these issues and by speaking to and for various concrete and sometimes marginalized constituencies. And there is the further claim that many do not give only at the office but take their work home and, through their individual efforts, carry it into the relevant communities. While these are interesting theses, they remain largely at the level of professional folklore. To the extent that they can be demonstrated, they may indicate something about a few individuals but do not tell us very much about the general structural relationship between political theory and politics. There is, however, a more significant point. In instances as diverse as nineteenth-century social science, various images of political science as policy analysis, critical theory, David Easton's announcement of a postbehavioral revolution, and Wolin's account of political theory as a vocation, the vision involved transcending the vagaries and unpredictability of individual action and establishing a professional cadre as an institutional social force that would carry authority and inform practice on a systematic basis.

Although, at least intellectually, if not professionally, political science and political theory had begun to go their separate ways by the early 1970s, both the mainstream discipline, represented by Easton's image of a "new revolution in political science" (Easton 1969), and theoretical dissidents, embracing Wolin's call to the vocation of political theory (1969), continued to grapple with the issue of the relationship between political theory and politics. Both Easton and Wolin made pleas for relevance, but neither Easton's call for the reconstruction of political science as public policy analysis nor Wolin's idea of political theory as a form of political education managed to transcend the tensions of the past. Easton's hope for a national federation of social science advisers was never realized, and Wolin's attempt, through the short-lived vehicle of *democracy,* to translate the academic idiom into the language of politics is an instructive example of the difficulties involved. But both of these visions raise issues long latent in the history of the social sciences. These include not only the general problem of the relationship between academic and political discourse but the compatibility of democracy and the claims of political theory.

One issue that received short shrift in Isaac's critique, and in the responses to his argument, was a consideration of whether political theory actually had anything to say about the events of 1989. I happened to be in Berlin, at an academic conference dealing with the historical origins of modern social science, the day that the "wall" came down. It was a profoundly moving event, and as usual, theorists were in awe at being so proximate to actual politics. What was most striking, however, was the general lack of any sense of the imminence of the event and the inability to provide more than the most mundane explanation of its occurrence. As people simultaneously danced on the wall and chipped away at it, several of us crossed, unhindered, into East Berlin. I asked an East German border guard, who was standing at attention in the middle of the bridge while being showered with rose petals and champagne, what he thought of it all. His answer was much the same as that of my colleagues: "Rationalität hat geseigt."

Finally, and maybe most important, there is the often neglected issue of justifying the very idea of theoretical intervention when there is a simultaneous commitment to democracy. This theme of the tension between science and democracy has been prominent, for example, in every attempt to recount the history of American political science (Smith 1997). There is a presumption that although such intervention may be difficult to achieve, it is, in principle, desirable, but the problem is not simply one of the conflict between science and democracy with respect to demands and commitments. The claim of second-order epistemic privilege is not easily reconciled with an image of democratic deliberation. And one can easily construe the history of political philosophy as affirming Hannah Arendt's observation that truth and politics are ultimately incompatible (1968). Two centuries of discussions of this matter with respect to the role of social science leave little doubt about the elitist attitudes of those who claim superiority for metapractical judgments. There is also a paradox attending many of those individuals that cry out from within the walls of the university for nothing less than the emancipation of humankind. Often their voices are situated in structures that are far from democratic. The academy and academic disciplines are often not models of democratic society. Academic freedom is freedom that is, in all senses of the word, academic. There is a folk music parody of the song "My Way" that is titled "Their Way" and relates the story of typical academic success from cowering student to oppressive full professor. It is instructive to remember that there are very few highly visible academic oppositional thinkers, on any part of the ideological spectrum, who have not, in the end, done it "their way." If academic intellectuals wish to democratize the world, they might well begin with the university.

It is easy to speak abstractly about the political responsibility of intellectuals, and there are probably few who would disagree with the general claim that those who, by the very vocation in which they are engaged, are devoted to the pursuit of truth and self-consciously concerned with standards of validity have a special responsibility to evoke these values in a wider public sphere (Maclean, Montefiore, and Winch 1990). But such a position does not answer a number of pragmatic questions regarding such matters as the capacity of academic intellectuals to engage in political

discourse, the extent to which they, any more than other citizens, are ideologically untainted and neutral seekers of truth and right, and the degree
to which they are in a position to exercise this responsibility. It is, in the
end, difficult to say what ethical imperatives should govern academic practices with respect to their relationship to politics as well as what constitutes authenticity in this relationship.

Much of what I have said will inevitably be read by many as, at best,
urging academic asceticism. The spirit that animates my basic argument,
however, is closer to what I take Wittgenstein to have meant when he said
that "philosophy may in no way interfere with the actual use of language;
it can in the end only describe it. It cannot give it any foundation either. It
leaves everything as it is" (1953:124). The point is not, I think, that describing, interpreting, explaining, evaluating, and other forms of metapractical
discourse may not, cannot, or should not have an effect on their object but
rather that they are different from the practices they talk about and are
contingently related to them. Maybe the greatest ethical lapse among
metapractices is not the failure to speak to or about certain events or address various moral issues but rather the refusal to come to terms with the
actual situation and character of the academic enterprise. Despite what
someone such as Lentricchia may suggest, Marx's point was that philosophy qua philosophy, that is, as a second-order practice, cannot change the
world. The answer is not the production of ever more finely grained epistemology and metaphysics—and maybe not even substantive, good reasons couched in academic discourse. In the end, the actions that we de-
plore are defeated by acting otherwise and, in various ways, convincing
others to do the same, and the academy is only one circumscribed arena
for such pursuits. There is a persistent, but often unreflective, assumption
that academicians, by simply doing what comes naturally, that is, practicing academic virtuosity, are somehow necessarily acting in other spheres—
politics, moral discourse, or the pursuit of human emancipation. The danger of such false consciousness is something that is ever present in the
very nature of metapractices. They both long to return to their origins and
yearn for authority over the universe from which they sprung. Much of
the talk about philosophers and political theorists speaking politically represents little more than the discursive residue of unrequited hope.

References

Adorno, Theodor W. et al. 1976. *The Positivist Dispute in German Sociology*. New York: Harper and Row.

Agger, Ben. 1992. *Cultural Studies as Critical Theory*. Washington, D.C.: Palmer Press.

Althusser, Louis. 1969. *For Marx*. London: Allen Lane.

Anderson, Martin. 1992. *Impostors in the Temple: The Decline of the American University*. New York: Simon and Schuster.

Anscombe, G. E. M. 1957. *Intention*. Ithaca: Cornell University Press.

———. 1958. "On Brute Facts." *Analysis* 18.

Apel, Karl-Otto. 1985. *Understanding and Explanation*. Cambridge: MIT Press.

Arendt, Hannah. 1958. *The Human Condition*. Chicago: University of Chicago Press.

———. 1968. *Between Past and Future*. New York: Viking.

Armstong, Karen. 1993. *A History of God*. New York: Knopf.

Aronson, J. L. 1984. *A Realist Philosophy of Science*. London: Macmillan.

Audi, Robert. 1993. *Action, Intention, and Reason*. Ithaca: Cornell University Press.

Aune, Bruce. 1977. *Reason and Action*. Boston: Reidel.

Austin, John L. 1962. *How to Do Things with Words*. Cambridge: Harvard University Press.

Ayer, A. J. 1967. "Man as a Subject of Science." In *Philosophy, Politics, and Society*, ed. Peter Lazlett and W. G. Runciman. New York: Barnes and Noble.

Ball, Terence, ed. 1987. *Idioms of Inquiry*. Albany: State University of New York Press.

Barnes, Barry. 1977. *Interests and the Growth of Knowledge*. London: Routledge and Kegan Paul.

Barnes, Barry, and David Bloor. 1982. "Relativism, Rationality, and the Sociology of Knowledge." In Hollis and Lukes, *Rationality and Relativism*.

Barry, Donald K. 1996. *Forms of Life and Following Rules*. Leiden: E. J. Brill.

Bauer, Henry H. 1992. *Scientific Literacy and the Myth of the Scientific Method*. Urbana: University of Illinois Press.

Bauman, Zygmunt. 1987. *Legislators and Interpreters*. Ithaca: Cornell University Press.

———. 1992. *Intimations of Postmodernity*. London: Routledge.

Bellah, Robert, et al. 1996. *Habits of the Heart*. Berkeley: University of California Press.

Bender, Thomas, 1993. *Intellectuals and Public Life*. Baltimore: Johns Hopkins University Press.

Bennett, Jonathan. 1976. *Linguistic Behaviour.* Cambridge: Cambridge University Press.

Bennington, Geoffrey, and Jacques Derrida. 1993. *Jacques Derrida.* Chicago: University of Chicago Press.

Berger, Peter, and T. Luckmann. 1966. *The Social Construction of Reality.* New York: Doubleday.

Bernstein, Richard. 1976. *The Restructuring of Social and Political Theory.* New York: Harcourt Brace Jovanovich.

————. 1983. *Beyond Objectivism and Relativism.* Philadelphia: University of Pennsylvania Press.

Bhaskar, Roy. 1973. *A Realist Theory of Science.* New York: Humanities Press.

————. 1979. *The Possibility of Naturalism: A Philosophical Critique of the Human Sciences.* Brighton, England: Harvester Press.

————. 1986. *Scientific Realism and Human Emancipation.* London: Verso.

Bilgrami, Akeel. 1992. *Belief and Meaning.* Oxford: Blackwell.

Binkley, Robert, Richard Bronaugh, and Ausonio Marras, eds. 1971. *Agent, Action, and Reason.* Toronto: University of Toronto Press.

Bishop, J. 1989. *Natural Agency.* New York: Cambridge University Press.

Bleicher, Josef. 1980. *Contemporary Hermeneutics: Hermeneutics as Method, Philosophy, and Critique.* London: Routledge and Kegan Paul.

Bloom, Allan. 1988. *The Closing of the American Mind.* New York: Simon and Schuster.

Bloom, Harold. 1993. In Edmundsen, *Wild Orchids and Trotsky.*

Bloor, David. 1976. *Knowledge and Social Inquiry.* London: Routledge and Kegan Paul.

Boggs, Carl. 1993. *Intellectuals and the Crisis of Modernity.* Albany: State University of New York Press.

Bourdieu, Pierre. 1976. *Outline of a Theory of Practice.* Cambridge: Cambridge University Press.

————. 1990. *The Logic of Practice.* Stanford: Stanford University Press.

Boyd, Richard, Philip Gasper, and J. D. Trout, eds. 1991. *Philosophy of Science.* Cambridge: MIT Press.

Brand, Myles, ed. 1970. *The Nature of Human Action.* Glenview, Ill.: Scott, Foresman.

————. 1984. *Intending and Action.* Cambridge, Mass.: MIT Press.

Brand, Myles, and Douglas Walton, eds. 1976. *Action Theory.* Dordrecht: Reidel.

Brantlinger, Patrick. 1990. *Crusoe's Footprints: Cultural Studies in Britain and America.* London: Routledge.

Bratman, Michael E. 1987. *Intention, Plans, and Practical Reason.* Cambridge: Harvard University Press.

Brink, David Owen. 1989. *Moral Realism and the Foundations of Ethics.* New York: Cambridge University Press.

Brown, D. E. 1991. *Human Universals.* New York: McGraw-Hill.

Brown, D. G. 1968. *Action.* Toronto: University of Toronto Press.

Brown, Richard Harvey. 1987. *Society as Text.* Chicago: University of Chicago Press.

————. 1989. *Social Science as Civic Discourse*. Chicago: University of Chicago Press.

————. 1994. "Reconstructing Social Theory after the Postmodern Critique." In Simons and Billig, *After Postmodernism*.

Brown, Wendy. 1997. "The Time of the Political." *Theory and Event* 1.

Bunge, Mario. 1996. *Finding Philosophy in Social Science*. New Haven: Yale University Press.

Care, Norman S., and Charles Landesman, eds. 1958. *Readings in the Theory of Action*. Bloomington: University of Indiana Press.

Castaneda, Hector. 1975. *Thinking and Doing*. Minneapolis: University of Minnesota Press.

Cavell, Stanley. 1979. *The Claim of Reason*. New York: Oxford University Press.

————. 1995. *Philosophical Passages*. Oxford: Blackwell.

Cheney, Lynne. 1995. *Telling the Truth*. New York: Simon and Schuster.

Cherniak, Christopher. 1986. *Minimal Rationality*. Cambridge: MIT Press.

Chisholm, Roderick. 1976. *Person and Object*. London: Allen and Unwin.

Churchland, Paul M., and Clifford A. Hooker, eds. 1985. *Images of Science*. Chicago: University of Chicago Press.

Clarke, Paul A. B. 1988. *The Autonomy of Politics*. Brookfield, England: Avebury.

Cohen, David, and Charles Lindblom. 1979. *Usable Knowledge*. New Haven: Yale University Press.

Collini, Stefan. 1985. "What Is Intellectual History?" *History Today* 35.

Connolly, William. 1991. *Identity and Difference*. Ithaca: Cornell University Press.

————. 1995. "The Uncertain Condition of the Critical Intellectual." *Political Theory* 23.

Cornman, J. 1975. *Perception, Commonsense, and Science*. New Haven: Yale University Press.

Cranach, Mario von, and Rom Harré, eds. 1982. *The Analysis of Action*. Cambridge: Cambridge University Press.

Culler, Jonathan. 1982. *On Deconstruction*. Ithaca: Cornell University Press.

Cushman, Phillip. 1995. *Reconstructing the Self, Reconstructing America*. Boston: Addison-Wesley.

Dallmayr, Fred. 1987. *Critical Encounters: Between Philosophy and Politics*. Notre Dame: University of Notre Dame Press.

Dallmayr, Fred, and Seyla Benhabib, eds. 1991. *The Communicative Ethics Controversy*. Cambridge: MIT Press.

Dallmayr, Fred, and Thomas A. McCarthy, eds. 1977. *Understanding and Social Inquiry*. Notre Dame: University of Notre Dame Press.

Danto, Arthur. 1965. "Basic Actions." *American Philosophical Quarterly* 2.

————. 1973. *Analytical Philosophy of Action*. New York: Cambridge University Press.

D'Arcy, Eric. 1963. *Human Acts*. Oxford: Clarendon Press.

Darnton, Robert. 1980. "Intellectual and Cultural History." In *The Past Before Us: Contemporary Historical Writing in the United States*, ed. Michael Kammen. Ithaca: Cornell University Press, 1980.

Davidson, Donald. 1963. "Actions, Reasons, and Causes." *Journal of Philosophy* 60.

———. 1971. "Agency." In Binkley, Bronaugh, and Marras, *Agent, Action, and Reason.*

———. 1980. *Essays on Actions and Events.* New York: Oxford University Press.

———. 1984. *Inquiries into Truth and Interpretation.* New York: Oxford University Press.

———. 1990. "The Structure and Content of Truth." *Journal of Philosophy* 87.

———. 1992. "The Second Person." *Midwest Studies in Philosophy* 17.

———. 1993. "The Third Man." *Critical Inquiry* 19.

———. 1994. "Post-Analytic Visions." In *The American Philosopher,* ed. Giovanna Borradori. Chicago: University of Chicago Press.

Davis, Lawrence. 1979. *Theory of Action.* Englewood Cliffs, N. J.: Prentice-Hall.

Deleuze, Giles, and Felix Guattari. 1994. *What Is Philosophy?* New York: Columbia University Press.

Dennett, Daniel. 1987. *The Intentional Stance.* Cambridge: MIT Press.

———. 1991. *Consciousness Explained.* Boston: Little, Brown.

———. 1995. *Darwin's Dangerous Idea.* New York: Simon and Schuster.

Derrida, Jacques. 1977. "Limited Inc." *Glyph* 2.

———. 1982. *Margins of Philosophy.* Chicago: University of Chicago Press.

———. 1987. *The Postcard: From Socrates to Freud and Beyond.* Chicago: University of Chicago Press.

Devitt, Michael. 1984. *Realism and Truth.* Oxford: Blackwell.

Dipert, Randall R. 1993. *Artifacts, Art Works, and Agency.* Philadelphia: Temple University Press.

Donagan, Alan. 1987. *Choice: The Essential Element in Human Action.* London: Routledge and Kegan Paul.

Downs, Anthony. 1957. *An Economic Theory of Democracy.* New York: Harper.

Dray, W. H. 1957. *Laws and Explanation in History.* Oxford: Oxford University Press.

Dretske, Fred. 1988. *Explaining Behavior in a World of Causes.* Cambridge: MIT Press.

Dreyfus, Herbert. 1986. "Why Studies of Human Capacities Modeled on Ideal Natural Science Can Never Achieve Their Goal." In *Rationality, Relativism, and the Human Sciences,* ed. J. Margolis, M. Krausz, and R. M. Burian. Boston: Nijhoff.

Drury, Shadia. 1997. *Leo Strauss and the American Right.* New York: St. Martin's Press.

D'Sousa, Dinesh. 1991. *Illiberal Education.* New York: Free Press.

Dummett, Michael. 1978. *Truth and Other Enigmas.* Cambridge: Harvard University Press.

———. 1991. *The Logical Basis of Metaphysics.* Cambridge: Harvard University Press.

Dworkin, R. M. 1977. *Taking Rights Seriously.* Cambridge: Harvard University Press.

Eagleton, Terry. 1976. *Criticism and Ideology: A Study in Marxist Literary Theory.* London: Verso.

————. 1983. *Literary Theory: An Introduction.* Minneapolis: University of Minnesota Press.

Easton, David. 1969. "The New Revolution in Political Science." *American Political Science Review* 63.

Eco, Umberto. 1976. *A Theory of Semiotics.* Bloomington: University of Indiana Press.

————. 1979. *The Role of the Reader.* Bloomington: University of Indiana Press.

————. 1984. *Semiotics and the Philosophy of Language.* Bloomington: University of Indiana Press.

————. 1990. *The Limits of Interpretation.* Bloomington: University of Indiana Press.

————. 1992. *Interpretation and Overinterpretation,* ed. Stefan Collini. New York: Cambridge University Press.

Edmundsen, Mark, ed. 1993. *Wild Orchids and Trotsky.* New York: Penguin.

Ellis, Brian. 1990. *Truth and Objectivity.* Oxford: Basil Blackwell.

Elster, Jon. 1983. *Sour Grapes.* New York: Cambridge University Press.

————. 1986. *Rational Choice.* New York: New York University Press.

Emmett, Dorothy. 1966. *Rules, Roles, and Relations.* London: Macmillan.

Evnine, Simon. 1991. *Donald Davidson.* Stanford: Stanford University Press.

Eyerman, Ron. 1994. *Between Culture and Politics.* Cambridge: Polity Press.

Farr, James. 1989. "Understanding Conceptual Change Politically." In *Political Innovation and Conceptual Change,* ed. Terence Ball, James Farr, and Russell L. Hanson. New York: Cambridge University Press.

Farrell, Frank B. 1994. *Subjectivity, Realism, and Postmodernism—The Recovery of the World.* New York: Cambridge University Press.

Feinberg, Joel. 1965. "Action and Responsibility." In *Philosophy in America,* ed. Max Black. Ithaca: Cornell University Press.

Feyerabend, Paul. 1970. "Against Method." In *Minnesota Studies in the Philosophy of Science,* vol. 1, ed. Michael Radner and Stephen Winokur. Minneapolis: University of Minnesota Press.

————. 1995. *Killing Time.* Chicago: University of Chicago Press.

Fink, Leon, Stephen Leonard, and Donald Reid, eds. 1996. *Intellectuals and Public Life.* Ithaca: Cornell University Press.

Fish, Stanley. 1980. *Is There a Text in This Class? The Authority of Interpretive Communities.* Cambridge: Harvard University Press.

————. 1989. *Doing What Comes Naturally.* Durham: Duke University Press.

————. 1995. *Professional Correctness.* Oxford: Oxford University Press.

Fodor, Jerry A. 1983. *Modularity of the Mind.* Cambridge: MIT Press.

————. 1985. "Précis of the *The Modularity of Mind.*" *Behavioral and Brain Sciences* 8.

Forguson, L. W. 1969. "Austin's Philosophy of Action." In *Symposium on J. L. Austin,* ed. K. T. Fann. New York: Humanities Press.

Foucault, Michel. 1979. *The Order of Things: An Archaeology of the Human Sciences.* New York: Vintage Books.

Freeland, Richard. 1992. *Academia's Golden Age: Universities in Massachusetts 1945–1970.* New York: Oxford University Press.

French, Peter, Theodore E. Vehling Jr., and Howard S. Wellstein. 1988. *Realism and Antirealism.* Minneapolis: University of Minnesota Press.

Friedman, Milton. 1953. *Essays in Positive Economics.* Chicago: University of Chicago Press.

Fuller, Steve. 1988. *Social Epistemology.* Bloomington: Indiana University Press.

Gadamer, Hans-Georg. 1975. *Truth and Method.* New York: Seabury Press.

———. 1976. *Philosophical Hermeneutics.* Berkeley: University of California Press.

Gaita, Raymond. 1990. *Value and Understanding.* London: Routledge.

Gallie, W. B. 1955–1956. "Essentially Contested Concepts." *Proceedings of the Aristotelian Society* 56.

Galston, William. 1993. "Political Theory in the 1980s: Perplexity Amidst Diversity." In *Political Science: The State of the Discipline II,* ed. Ada Finifter. Washington, D.C.: American Political Science Association.

Gandy, Richard. 1973. "Reference, Meaning, and Belief." *Journal of Philosophy* 70.

Gasché, Rodolphe. 1986. *The Tain of the Mirror.* Baltimore: Johns Hopkins University Press.

Geertz, Clifford. 1975. *Kinship in Bali.* Chicago: University of Chicago Press.

———. 1989. "Anti Anti-Relativism." In Krausz, *Relativism.*

Geiger, Roger. 1993. *Research and Relevant Knowledge: American Research Universities Since World War II.* New York: Oxford University Press.

Gellner, Ernest. 1968. "The New Idealism." In *Problems in the Philosophy of Science,* ed. Imre Lakatos and Alan Musgrave. Amsterdam: North-Holland.

———. 1973. *Cause and Meaning in the Social Sciences.* London: Routledge and Kegan Paul.

———. 1985. *Relativism and the Social Sciences.* New York: Cambridge University Press.

Gibson, Roger. 1982. *The Philosophy of W. V. O. Quine.* Tampa: University of South Florida Press.

Giddens, Anthony. 1976. *New Rules of Sociological Method.* New York: Basic Books.

———. 1977. *Studies in Social and Political Theory.* New York: Basic Books.

———. 1984. *The Constitution of Society: Outline of the Theory of Structuration.* Berkeley: University of California Press.

Gilbert, Margaret. 1989. *On Social Facts.* London: Routledge.

Gillespie, Michael. 1995. "Beyond East and West." *Political Theory* 23.

Gillespie, Norman, ed. 1986. *Moral Realism. Southern Journal of Philosophy* 24 (supp.).

Ginet, Carl. 1990. *On Action.* Cambridge: Cambridge University Press.

Glymour, Clark. 1980. *Theory and Evidence.* Princeton: Princeton University Press.

Goldman, Alvin. 1970. *A Theory of Human Action.* Englewood Cliffs, N. J.: Prentice-Hall.

Goodman, Nelson. 1972. "The Way the World Is." In *Problems and Projects.* Goodman, Nelson. Indianapolis: Hackett.

———. 1978. *Ways of Worldmaking.* Indianapolis: Hackett.

———. 1992. "Seven Strictures on Similarity." In *How Classification Works: Nelson Goodman Among the Social Sciences,* ed. Mary Douglas and David Hull. Edinburgh: Edinburgh University Press.

Gopnik, Adam. 1996. "Man Without a Plan." *New Yorker.* October.

Gracia, Jorge J. E. 1995. *A Theory of Textuality: The Logic and Epistemology.* Albany: State University of New York Press.

Green, Donald, and Ian Shapiro. 1994. *Pathologies of Rational Choice.* New Haven: Yale University Press.

Greenleaf, W. H. 1964. *Order, Empiricism, and Politics.* London: Oxford University Press.

Grice, H. P. 1957. "Meaning." *Philosophical Review* 78.

Grossberg, Lawrence, Cary Nelson, and Paula A.Treichler. 1992. *Cultural Studies.* New York: Routledge.

Gunnell, John. 1968a. *Political Philosophy and Time.* Middletown, Conn.: Wesleyan University Press (new edition, University of Chicago Press, 1987).

———. 1968b. "Social Science and Political Reality: The Problem of Explanation." *Social Research* 34.

———. 1973. "Political Inquiry and the Concept of Action: A Phenomenological Analysis." In *Phenomenology and the Social Sciences,* vol. 2, ed. Maurice Natanson. Evanston, Ill.: Northwestern University Press.

———. 1975. *Philosophy, Science, and Political Inquiry.* Morristown, N.J.: General Learning Press.

———. 1979a. *Political Theory: Tradition and Interpretation.* Cambridge, Mass.: Winthrop.

———. 1979b. "Political Science and the Theory of Action: Prolegomena." *Political Theory* 7.

———. 1980. "Method, Methodology, and the Search for Traditions in the History of Political Theory." *Annals of Scholarship* 1.

———. 1981. "Political Theory and the Theory of Action." *Western Political Quarterly* 34.

———. 1982. "Interpretation and the History of Political Theory: Apology and Epistemology." *American Political Science Review* 76.

———. 1983. "Political Theory: The Evolution of a Sub-field." In *Political Science: The State of the Discipline,* ed. Ada Finifter. Washington, D.C.: American Political Science Association.

———. 1986a. *Between Philosophy and Politics: The Alienation of Political Theory.* Amherst: University of Massachusetts Press.

———. 1986b. "Annals of Political Theory." In Nelson, *Tradition, Interpretation, and Science.*

———. 1986c. "History and Theory." *American Political Science Review* 80.

———. 1993. *The Descent of Political Theory: The Genealogy of an American Vocation.* Chicago: University of Chicago Press.

———. 1997. "Paradoxos Theoretikos." In *Contemporary Empirical Political Theory,* ed. Kristen Monroe. Berkeley: University of California Press.

———. In press. "Political Theory as a Metapractice." In *Political Theory and Partisan Politics,* ed. Edward Portis, Adolph Gunderson, and Ruth Shively. Albany: State University of New York Press.

Haan, Norma et al., eds. 1983. *Social Science as Moral Inquiry.* New York: Columbia University Press.

Habermas, Jürgen. 1970. "Towards a Theory of Communicative Competence." *Inquiry* 13.

———. 1984. *The Theory of Communicative Action*. Vol. 1, *Reason and the Rationalization of Society*. Boston: Beacon Press.

———. 1987. *The Philosophical Discourse of Modernity*. Cambridge: MIT Press.

Hacking, Ian. 1982. "Language, Truth, and Reason." In Hollis and Lukes, *Rationality and Relativism*.

———. 1983. *Representing and Intervening*. Cambridge: Cambridge University Press.

Hampshire, Stuart. 1960. *Thought and Action*. London: Chatto and Windus.

Harman, Gilbert. 1977. *The Nature of Morality*. New York: Oxford University Press.

Harré, Rom. 1986. *Varieties of Realism*. Oxford: Basil Blackwell.

Harré, Rom, and Michael Krausz. 1996. *Varieties of Relativism*. Oxford: Blackwell.

Harris, James F. 1992. *Against Relativism*. La Salle, Ill.: Open Court.

Harvey, Irene. 1986. *Derrida and the Economy of Differance*. Bloomington: University of Indiana Press.

Hauptmann, Emily. 1996. *Putting Choice Before Democracy*. Albany: State University of New York Press.

Heisenberg, Werner. 1958. *Physics and Philosophy*. New York: Harper.

Hempel, Carl. 1965. *Aspects of Scientific Explanation*. New York: Free Press.

Hesse, Mary. 1980. *Revolutions and Reconstructions in the Philosophy of Science*. Bloomington: University of Indiana Press.

Hindess, Barry. 1971. *Philosophy and Methodology in the Social Sciences*. Sussex, England: Harvester Press.

Hirsch, David. 1991. *The Deconstruction of Literature: Criticism After Auschwitz*. Hanover: University Press of New England/Brown University Press.

Hirsch, E. D. Jr. 1967. *Validity in Interpretation*. New Haven: Yale University Press.

———. 1976. *The Aims of Interpretation*. Chicago: University of Chicago Press.

Hollis, Martin. 1977. *Models of Man*. Cambridge: Cambridge University Press.

———. 1982. "The Social Destruction of Reality." In Hollis and Lukes, *Rationality and Relativism*.

Hollis, Martin, and Stephen Lukes, eds. 1982. *Rationality and Relativism*. Cambridge: MIT Press.

Holmwood, John, and Alexander Stewart. 1991. *Explanation and Social Theory*. London: Macmillan.

Hookway, Christopher, and Philip Pettit, eds. 1978. *Action and Interpretation*. Cambridge: Cambridge University Press.

Horkheimer, Max. 1972. *Critical Theory*. New York: Herder and Herder.

Hornsby, Jennifer. 1980. *Actions*. London: Routledge and Kegan Paul.

Hoyningen-Huene, Paul. 1993. *Reconstructing Scientific Revolutions*. Chicago: University of Chicago Press.

Hull, David. 1994. *Richard Rorty: Prophet of the New Pragmatism*. Albany: State University of New York Press.

Isaac, Jeffrey C. 1987. "After Empiricism: The Realist Alternative." In Terence Ball, *Idioms of Inquiry*.

————. 1990. "Realism and Reality: Some Realistic Considerations," *Journal for the Theory of Social Behavior* 20.

————. 1995. "The Strange Silence of Political Theory." *Political Theory* 23.

Jacoby, Russell. 1988. *The Last Intellectuals.* New York: Basic Books.

————. 1996. "America's Professoriate: Politicized, Yet Apolitical." *Chronicle of Higher Education,* April 12.

Jarvie, I. C. 1970. "Understanding and Explanation in Sociology and Social Anthropology." In *Explanation in the Behavioural Sciences,* ed. Robert Borger and Frank Cioffi. Cambridge: Cambridge University Press.

————. 1972. *Concepts and Society.* London: Routledge and Kegan Paul.

————. 1984. *Rationality and Relativism.* London: Routledge and Kegan Paul.

Jay, Martin. 1989. "The Morals of Genealogy: Or Is There a Post-Structuralist Ethics?" *Cambridge Review* 110.

Johnson, Paul. 1988. *Intellectuals.* New York: Harper and Row.

Juhl, P. D. 1980. *Interpretation.* Princeton: Princeton University Press.

Kant, Immanuel. 1983. *Perpetual Peace and Other Essays on Politics, History, and Morals,* trans. Ted Humphrey. Indianapolis: Hackett.

Keat, Russell, and John Urry. 1975. *Social Theory as Science.* London: Routledge.

Kenny, Anthony. 1963. *Action, Emotion, and Will.* London: Routledge and Kegan Paul.

Kimball, Roger. 1990. *Tenured Radicals: How Politics Has Corrupted Our Higher Education.* New York: Harper and Row.

Knapp, Steven H., and Walter Benn Michaels. 1982. "Against Theory." *Critical Inquiry* 8.

Koerner, Stephán. 1966. *Experience and Theory.* New York: Humanities Press.

Kolenda, Konstantin. 1990. *Rorty's Humanistic Pragmatism.* Tampa: University of South Florida Press.

Koselleck, Reinhart. 1988. *Critique and Crisis: Enlightenment and the Pathogenesis of Modern Society.* Cambridge: MIT Press.

Krausz, Michael, ed. 1989. *Relativism: Interpretation and Confrontation.* Notre Dame: University of Notre Dame Press.

Kripke, Saul A. 1982. *Wittgenstein on Rules and Private Language.* Oxford: Blackwell.

Kuhn, Thomas. 1962. *The Structure of Scientific Revolutions.* Chicago: University of Chicago Press.

————. 1977. *The Essential Tension.* Chicago: University of Chicago Press.

————. 1991. "The Natural and the Human Sciences." In *The Interpretive Turn,* ed. D. R. Hiley, J. F. Bohman, and R. Shusterman. Ithaca: Cornell University Press.

————. 1993a. "Foreword." In Hoyningen-Huene, *Reconstructing Scientific Revolutions.*

————. 1993b. "Afterwords." In *World-Changes: Thomas Kuhn and the Nature of Science,* ed. Paul Horwich. Cambridge: MIT Press.

Laclau, Ernesto. 1990. *New Reflections on the Revolution of Our Time.* London: Verso.

Laclau, Ernesto, and Chantal Mouffe. 1986. *Hegemony and Social Theory: Towards a Radical Democratic Politics.* London: Verso.

Lakatos, Imre. 1970. "Falsification and the Methodology of Scientific Research Programmes." In *Criticism and the Growth of Knowledge,* ed. Imre Lakatos and Alan Musgrave. Cambridge: Cambridge University Press.

Landesman, Charles. 1969. "Actions as Universals: An Inquiry into the Metaphysics of Action." *American Philosophical Quarterly* 6.

————. 1972. *Discourse and Its Presuppositions.* New Haven: Yale University Press.

Laudan, Larry. 1977. *Progress and Its Problems.* Berkeley: University of California Press.

————. 1981. *Science and Hypothesis.* Dordrecht: Reidel.

————. 1990. *Science and Relativism.* Chicago: University of Chicago Press.

Layder, Derek. 1990. *The Realist Image in Social Science.* London: Macmillan.

Lehman, David. 1991. *Signs of the Times.* New York: Poseidon Press.

Lemert, Charles C., ed. 1991. *Intellectuals and Politics.* Newbury Park, Calif.: Sage.

Lenin, V. I. 1950. *Materialism and Empirio-criticism.* London: Laurence and Wishart.

Lennon, Kathleen. 1990. *Explaining Human Action.* London: Duckworth.

Lentricchia, Frank. 1983. *Criticism and Social Change.* Chicago: University of Chicago Press.

Leplin, Jarrett, ed. 1984. *Scientific Realism.* Berkeley: University of California Press.

LePore, Ernest, and Brian McLaughlin, eds. 1985. *Action and Events.* Oxford: Blackwell.

————. 1986. *Truth and Interpretation.* Oxford: Blackwell.

Levine, G., ed. 1993. *Realism and Representation: Essays on the Problem of Realism in Relation to Science, Literature, and Culture.* Madison: University of Wisconsin Press.

Lewis, David K. 1969. *Convention: A Philosophical Study.* Cambridge: Harvard University Press.

————. 1986. *On the Plurality of Worlds.* Cambridge: Blackwell.

Lindblom, Charles. 1990. *Inquiry and Change.* New Haven: Yale University Press.

Lukes, Stephen. 1982. "Relativism in Its Place." In Hollis and Lukes, *Rationality and Relativism.*

Lyotard, Jean-François. 1984. *The Postmodern Condition.* Minneapolis: University of Minnesota Press.

Macdonald, Graham, and Phillip Pettit. 1981. *Semantics and Social Science.* London: Routledge and Kegan Paul.

MacIntyre, Alasdair. 1970. "The Idea of a Social Science." In Wilson, *Rationality.*

————. 1982. *After Virtue.* Notre Dame: University of Notre Dame Press.

————. 1984. "The Relationship of Philosophy to Its Past." In *Philosophy in History,* ed. Richard Rorty, J. B. Schneewind, and Quentin Skinner. New York: Cambridge University Press.

————. 1986. "The Intelligibility of Action." In *Rationality, Relativism, and the Human Sciences,* ed. J. Margolis, M. Krausz, and R. M. Burian. Boston: Nijhoff.

————. 1989. "Relativism, Power, and Philosophy." In Krausz, *Relativism.*

Mackinnon, Edward. 1974. *The Problem of Scientific Realism.* Englewood Cliffs, N. J.: Prentice-Hall.

————. 1978. "Scientific Realism: The New Debates." *Philosophy of Science* 46.

Maclean, Ian, Alan Montefiore, and Peter Winch, eds. 1990. *The Political Responsibility of Intellectuals.* Cambridge: Cambridge University Press.

Malcolm, Norman. 1963. *Knowledge and Certainty.* Englewood Cliffs, N.J.: Prentice-Hall.

Malpas, J. E. 1992. *Donald Davidson and the Mirror of Meaning.* Cambridge: Cambridge University Press.

Mandelbaum, Maurice. 1982. In Meiland and Krausz, *Relativism.*

Manicas, Peter. 1987. *A History and Philosophy of the Social Sciences.* Oxford: Basil Blackwell.

———. 1989. "Explanation and Quantification." In *The Qualitative-Quantitative Distinction in Social Science,* ed. Barry Glassner and Jonathan D. Moreno. Boston: Kluwer Academic.

March, James G., and John P. Olsen. 1989. *Rediscovering Institutions: The Organizational Basis of Politics.* New York: Free Press.

Margolis, Joseph. 1986. *Pragmatism Without Foundations: Reconciling Realism and Relativism.* Oxford: Basil Blackwell.

———. 1991. *The Truth About Relativism.* Oxford: Blackwell.

Martin, Bill. 1992. *Matrix and Line: Derrida and the Possibilities of Postmodern Social Theory.* Albany: State University of New York Press.

Masters, Roger D. 1989. *The Nature of Politics.* New Haven: Yale University Press.

McDermott, Patrice. 1994. *Politics and Scholarship.* Urbana: Illinois University Press.

Meiland, Jack W., and Michael Krausz, eds. 1982. *Relativism: Cognitive and Moral.* Notre Dame: University of Notre Dame Press.

Melden, A. I. 1961. *Free Action.* New York: Humanities Press.

Mele, Alfred R. 1992. *Springs of Action.* Oxford: Oxford University Press.

Michelfelder, Diane P., and Richard Palmer, eds. 1989. *Dialogue and Deconstruction: The Gadamer-Derrida Encounter.* Albany: State University of New York Press.

Miller, Richard W. 1987. *Fact and Method.* Princeton: Princeton University Press.

Mischel, Theodore, ed. 1969. *Human Action.* New York: Academic Press.

Mitchell, W. J. T., ed. 1983. *The Politics of Interpretation.* Chicago: University of Chicago Press.

Moser, Paul K. 1993. *Philosophy After Objectivity.* New York: Oxford University.

Munch, Richard. 1987. *Theory of Action: Toward a New Synthesis Going Beyond Parsons.* London: Routledge and Kegan Paul.

Nagel, Ernest. 1961. *The Structure of Science.* New York: Harcourt, Brace, and World.

Nagel, Thomas. 1986. *The View from Nowhere.* Oxford: Oxford University Press.

Nelson, John S., ed. 1986. *Tradition, Interpretation, and Science.* Albany: State University of New York Press.

Nelson, John, Allan Megill, and Donald N. McCloskey, eds. 1987. *The Rhetoric of the Human Sciences.* Madison: University of Wisconsin Press.

New Literary History. 1981. 1983. Vols. 13, 14.

Newton-Smith, William. 1981. *The Rationality of Science.* London: Routledge.

———. 1982. "Relativism and the Possibility of Interpretation." In Hollis and Lukes, *Rationality and Relativism.*

Nielsen, Kai. 1991. *After the Demise of the Tradition.* Boulder: Westview Press.

———. 1995. *On Transforming Philosophy.* Boulder: Westview Press.

Nietzsche, Friedrich. 1967. *The Will to Power.* New York: Random House.

Nordernfelt, Lennart. 1974. *The Explanation of Human Actions.* Uppsala, Sweden: University of Uppsala Press.

Norris, Christopher. 1985. *The Contest of Faculties: Philosophy and Theory After Deconstruction.* London: Macmillan.

———. 1987. *Derrida.* Cambridge: Harvard University Press.

———. 1990. *What Is Wrong with Postmodernism?* Baltimore: Johns Hopkins University Press.

———. 1996. *Reclaiming Truth.* Durham, N.C.: Duke University Press.

Novick, Peter. 1988. *That Noble Dream: The "Objectivity Question" and the American Historical Profession.* New York: Cambridge University Press.

Oakeshott, Michael. 1962. *Rationalism in Politics, and Other Essays.* New York: Basic Books.

———. 1975. "On Understanding Human Conduct." In *On Human Conduct.* Oakeshott, Michael. Oxford: Clarendon Press.

Ormisten, Gayle L., and Alan D. Schrift, eds. 1990a. *The Hermeneutic Tradition: From Ast to Ricoeur.* Albany: State University of New York Press.

———. 1990b. *Transforming the Hermeneutic Context: From Nietzsche to Nancy.* Albany: State University of New York Press.

Orwell, George. 1968. *The Collected Essays, Journalism, and Letters of George Orwell.* Vol 4, *In Front of Your Nose.* New York: Harcourt, Brace and World.

Outhwaite, William. 1975. *Realism, Hermeneutics, and Critical Theory.* New York: St. Martin's Press.

———. 1987. *New Philosophies of Social Science: Realism, Hermeneutics, and Critical Theory.* New York: St. Martin's Press.

Palmer, Richard E. 1969. *Hermeneutics: Interpretation Theory in Schleiermacher, Dilthey, Heidegger, and Gadamer.* Evanston, Ill.: Northwestern University Press.

Parsons, Talcott. 1937. *The Structure of Social Action.* New York: Free Press.

———. 1977. *Social Systems and the Evolution of Action Theory.* New York: Free Press.

———. 1978. *Action Theory and the Human Condition.* New York: Free Press.

Parsons, Talcott, and Edward A. Shils, eds. 1949. *Toward a General Theory of Action.* Glencoe, Ill.: Free Press.

Peters, R. S. 1958. *The Concept of Motivation.* London: Routledge and Kegan Paul.

Pihlström, Sami. 1996. *Structuring the World.* Helsinki: Philosophical Society of Finland.

Pinker, Steven. 1994. *The Language Instinct.* New York: Morrow.

Pocock, J. G. A. 1971. *Politics, Language, and Time.* New York: Atheneum.

———. 1980. "A Salute to John Gunnell." *Annals of Scholarship* 1.

Popper, Karl. 1965. *Conjectures and Refutations.* New York: Basic Books.

———. 1970. "Normal Science and Its Dangers." In *Criticism and the Growth of Knowledge,* ed. Imre Lakatos and Alan Musgrave. Cambridge: Cambridge University Press.

———. 1972. *Objective Knowledge.* Oxford: Clarendon Press.

———. 1976. "Reason or Revolution?" In Adorno et al., *The Positivist Dispute in German Sociology.*

———. 1992. *Unended Quest: An Intellectual Autobiography.* London: Routledge.

Powell, Betty. 1967. *Knowledge of Actions.* New York: Humanities Press.

Prado, C. G. 1987. *The Limits of Pragmatism.* Highlands, N. J.: Humanities Press.

Putnam, Hilary. 1978. *Meaning and the Moral Sciences.* New York: Routledge and Kegan Paul.

―――. 1981. *Reason, Truth, and History.* Cambridge: Cambridge University Press.

―――. 1983. *Realism and Reason.* New York: Cambridge University Press.

―――. 1987. *The Many Faces of Realism.* La Salle, Ill.: Open Court.

―――. 1988. *Representation and Reality.* Cambridge: MIT Press.

―――. 1990. *Realism with a Human Face.* Cambridge: Harvard University Press.

―――. 1992. *Renewing Philosophy.* Cambridge: Harvard University Press.

―――. 1994. *Words and Life.* Cambridge: Harvard University Press.

―――. 1995. *Pragmatism.* Cambridge: Blackwell.

Quine, W. V. O. 1953. *From a Logical Point of View.* Cambridge: Harvard University Press.

―――. 1960. *Word and Object.* Cambridge: MIT Press.

―――. 1969. *Ontology Naturalized and Other Essays.* New York: Columbia University Press.

―――. 1975. "On Empirically Equivalent Systems of the World." *Erkenntnis* 9.

―――. 1981. *Theories and Things.* Cambridge: Harvard University Press.

―――. 1995. *From Stimulus to Science.* Cambridge: Harvard University Press.

Quinton, Anthony. 1974–1975. "Social Objects." *Proceedings of the Aristotelian Society.* 75.

Rabinow, P., and W. Sullivan, eds. 1979. *Interpretative Social Science.* Berkeley: University of California Press.

Rajchman, John, and Cornel West, eds. 1985. *Post-Analytic Philosophy.* New York: Columbia University Press.

Ramberg, Bjørn. 1989. *Donald Davidson's Philosophy of Language.* Oxford: Basil Blackwell.

Raven, Diederick, Lieteke van Vucht Tijssen, and Jan de Wolf, eds. 1992. *Cognitive Relativism and Social Science.* New Brunswick, N. J.: Transaction.

Rawls, John. 1971. *A Theory of Justice.* Cambridge: Harvard University Press.

Rescher, Nicholas. 1987. *Scientific Realism: A Critical Appraisal.* Boston: Reidel.

Richter, Melvin. 1995. *The History of Political and Social Concepts: A Critical Introduction.* Oxford: Oxford University Press.

Ricoeur, Paul. 1971. "The Model of the Text." *Social Research* 38.

―――. 1976a. *Interpretation Theory, Discourse, and the Surplus of Meaning.* Fort Worth: Texas Christian University Press.

―――. 1976b. "History and Hermeneutics." *Journal of Philosophy.* 73.

―――. 1986. *Lectures on Ideology and Utopia.* New York: Columbia University Press.

Robbins, Bruce, ed. 1990. *Intellectuals: Aesthetics, Politics, Academics.* Minneapolis: University of Minnesota Press.

Rorty, Amelie Oksenberg. 1989. "Relativism, Person, and Practices." In Krausz, *Relativism.*

Rorty, Richard. 1972. "The World Well Lost." *Journal of Philosophy* 69.

————. 1979. *Philosophy and the Mirror of Nature.* Princeton: Princeton University Press.

————. 1982. *The Consequences of Pragmatism.* Minneapolis: University of Minnesota Press.

————. 1989. "Solidarity or Objectivity?" In Krausz, *Relativism.*

————. 1992. "The Pragmatist's Progress." In Umberto Eco et al., *Interpretation and Overinterpretation,* ed. Stefan Collini. New York: Cambridge University Press.

————. 1994. "After Philosophy, Democracy." In *The American Philosopher,* ed. Giovanna Borradori. Chicago: University of Chicago Press.

Rosenau, Pauline. 1992. *Post-Modernism and the Social Sciences.* Princeton: Princeton University Press.

Roth, Paul A. 1987. *Meaning and Method in the Social Sciences: A Case for Methodological Pluralism.* Tampa: University of South Florida Press.

Rudner, Richard. 1966. *Philosophy of Social Science.* Englewood Cliffs, N. J.: Prentice-Hall.

Ryle, Gilbert. 1949. *The Concept of Mind.* New York: Barnes and Noble.

————. 1968a. "Thinking and Reflecting." In *The Human Agent.* London: Macmillan.

————. 1968b. "A Puzzling Element in the Notion of Thinking." In *Studies in the Philosophy of Thought and Action,* ed. P. F. Strawson. Oxford: Oxford University Press.

Said, Edward. 1993. In Edmundsen, *Wild Orchids and Trotsky.*

————. 1994. *Representations of the Intellectual.* New York: Pantheon.

Sankey, Howard. 1997. *Rationality, Relativism, and Incommensurability.* Sydney: Ashgate.

Satz, Debra, and John Ferejohn. 1994. "Rational Choice." *Journal of Philosophy* 91.

Savigny, Eike von. 1988. *The Social Foundations of Meaning.* New York: Springer-Verlag.

Sayre-McCord, Geoffrey, ed. 1988. *Essays on Moral Realism.* Ithaca: Cornell University Press.

Schatzki, Theodore R. 1996. *Social Practices.* New York: Cambridge University Press.

Schick, Frederic. 1991. *Understanding Action.* Cambridge: Cambridge University Press.

Schiffer, Stephen. 1987. *Remnants of Meaning.* Cambridge: MIT Press.

Schmitt, Carl. 1976. *The Concept of the Political,* trans. George Schwab and including Leo Strauss's "Comments." New Brunswick, N.J.: Rutgers University Press.

Searle, John R. 1969. *Speech Acts: An Essay in the Philosophy of Language.* Cambridge: Cambridge University Press.

————. 1977. "Reiterating the Differences: A Reply to Derrida." *Glyph* 1.

————. 1979. *Expression and Meaning: Studies in the Theory of Speech Acts.* Cambridge: Cambridge University Press.

————. 1983. *Intentionality: An Essay in the Philosophy of Mind.* New York: Cambridge University Press.

————. 1992. *The Rediscovery of the Mind.* Cambridge: MIT Press.

————. 1995. *The Construction of Social Reality.* New York: Free Press.

Sellars, Wilfrid. 1963. *Science, Perception, and Reality.* New York: Humanities Press.

Shapiro, Ian. 1990. *Political Criticism.* Berkeley: University of California Press.

Shapiro, Ian, and Judith Wagner DeCew, eds. 1995. *Theory and Practice: Nomos XXXVII.* New York: New York University Press.

Shwayder, David. 1965. *The Stratification of Behavior.* New York: Humanities Press.

Siegel, Harvey. 1987. *Relativism Refuted.* Dordrecht: Reidel.

Simons, Herbert W., and Michael Billig, eds. 1994. *After Postmodernism.* Thousand Oaks, Calif.: Sage.

Skinner, Quentin. 1969. "Meaning and Understanding in the History of Ideas." *History and Theory* 8.

———. 1970. "Conventions and the Understanding of Speech Acts." *Philosophical Quarterly* 20.

———. 1971. "On Performing and Explaining Linguistic Actions." *Philosophical Quarterly* 21.

———. 1972a. " 'Social Meaning' and the Explanation of Social Action." In *Philosophy, Politics, and Society,* ed. Peter Laslett, W. G. Runciman, and Quentin Skinner. Oxford: Oxford University Press.

———. 1972b. "Motives, Intentions, and the Interpretation of Texts." *New Literary History* 3.

———. 1974. "Some Problems in the Analysis of Political Thought and Action." *Political Theory* 2.

———. 1975–1976. "Hermeneutics and the Role of History." *New Literary History* 7.

———. 1978a. *Foundations of Modern Political Thought,* vol. 1. Cambridge: Cambridge University Press.

———. 1978b. "Action and Context." *Proceedings of the Aristotelian Society* 52 (supp).

———. 1985. "What Is Intellectual History?" *History Today* 35.

———. 1988. "A Reply to My Critics." In *Meaning and Context: Quentin Skinner and His Critics,* ed. James Tully. Princeton: Princeton University Press.

Smith, Rogers M. 1997. "Still Blowing in the Wind: The American Quest for a Scientific Study of Politics." *Daedalus* 126.

Stegmuller, William S. 1976. *The Structure and Dynamics of Theories.* New York: Springer-Verlag.

Stitch, Stephen. 1990. *The Fragmentation of Reason.* Cambridge: MIT Press.

Strauss, Leo. 1953. *Natural Right and History.* Chicago: University of Chicago Press.

———. 1961. "Relativism." In *Relativism and the Study of Man,* ed. Helmut Schoeck and James W. Wiggins. Princeton: Van Nostrand.

———. 1976. "Comments." In Schmitt, *The Concept of the Political.*

Strawson, Frederick. 1963. *Individuals: An Essay in Descriptive Metaphysics.* Garden City, N. J.: Doubleday.

Stroud, Barry. 1984. *The Significance of Philosphical Skepticism.* Oxford: Oxford University Press.

Suppe, Frederick. 1977. *The Structure of Scientific Theories.* Urbana: University of Illinois Press.

———. 1989. *The Semantic Conception of Scientific Theories and Scientific Realism.* Urbana: University of Illinois Press.

Tännsjö, Torbjörn. 1990. *Moral Realism.* Savage, Md.: Rowman & Littlefield.

Tarski, Alfred. 1949. "The Semantic Conception of Truth." In *Readings in Philosophical Analysis,* ed. H. Feigl and W. Sellars. New York: Appleton-Century-Crofts.

————. 1956. *Logic, Semantics, and Mathematical Objects.* Oxford: Clarendon Press.

Taylor, Charles. 1964. *The Explanation of Behaviour.* London: Routledge and Kegan Paul.

————. 1970a. "Explaining Action." *Inquiry* 13.

————. 1970b. "The Explanation of Purposive Behaviour." In *Explanation in the Behavioural Sciences,* ed. Robert Borger and Frank Cioffi. Cambridge: Cambridge University Press.

————. 1971. "Interpretation and the Sciences of Man." *Review of Metaphysics* 25.

————. 1982. "Rationality." In Hollis and Lukes, *Rationality and Relativism.*

————. 1984. "Philosophy and Its History." In *Philosophy in History,* ed. Richard Rorty, J. B. Schneewind, and Quentin Skinner. New York: Cambridge University Press.

Taylor, Charles Alan. 1996. *Defining Science.* Madison: University of Wisconsin Press.

Taylor, Richard. 1966. *Action and Purpose.* Englewood Cliffs, N.J.: Prentice-Hall.

Thalberg, Irving. 1972. *Enigmas of Agency.* New York: Humanities Press.

————. 1977. *Perception, Emotion, and Action.* Oxford: Basil Blackwell.

Thomas, David. 1979. *Naturalism and Social Science: A Post-Empiricist Philosophy of Social Science.* Cambridge: Cambridge University Press.

Thompson, E. P. 1971. "Anthropology and the Discipline of Historical Context." *Midland History* 1.

Thomson, Judith. 1977. *Acts and Other Events.* Ithaca: Cornell University Press.

Toulmin, Stephen. 1972. *Human Understanding.* Oxford: Oxford University Press.

Trigg, Roger. 1985. *Understanding Social Science.* Oxford: Basil Blackwell.

————. 1989. *Reality at Risk.* New York: Harvester Wheatsheaf.

Trilling, Lionel. 1965. *Beyond Culture: Essays on Literature and Learning.* New York: Viking.

Tully, James, ed. 1988. *Meaning and Context: Quentin Skinner and His Critics.* Cambridge: Polity Press.

Tuomela, Raimo. 1973. *Theoretical Concepts.* New York: Springer-Verlag.

————. 1977. *Human Action and Its Explanation.* Dordrecht: Reidel.

————. 1984. *A Theory of Social Action.* Boston: Reidel.

————. 1995. *The Importance of Us.* Stanford: Stanford University Press.

van Fraasen, Bas. 1980. *The Image of Science.* Oxford: Oxford University Press.

Vermagen, Bruce, and M. Hintikki, eds. 1985. *Essays on Davidson.* Oxford: Clarendon Press.

von Wright, Georg Henrik. 1971. *Explanation and Understanding.* Ithaca: Cornell University Press.

Walzer, Michael. 1987. *Interpretation and Social Criticism.* Cambridge: Cambridge University Press.

————. 1988. *The Company of Critics.* New York: Basic Books.

White, Alan, ed. 1968. *The Philosophy of Action*. New York: Oxford University Press.

White, Stephen K. 1991. *Political Theory and Postmodernism*. New York: Cambridge University Press.

Whittemore, Robert C., ed. 1979. *Studies in Action Theory*. New Orleans: Tulane University Press.

Williams, Bernard. 1985. *Ethics and the Limits of Philosophy*. Cambridge: Harvard University Press.

Williams, Michael. 1991. *Unnatural Doubts: Epistemological Realism and the Basis of Skepticism*. Oxford: Blackwell.

Wilson, Bryan, ed. 1970. *Rationality*. Oxford: Oxford University Press.

Wilson, George M. 1989. *The Intentionality of Human Action*. Stanford: Stanford University Press.

Winch, Peter. 1958. *The Idea of a Social Science and Its Relationship to Philosophy*. London: Routledge and Kegan Paul.

———. 1959–1960. "Nature and Convention." In *Proceedings of the Aristotelian Society* 60.

———. 1964. "Understanding a Primitive Society," *American Philosophical Quarterly* 1.

———. 1972. *Ethics and Action*. London: Routledge and Kegan Paul.

Wittgenstein, Ludwig. 1933. *Tractatus Logico-Philosophicus*. London: Routledge and Kegan Paul.

———. 1953. *Philosophical Investigations*. New York: Macmillan.

———. 1958. *The Blue and Brown Books*. New York: Harper and Row.

———. 1961. *Notebooks, 1914–1916*. New York: Harper.

———. 1967. *Zettel*. Berkeley: University of California Press.

Wolin, Richard. 1992. *The Terms of Cultural Criticism*. New York: Columbia University Press.

Wolin, Sheldon. 1960. *Politics and Vision*. Boston: Little, Brown.

———. 1969. "Political Theory as a Vocation." *American Political Science Review* 63.

———. 1997. "What Time Is It?" *Theory and Event* 1.

Wood, David, ed. 1992. *Derrida: A Critical Reader*. Oxford: Oxford University Press.

Wright, Crispin. 1987. *Realism, Meaning, and Truth*. Oxford: Basil Blackwell.

Index

absolute text: fallacy of, 178
academic freedom, 220
academicians, 199, 216
academic intellectuals, 196, 201
academic political theory, 196–211, 215–21
academics, 217
accordion effect, 77
action, 72–74; communicative, 51; conventional, 72–74; explanation of, 164; man of, 67; phenomenology of, 9; primitive, 77; rational, 164; talk about, 75; theory of, 9–10, 50–51, 57–63, 72–74
Adorno, Theodor, 90
aestheticism: neo-Romantic, 92
alienation of political theory, xi–xii
American political theory, 211–15
American scholar, 196
American university, 216–18
analysis: ordinary language, 48; postanalytic philosophy, xi; Wittgensteinian, x
analytical context, 168–69
anarchists, epistemological, 15
anarchy, 172
antifoundationalism, 94–95, 97, 153, 207; fundamental claim of, 208–9
antirationalism, 106
antirealism, 143, 145; global, 145
antisymmetry, 28–30
Apel, K.-O., 103
archewriting, 182–83

Arendt, Hannah, 85, 220
Aristotle, 63, 209–10
artifact (term), 50
attitudes, propositional, 59
Audi, Robert, 60
Austin, J. L., xiii, 9, 51, 57, 65, 76, 118, 157, 164, 177, 182, 184
author: animus of, 187; banishment of, 171; will and mind of, 171
authority: of metanarratives, 102; moral, 95
autonomy: of local concepts, 86; of the political, 85; of politics, 86–87; semantic, 171, 178; of text, 14, 32, 178, 184–85
Ayer, A. J., 58
Azande, 103

background, 56
Bacon, Francis, 128
behavior: brute facts of, 11; concept of, 63; conformative, 68; postbehavioral revolution, 219; rule-following, 102; social, 49
behavioralism, 124; postbehavioralism, 125
behavioral political science, ix–x
behaviorism, 65
Bender, Thomas, 216
Berlin School, 132
Berlin wall, 211, 219–20
Bhaskar, Roy, 150–52
Bible, 158

241

Deleuze, Gilles, 6
de Man, Paul, 191
democracy, 219
Dennett, Daniel, 61
Derrida, Jacques, 15, 56, 92, 95, 99, 108, 156, 180–84
Descartes, 128
Dewey, John, 124
différance, 182
Dilthey, Wilhelm, 158–59
discourse(s): civic, 214; first-order, 19–20, 32, 102; foreign elements, 26; levels of, 183–92; metadiscourses, 19, 21–23; metapractical, 21; objective aspect of, 178; orders of, x, 18, 25–26, 34–36; vs practice, 18; second-order, 22–23, 33, 43, 91, 96, 101–2, 120, 197–98, 210–11; talk about actions, 75; third-order, 24, 35; types of, 19
discursive regimes, 18
distanciation, 178
diversity: fear of, 96
doing(s), 3, 75, 77
Downs, Anthony, 52
Duhem, Pierre, 131
Dworkin, Ronald, 90

Easton, David, 84
Eco, Umberto, 158, 191
Eddington, A. S., 132
Einstein, Albert, 132, 206
Eliot, T. S., 190
Elster, Jon, 52
empirical ontology, 40
empiricism, 131; constructive, 146; dogmas of, 135, 140; logical, 36, 122–27, 132; postempiricism, 109; vs realism, 141–47; third dogma of, 110; two dogmas of, 109

Empson, William, 190
England, 205
epistemological anarchists, 15
epistemological fanaticism, 158
epistemological quest, 5, 208
epistemological realism, convergent, 145
epistemological skepticism, 144
epistemology: external, 24; internal, 24; partisan science of, 150; in philosophy, 166; role of, 24; theory as, 200–201; theory vs, 166
essentialism, 83
ethics, 104; of language, 171–72; philosophical realism in, 149–50; universalism in, 106
evolutionary theory of scientific truth, 137
explanation, 80, 179
extension, 72–74

facts, 134–35, 147; brute, 11, 55–57; in first-order practices, 42–43; mental, 57; social, 54–55; of social science, 42
fallacy: of absolute text, 178; intentional, 178
fanaticism, epistemological, 158
fear: of diversity, 96; of relativism, 96
feigned realism, 144
feminist theory, 203
Feyerabend, Paul, 6, 119, 132–33, 140, 144
First Commandment, 157
first-order discourses, 19–20, 32, 102
first-order practices, 19–20; facts in, 42–43; metapractices vs, 22
first world, 138
Fish, Stanley, 14, 184–85, 202, 217

theology, philosophical, 208–9
theoretical culture, 107
theoretical instrumentalism, 139
theoretical physics, 37
theoretical pluralism, 39
theoretical realism, 40, 121–53;
  contemporary period, 134–41
theoretician's dilemma, 122
theoria, 40
theorists, xiii; as connected critic,
  215
theory, 19, 81, 134; of action, 9–
  10, 50–51, 57–63; concept of,
  37–46, 52; of conventional
  objects, 9, 185–86; critical, 207;
  critical race, 204; as epistemology, 200–201; vs epistemology,
  166; feminist, 203; history of,
  134; of institutions, 80; of
  language, 51; legal, 149–50;
  meaning of, 160; metatheory, x,
  xiv, 51, 149; in philosophy, 166;
  in philosophy of science, 134;
  of politics, 8, 12, 45, 53, 82; and
  practice, 3, 100; vs practice,
  203–5; rational choice, 52, 60;
  realizing, 134; scientific, 134; in
  second-order practices, 42; as
  set of principles of inquiry,
  200–201; social choice, 52; in
  social phenomena, 43; of social
  phenomena, 43; of
  structuration, 81; of structures,
  80; substantive, 51; traditional
  vs critical, 37. *See also* political
  theory
theory (term), 40, 43, 134
theory construction, 122
theory/practice problem, 204–5,
  210–11
thinking, 65–66
third-order discourses, 24, 35

third-order practices, 22, 35
third world, 138
thought(s), 65–66; concept of, 66;
  as linguistic episodes, 66
Torah, 157
Toulmin, Stephen, 133, 138
tradition, 15, 212
transcendental illusion, 5
transcendentalism, 93; imminent,
  90
translation, 115, 117, 186–87
trickle-down hypothesis, 218
truth(s), 98–99, 114, 143; criteria
  of, 105–6; definition of, 147;
  evolutionary theory of, 137; and
  politics, 220; of science, 135;
  scientific, 134; Tarski's semantic
  theory of, 112, 137; of texts,
  175
T-sentence, 112
Tuomela, Raimo, 59–60

underlabourer view of philosophy,
  3
understanding, 1, 80, 175, 186–87;
  historical, 1; positive, 48
understanding language, 186
Universal Grammar, 62
universalism, 106
universals, 72
university: American, 216–18; and
  politics, 215–21
usable knowledge, 215

Vienna Circle, 131, 137
vocation, 212, 219

Walzer, Michael, 215
Wayne, John, 67
Weber, Max, 9, 162, 197
Weimar culture, 93
Whewell, William, 130

About the Author

John G. Gunnell is Distinguished Professor of Political Science in the Graduate School of Public Affairs at the State University of New York at Albany. He has written widely on various aspects of political theory and political philosophy as well as on the history of political science. His latest book, prior to the present volume, is the *Descent of Political Theory: The Genealogy of an American Vocation* (University of Chicago Press, 1993).

① what question are you answering?

② why is this question important?

③ no Ceaser

④ what real difference
does it make what level
of abstraction ideas occur

⑤ ⓐ Meta — before

ⓑ meta — epi phenomenal

⑥ An action is not a discourse

⑦ Ideas do influence actions 92

⑧ Hegel... |||| |||| | No evidence give Assents.
Enlightenment → collap.
Not even anecdotal

⑨ Social scientists want a claim to
rule, that claim is bound a destroy
the old order — but the ground of
destroying the old order, relation — my